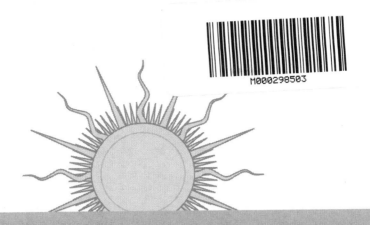

This series provides a forum for theoretical and empirical investigations of social phenomena. It promotes works that focus on the interactions among cognitive processes, individual behavior, and social outcomes. It is especially open to interdisciplinary books that are genuinely integrative.

Editor: Timur Kuran
Editorial Board: Tyler Cowen   Avner Greif
                    Diego Gambetta   Viktor Vanberg

Titles in the Series

(continues on last page of the book)

Markets and Cultural Voices

LIBERTY VS. POWER IN THE LIVES OF
MEXICAN AMATE PAINTERS

Tyler Cowen

THE UNIVERSITY OF MICHIGAN PRESS

Ann Arbor

2008   2007   2006   2005   4   3   2   1

A CIP catalog record for this book is available from the British Library.

Library of Congress Cataloging-in-Publication Data

Cowen, Tyler.
    Markets and cultural voices : liberty vs. power in the lives of
Mexican Amate painters / Tyler Cowen.
        p.   cm. — (Economics, cognition, and society)
    Includes bibliographical references.
    ISBN 0-472-09889-6 (cloth : alk. paper) — ISBN 0-472-06889-X
(pbk. : alk. paper)
    1. Nahuas—Mexico—San Agustín Oapan—Economic
conditions.   2. Nahuas—Mexico—San Agustín Oapan—Industries.
3. Nahua art—Mexico—San Agustín Oapan.   4. Folk art—Mexico—San
Agustín Oapan.   5. Indian business enterprises—Mexico—San Agustín
Oapan.   6. Paper, Handmade—Mexico—San Agustín Oapan.   7. Amate
(Plant)—Economic aspects—Mexico—San Agustín Oapan.   8. San
Agustín Oapan (Mexico)—Social conditions.   9. San Agustín Oapan
(Mexico)—Economic conditions.   I. Title.   II. Series.

F1221.N3C69   2004
338.4'7745—dc22
                                                          2004017200

ISBN13 978-0-472-09889-7 (cloth : alk. paper)
ISBN13 978-0-472-06889-0 (pbk. : alk. paper)
ISBN13 978-0-472-02412-4 (electronic)

To Natasha and Yana, two fellow lovers of Mexican art

Contents

Acknowledgments

THE MATERIAL IN THIS BOOK is based on many conversations and interviews in addition to the formal bibliography. I would like to thank (in no particular order): Marcial Camilo Ayala, Juan Camilo Ayala, Felix Camilo Ayala, Roberto Mauricio, Abraham Mauricio, Felix Jimenez Chino, Inocencio Jimenez Chino, his wife Florencia, Leonardo Camilo Altamirano, Claudia Altamirano, Felipe de la Rosa, Julio de la Rosa, Clemente de la Rosa, Pedro de la Rosa, Angel Dominguez, Martina Adame, Joel Adame, Maria Ayala Ramirez, Carmen Camilo Ayala, Amalia Camilo Ayala, Alcividiades Camilo Altamirano, Nicolás de Jesús, Eusebio Diaz, Cristino Flores Medina, Felix Venancio, Salomón Ramírez Miranda, Carlos Ortiz, Jose Rutilo, Carlos Tolentino, Alfonso Lorenzo, Francisco Lorenzo Ramirez, Ed Rabkin and Carolyn Mae Lassiter, Jonathan Amith, Max Kerlow, Felipe Ehrenberg, Gobi Stromberg, Larry Kent, Gloria Frank, Laurie Carmody, Leonore Thomas, Bill Negron, Martin Kroll, Maureen Kelley, Maria Walsh, Steven Clark, Sydney Jenkins, France Chancellor, Señor Watanabe, Carol Lamb Hopkins, Alexander Benitez, Dominique Raby, Enrique, Scott Guggenheim, Thomas Bird, Renata Madero, Randall Kroszner, Cathy Good, Peggy Golde, Ralph White, Janie Burke, Lilia Quiroz, Florence Browne, Ute Stebich, Albert Wuggetzer, Selden Rodman, Carole Rodman, Carla Rodman, Davis Mather, Sheri Cavin, and Randall Morris. Many of these individuals helped me a great deal, and I apologize if anyone feels slighted at being included in such a long list and not receiving especial thanks. Many of the people on this list deserve a special commendation.

In terms of comments and assistance, my debts are many. Without Ed Rabkin and Selden Rodman, the book could not exist. Anthropologist Jonathan Amith has been helpful beyond the call of duty. This study would not have been possible without his pioneering anthropological efforts and without the earlier work of Cathy Good—in particular her unpublished doctoral dissertation. Maureen Kelley encouraged me to write this book. Mary Hirschfeld offered especially useful comments. Bryan Caplan, Natasha Cowen, Kevin Grier, Robin Grier, and Robin Hanson offered helpful comments as well. Eric Crampton, Chris Coyne, and T. Clark Durant offered useful research assistance. Andres Marroquìn helped with the Spanish. Most of all, I am indebted to the artists, who have given so freely of their time and energy. Marcial Camilo had the good patience to sit for three days and offer corrections while I read him a Spanish translation of the entire story; the other artists have heard and responded to parts of the story as well.

I spell the artists' names as they do, which in some cases means leaving off the diacritical marks that one would otherwise expect in Spanish. The artists are familiar with these marks and have made conscious decisions not to use them.

1 • Introduction

WHAT HAPPENS WHEN poor, Nahuatl-speaking Mexican artists enter global art markets? What choices do they face? What is required for them to succeed? I will address these questions in this book by tracing the theme of liberty versus power in the lives of several Mexican painters, three of them brothers. These individuals have painted both on amate paper (bark paper) and on board—in both cases, for sale abroad and to North Americans in Mexico. They all hail from the small, rural pueblo of San Agustín Oapan in the state of Guerrero in central Mexico.

Throughout this study, the theme of liberty versus power will interlock with two primary topics: (1) how poor rural communities develop and grow richer and (2) how the globalization of culture affects diversity and the cultural voices of the poor.

Economic Development

By the term *liberty*, I mean the positive ability of individuals to control their lives, support their families, shape their cultures, and speak their minds. Liberty requires wealth, and questions arise about how wealth is created and distributed.

The stories of the artists featured here and the broader story of amate painting present a microcosm of successful economic development.

The amate and crafts merchants have succeeded through intense training; investment in unique, nonreplicable skills; marketing to outsiders; and the cultivation of trade networks. The residents of Oapan have developed a "cluster of creativity" to drive their development. Michael Porter, in his *Competitive Advantage of Nations* (1998), cited such clusters as critical to the economic success of advanced nations; the Japanese electronics industry, Italian shoe making, and Swiss pharmaceuticals are classic examples.

Spatial concentration matters for the developing world as well, arguably to a greater degree. In Mexico (and many other places), it is common that a single art form will be found in one village or a small number of villages and nowhere else. This geographic clustering implies not only that the underlying conditions for creativity are fragile but also that small communities can be extremely dynamic. A village can take off if it captures these artistic and economic synergies. The history of the arts in Oapan shows both such dynamism and such fragility and thus offers a case study in the evolution of a successful creative cluster. Oapan's ability to generate such a cluster has been essential to its economic growth and thus to the liberty of its residents.

Creative clusters have improved the quality of life in Oapan significantly over the last forty years. The extension of the market nexus to the pueblo, rather than impoverishing the community, has provided dramatic boosts in the standard of living. Whether we look at health, food, transportation, household conveniences, or entertainment, village residents are far better off than they were in times past. Amate painting and the general growth of trade in Oapan illustrate the payoffs from successful "indigenous" entrepreneurship. The episode at hand gives us reasons to be optimistic about economic development out of rural poverty.

The story presented in this book is not, however, one of liberty alone. The market means of producing wealth must be distinguished from the use of political power to extract wealth from unwilling victims. The history of the Mexican poor reflects an ongoing race between these differing forces.

Sociologist Stanislav Andreski, in his 1966 book *Parasitism and Subversion*, puts this distinction at the center of the Latin American predicament. He draws on Franz Oppenheimer's earlier *The State* ([1908] 1999)—a formative work in German sociology—which developed the theme of liberty versus power. Economist Gordon Tullock (1967) provided a more general contrast between voluntary exchange and predatory "rent-seeking" behavior, which seeks to grab resources from others in lieu of producing wealth. More recently, Hernando de Soto (*The Other Path*, 1989) has written on wealth creation in indigenous communities. He argues that well-defined property rights and protection against arbitrary confiscations can mobilize indigenous entrepreneurship and raise living standards.

I present the case studies of this book as illustrating these intellectual traditions. The lives of the Oapan painters illustrate the continuing relevance of the distinction between production and predation. While markets have become increasingly important in Oapan, politics has played a significant role as well. Chapter 2 will show how corrupt police have proven an enemy of the amate painters. Chapter 5 will focus on politics and examine the forces that have sought to confiscate the land and wealth of Oapan—to the detriment of the community, its prosperity, and its creativity. Nonetheless, the story of the Oapan painters is on the whole a positive and optimistic one, featuring growth in living standards and creative achievements.

Cultural Globalization

Liberty is not just about wealth; it also concerns having a cultural voice. But a cultural voice requires access to markets, access to audiences, and some degree of financial—and thus creative—independence.

Globalization has enabled the Oapan community and the amate painters to find their cultural voices. High-quality amate painting, despite being tightly clustered in four neighboring rural Mexican villages, relies on global markets. North American buyers, patrons, and technologies have been essential to amate painting since the beginnings of the art in the 1960s. Whatever difficulties and compromises the painters have had to face, amate painting has given them the means to develop a new cultural tradition and express their older cultural identities.

While the amate arts are but a single example, they suggest how a U.S.-Mexico cultural partnership might be fruitful and at least partially supportive of indigenous cultures. Critics frequently charge that poorer indigenous societies are corroded or ruined by outside contact with larger and richer societies. Amate markets, a case study in globalization, show how cross-cultural contact can mobilize creative energies.

The history of amate production does not fit the usual story about how globalization or cross-cultural exchange wipes out the artistic production of smaller indigenous societies. Oapan residents tend to look favorably on their contacts with the United States, which they view as providing a counterweight to the larger national Mexican culture surrounding them. Selling to foreigners has helped them maintain, extend, and preserve their cultural achievements. In essence, the very large culture (United States) is helping the very small culture (Oapan) survive against a larger surrounding culture, mestizo Mexico.[1]

The history of amate illustrates another twist on standard accounts of globalization. Very small cultures often need to trade and exchange ideas with their immediate neighbors—namely, other very small cultures—to realize their cultural voices. Much larger cultural units, such as Mexico and the United States, can support such a trade of ideas across the smaller cultural units. The spread of high-quality amate painting from Ameyaltepec to Oapan shows this mechanism at work. The two pueblos are very close together, both in space and in terms of cultural origins. Yet the painting of complex amate "stories" (*historias*) spread from one pueblo to the other only in the environments of Taxco, Cuernavaca, Acapulco, and Mexico City, where larger marketplaces brought indigenous painters together and helped them share ideas.

The history of amate also suggests that it is hard to draw a clear distinction between forces preserving indigenous communities and forces corrupting them. In this instance, contact with the outside world, trading for the amate paper itself (from the San Pablito Indians), transportation to Cuernavaca, and sales to American tourists all mobilized the creative achievements of San Agustín artisans. Forces of this kind, however, also led to subsequent cultural declines. A ten-hour trip on burro, from the pueblo to the city, has become a three-hour trip in a car, truck, or bus. As the citizens of Oapan have had more contact with the outside world, they have taken less care to preserve their native traditions, such as dances and mask making. Social customs have changed or eroded. Many people have left the community, either for larger Mexican cities or for the United States, never to return on a permanent basis. Amate production itself has ended up as largely unprofitable for many of the artists (see chapter 6).

Oapan thus provides one indication of how cross-cultural contact mobilizes the creative fruits of a society before transforming that society beyond recognition. In an earlier work, *Creative Destruction: How Globalization Is Changing the World's Cultures* (2002), I examined this phenomenon more generally and noted a common pattern (the "Minerva model"). An initial meeting of cultures often produces a creative boom, as individuals trade materials, technologies, and new ideas. In many cases, a richer culture will hire the creative labor of the poorer culture and provide financial support for its creations. Temporarily we have the best of both worlds, at least from a cultural point of view: the core of the smaller or poorer culture remains intact, while it benefits from trade and markets its unique worldview. Over time, however, the larger and wealthier culture upsets the creative wellsprings of the poorer culture. The poorer culture is so small, relative to the larger culture, that it cannot remain insulated. The poorer culture ends up more modern, richer, and often better off, but it is also less creative, if only because it is less unique.

The question, therefore, is not whether cross-cultural contact is either uplifting or destructive, for frequently it is both. Cross-cultural contact often "cashes in" the potential creativity embedded in a culture. By accepting the eventual decline of that culture, we are also mobilizing its creative forces to unprecedented levels, at least for a while.

The field of cultural economics typically focuses on institutions in those countries where it has evolved, namely, the United States and Europe. It neglects poorer societies and the special problems (and opportunities) they face in producing and funding their creative outputs. I part from mainstream cultural economics by examining what is sometimes called "folk art," "outsider art," or "naive art." Whatever we may take these terms to mean, the creative activities at hand fit neither the model of Western high art nor that of Western popular culture.[2]

In the case of amate, we have an art popular in its society but sold almost exclusively to wealthier outsiders. Unlike high culture, the amate arts do not have many close or direct links with institutional gatekeepers, such as museums, fund-raising networks, government sub-sidies, and historical scholarship and canonization. In these regards, the amate arts resemble folk art. The amate arts are not, however, a mere generic repetition of given themes and techniques, as are many folk arts. Many amate artists produce works of two different kinds: (1) cheaper generic works for immediate sale to uninformed audiences and (2) higher-quality original creative works (often commissioned in advance) for patrons and better-informed clients.

Method

Amate painting, like so many Mexican commercial enterprises, is organized in terms of the individual artistic entrepreneur and the entrepreneurial family. Amate painters typically do not work through larger firms or cultural organizations. My investigation therefore uses the medium of economic biography, a neglected method in cultural economics. Economists profess a strong interest in "methodological individualism," but rarely do they take these strictures literally. Many empirical investigations of culture move quickly to larger institutions, such as museums or multinational entertainment corporations. In sta-tistical work, economists measure the actions of particular individuals (through panel data sets), but they commonly ignore individual histo-ries and biographies.[3]

Unlike many artistic biographies, this book looks at failure as well as success. History uses paper trails, which favor well-known artistic episodes and highly literate eras, such as French Impressionism and the Italian Renaissance. In reality, most artists do not have their lives recorded on paper and do not achieve widespread celebrity, even when their work is of high quality. This study examines how some lesser-known creators try to survive as artists—and the choices they face in seeking to pursue their art and earn a living. Such a focus illuminates aspects of art markets that a study of Michelangelo or Monet does not.[4]

The narratives presented here attempt to reflect broader truths about questions of general interest. The stories concern only one small part of Mexico and offer no proof of generality per se. Nonetheless, the case study and biographical methods speak to generality in a number of ways.

Consider, for instance, the issues surrounding foreign buyers, cultural imperialism, and the supposed corruption of indigenous art forms. A narrative can offer general insight in a number of ways. First, particular cases can weaken the plausibility of general claims to the contrary. For instance, if it is argued that wealthy American customers corrupt third world artisans and silence their cultural voices, the history of amate painting offers a useful corrective. Second, cases show us what to look for in other investigations. For instance, in a globalizing world, we find an important role for foreign buyers in Australian Aboriginal art, Persian carpets, reggae music, and many other creative art forms (Cowen 2002). Third, particular cases teach us how general mechanisms operate. We learn how the existence of foreign buyers confers prestige on amate art and partially counteracts negative ethnic stereotypes within Mexico; we see that many painters start trying to market themselves to the foreign buyers as "Aztec" and "exotic"; we better understand the role of tourist centers, such as Cuernavaca, in bringing together buyers and artists; and so on. Studying cases allows us to take general mechanisms and make them institutionally richer and more persuasive.

This investigation thus stands in a broader methodological tradition. Several essays in the volume *Social Mechanisms* edited by Peter Hedström and Richard Swedberg (1998) have fleshed out the idea of mechanisms as a central part of social science. Hedström and Swedberg there call for "an analytical approach that systematically seeks to explicate the social mechanisms that generate and explain observed associations between events" (1). Jon Elster there defines a mechanism as "intermediate between laws and descriptions." He explains, "Roughly speaking, mechanisms are *frequently occurring and easily recognizable causal patterns that are triggered under generally unknown conditions or with indeterminate consequences*" (45).

Social science mechanisms of this kind stand on a middle ground between pure theory and pure descriptive empirics. They tell us how theory regulates the relationships between variables in a setting with some institutional richness. To better understand these mechanisms, we need to see how they operate in practice. More specifically, we cannot understand the theme of liberty versus power in a purely abstract setting. This bring us back to concrete histories and stories, informed by a broader theoretical understanding; in this context, it brings us back to the lives of the amate painters.[5]

The Protagonists

Marcial Camilo Ayala • Marcial was born in San Agustín Oapan, a small and remote Mexican village in Guerrero populated by indigenous Nahuas. Since the 1960s, most households have been involved in producing amate (bark paper) paintings and ceramics for sustenance.

Marcial is the leading amate painter in the region and the only family member who is fully literate. Born in 1951, Marcial taught himself Spanish in his early twenties, working from a Spanish-Nahuatl dictionary. He used Carlos Castaneda's *Teachings of Don Juan*—still a favorite book of his—as his reading text. Marcial reads voraciously, at least when he has free time from art and from village politics and when his diabetic condition does not interfere. He has read Dante's *Divine Comedy* twice and has several times painted his vision of the Inferno, Purgatory, and Paradise. He has painted the cave allegory from Plato's *Republic* as well. Marcial loves Beethoven (his favorite), Mozart, Dvorák, and Bach. Marcial is a political leader in Oapan, in part because of his eloquence at town meetings, and he is a strong advocate for the rights of indigenous cultures.

Marcial admires Renaissance art, Picasso, the Mexican muralists, the Mexican surrealists (especially Remedios Varro), Henri Rousseau, and Haitian naive art. His paintings and amates reflect these influences, as he has gone—more than any other artist—beyond the original artistic traditions of the pueblo. For many years, he has worked on both his technical proficiency and his ability to innovate conceptually.

Marcial is the only member of his family who has been to the United States. He has visited Santa Fe (several times), Miami, Chicago, Los Angeles, and Washington—sometimes in connection with art exhibits, once for a television program with Kevin Costner about indigenous peoples (*Five Hundred Nations*, produced in Los Angeles in the 1990s), and once to consult for the Smithsonian Institution (Washington).

Marcial now lives in Cuernavaca, where he has a studio for painting. His wife and four children live in nearby Taxco. In the summer and fall, he spends time in Oapan working in the fields and doing odd jobs, such as protecting his crops against rampaging local animals. He claims that fieldwork brings him closer to nature and keeps his inspiration fresh for painting.

Though Marcial will claim to be shy, he has the personality of a natural leader. His long-time North American friend Florence Browne cites lack of fear as his strongest and most memorable personal quality.[6]

Marcial's work enjoyed a burst of attention in the mid- to late 1970s, but it had been neglected for many years. Recently, interest has grown. The Smithsonian commissioned several Marcial amates for the opening exhibit of the National Museum of the American Indian (which will include Mexico) which opened in September 2004 on the Mall in Washington. Amates had two shows in France in 2002, were included in several New York City art shows, and were exhibited at Ramapo College in New Jersey.

Marcial's life reflects the tensions between freedom and cultural preservation. Marcial, of the three painting brothers, is by far the most concerned with preserving the traditions of the village. He regards cultural preservation as close to a sacred duty. Yet he has spent most of the last thirty years living outside the village. In the 1970s, he lived with Ed Rabkin in Cuernavaca, and in the early 1990s, he moved to Taxco, largely because he could not tolerate the isolation, petty politics, and lack of markets in Oapan. In his unguarded moments, he will admit he cannot stand living in the village for any length of time. Marcial subsequently found even Taxco (with a population of fifty-two thousand) to be too small and too stifling, and he was glad to move back to Cuernavaca in 2001.

Marcial and his brothers complain that the traditional dances are vanishing, yet none of the brothers wishes to partake in such dances. They claim it is too much work and too exhausting and that perfecting the dances involves too much time away from their own commitments, which of course include selling amates to the outside world.

Juan Camilo Ayala • Juan Camilo, older brother of Marcial, still lives in the pueblo. Unlike Marcial, Juan is not fully fluent in Spanish. He works every year in the fields for several months, harvesting the family crop. In his extra time and during the winter months, he paints on amate paper and board. Juan is quiet and soft-spoken yet powerful in effect, carrying the air of an influential and benevolent paterfamilias. He has five surviving children, all of whom he has taught or is teaching how to paint. Everyone in the household contributes to the family craft business.

Juan prefers to stay at home in Oapan, though he sometimes travels to Oaxaca or Puerto Escondido for a month or two to sell his artworks, usually to North Americans and Europeans. His life consists of hard work, his art, and time spent with family. In his free time, he enjoys walking around the nearby countryside and envisioning scenes to paint. He has maintained a traditional artistic style and almost always paints the pueblo, a fiesta, or a nearby landscape, typically using a celebratory style. Unlike Marcial, he has never painted *sueños* (his dreams), as his brothers refer to works of the imagination.

Juan, like Marcial, adheres to an extreme work ethic. After a hard day of work in the fields, he is still able to come home and concentrate on his painting.

Felix Camilo Ayala • At forty-five years old, Felix Camilo is the youngest of the three painting brothers. He lives in the pueblo. His wife died of fever in 1998, so he is solely responsible for raising a family of seven children. He is very protective and loving of his family. He comes across as sad and world-weary, although his friends claim he was very different before his wife's illness.

Felix spends most of his time at home and works in the fields only rarely. Most of Felix's artwork is now on a small scale. He paints amates and small pieces on board, typically of the twelve-by-twelve-inch size, as much for his own pleasure as for sale. Given that the amates and paintings no longer yield much of a living, he concentrates his time on painting pottery and laminated crosses, typically for street sale to tourists in Taxco, Cuernavaca, and Acapulco. Unlike with Marcial and Juan, doing the highest quality of art does not seem very important to him. Marcial and Juan think of themselves as artists, in a very self-conscious manner, but Felix still thinks of himself as a craftsperson or a village artisan and indeed appears more comfortable with this self-image. When he shows his art, it is almost with apology, whereas for Marcial and Juan it is more an act of boasting and self-congratulation.

The last of the trio to start painting, Felix has always felt the shadow of his brothers and has been reluctant to compete on their terms. Nonetheless, his talent has won recognition. When the group was given a large show in Connecticut in 1981, Felix was represented more prominently than any other group member.

Felix is quiet and does not show obvious charisma. Yet he is keenly intelligent and has a strong sense of irony, and his advice is valued greatly by his friends. He gets along with just about everybody, is removed from village politics, and is universally considered to be sweet.

Inocencio Jimenez Chino, Felix Jimenez Chino, Roberto Mauricio Salazar, and Abraham Mauricio Salazar • Along with the Camilo brothers, these two pairs of brothers are considered the artistic leaders of San Agustín. For a number of years, they formed a "collaborative circle" (Farrell 2001) with the Camilos, painting for foreign clients under the tutelage of Ed Rabkin, a North American supporter of the group.

The Pueblo: San Agustín Oapan • San Agustín Oapan lies in the center of the Mexican state of Guerrero, along the Rio Balsas. The pueblo is five hundred to six hundred meters above sea level, where the terrain is mountainous and extremely dry, with many canyons, large cactuses, some deciduous trees, and a large amount of scrub. The village has three to four thousand people in the rainy season—when the crops are planted—and many fewer otherwise.[7]

The pueblo consists almost exclusively of private homes. Oapan has no hotels, restaurants, or full-size stores to speak of, though there are several one-room cantinas, a few outdoor commercial stalls, and several homes that devote a few shelves of space to canned goods and local foodstuffs. The other large-scale structures are not commercial in nature. A large Catholic church in an open plaza marks the center of town. On one side of the plaza is the *comisario* building, containing both the town hall and two small jail cells. On the other side of the square is a bus stop (with the name of the town painted on a small sign) and an elevated building where visiting priests rest and store their materials. The elevated building is built on top of a small pre-Hispanic pyramid, many of whose stones remain visible underneath the more modern structure.

The name of the village reflects its cross-cultural heritage. The first two words of the pueblo's name, *San Agustín*, date from the sixteenth century, when the Augustinian religious order attempted to homestead the religious loyalties of numerous Mexican villages. The third word, *Oapan*, predates the Spanish conquest and, in Nahuatl, the native language, means "where the green maize stalk abounds." The villagers often refer simply to "Oapan" rather than using the full name of the pueblo.[8]

San Agustín Oapan is part of a larger ethnic community. Along the Rio Balsas, fifteen small pueblos share a broadly common microculture—made up of about thirty-five thousand individuals—known as Alto Balsas Nahua. San Agustín is the historic center of these communities, the oldest and still the largest pueblo of the group.

Marcial Camilo Ayala, untitled, 15″ x 22.5″. This is one of Marcial's earliest amates. Rabkin bought it from him in 1972 in the streets of Cuernavaca. The figure is walking along a muddy Rio Balsas, near San Agustín. Collection of the author, purchased from Ed Rabkin. *The original works are in color unless otherwise noted.*

Roberto Mauricio, untitled, painted on board, approximately 25″ x 31″. This early painting of Roberto's portrays himself walking along a path in the nearby canyons. Collection of Carole Rodman, bought by Selden Rodman from Ed Rabkin.

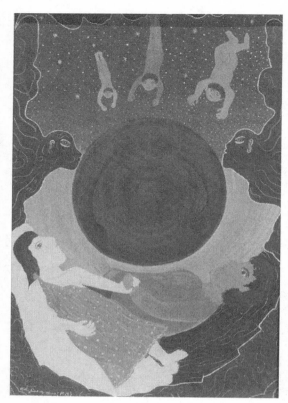

Felix Jimenez Chino, *Lovers*, painted on board, 20″ x 14″. Private collection.

Felix Jimenez Chino, *Walk at Night*, painted for Maria Walsh in the 1970s, 15″ x 22.5″. Private collection.

Marcial Camilo Ayala in Taxco, 2001. He is holding his picture *Electrification of the Village*, painted on canvas, 30″ x 23″. Collection of the author.

Juan Camilo Ayala and family, 2001. *Left to right:* Juan's wife, Claudia Altamirano; his daughters, Alcividiades and Aide; his son Leonardo; and Juan. Photo taken by the author.

Bus stop in San Agustín Oapan, 2001. On the left side of the picture is the building where the visiting priests stay; the stones on the bottom are the remnant of a pre-Hispanic pyramid. Note the satellite antenna in the background.

Marcial Camilo Ayala, *Corrupt Bureaucrats*, 2000, black-and-white amate, 15″ x 22.5″. Marcial here portrays his vision of Mexican politics. Collection of Randall Kroszner.

Marcial Camilo Ayala, *March of Cortés*, 2003, 15″ x 22.5″. This is part of Marcial's sixteen-amate series on the history of the Nahua people in Mexico. Collection of the author.

Marcial Camilo Ayala, *Oliva Sleeping*, 1990, 23″ x 23″. Oliva is Marcial's daughter; he painted her at the age of eight. This was one of his latter pictures for Ed Rabkin. Collection of the author.

Marcial Camilo Ayala, *Easter Scene*, 2000, painted on board, 23″ x 31″. In this scene, a preacher is speaking to an Oapan crowd in the center of town. Art dealer Gloria Frank purchased this painting from Marcial; it is now held in the collection of Rosemary and Stephen Schmelkin.

Felix Camilo Ayala, *Flight from Egypt*, 2000, painted on board, 11″ x 8.5″. Collection of the author.

Felix Camilo Ayala holding a recent painting, 2002. Collection of the artist.

2 • Early Years and the Quest for Markets

THE HISTORY OF OAPAN shows a growing role for the market means of producing wealth. This chapter presents the origins of the relevant markets and explains how the artists started in a family setting and then stepped into broader commercial transactions. We will see that the broader community, including the artists, has grown richer. At the end of the chapter, we will see how the artists have had to struggle with forces of predation, usually in the form of the corrupt Mexican police.

Numerous writers suggest that markets and globalization do not much improve the lot of the poor, especially in the developing world. June C. Nash (2001, 9) summarizes a common view: "Even with recovery in the early 1990s, the sectoral imbalances in Latin America remained, with the 33 percent below the poverty line in 1980 rising to 39 percent in 1985 and hovering at the same proportion in the early 1990s. . . . The postrecovery trends show: 1) a rise in unemployment, 2) a decline in social welfare . . . 3) persistence of unemployment, 4) the worldwide drop in real wages." Nash writes also of Mexicans looking for an alternative to "being subsumed in global capitalist circuits as 'people without faces and without voices' " (1).[1]

The history of Oapan, however, suggests an alternative vision more favorable to markets and globalization. Over the last thirty-five years, Oapan has been brought successively into the orbit of the Mexican economy and, to some extent, the world economy. At the same time, the microdata of material culture show a booming economy, neither an immiseration nor a slow process of trickle down. A comparison of the lives described in this chapter and of those same lives as described in chapter 4 ("The Lives Today") shows ongoing and rapid improvements in just about every sphere of life. The areas of progress include trans-portation, medicine, entertainment, electricity, ease of obtaining water, clothing, food choice and storage, ability to travel, and literacy. Most of all, starvation is no longer a regular worry, unlike forty years ago. However impoverished modern Oapan may appear to the North American observer, it was formerly far, far poorer. We shall see that global markets helped this culture to obtain a recognized voice, rather than taking it away from them.

Oapan is only a single example, and it does not prove any conclu-sions about all of Latin America or Mexico. Nonetheless, it shows how globalization can serve as a force for the better, in both material and cultural terms. It is a model for how growing trade relations can benefit a poor and indigenous village.

The overall region has been poor for a long time. Guerrero has been one of the last states of Mexico to develop. A survey from the 1950s examined all thirty-two Mexican states and found that Guer-rero ranked twenty-ninth in terms of industrialization, twenty-fifth in terms of productivity, twenty-seventh in electricity capacity, thir-tieth in kilometers of railroad, thirtieth in terms of teachers per capita, thirty-first in terms of minimum wage, thirtieth in terms of cars per capita, and first in terms of the percentage of the population occupied in agriculture. Oapan, in turn, is in one of the poorer parts of Guerrero.[2]

The able male villagers in Oapan, whether artisans or not, for many generations spent a good portion of their lives working the land. They grow corn, beans, pumpkins, chiles, watermelons, canteloupes, sesame, green beans, squash, herbs, and onions. Agriculture is primarily for family subsistence and for small-scale trade within the immediate area, rather than for sale to an outside market. Especially in earlier times, Oapan residents identified themselves first and foremost as growers of corn. The agriculture is not mechanized, and the fields are plowed by human labor, assisted by burro and formerly by oxen. The *coa*, a dig-ging stick originating in pre-Hispanic times, remains common. Nonetheless, the influence of cross-cultural contact is to be seen every-where. The Spanish brought the plow, numerous domesticated animals, the steel knife, and the potter's wheel and kiln, all of which became central to village life.[3]

The food staples of Oapan—grown in or near the village—are tortillas, beans, tamales, and chiles. Tortillas, made by hand every day by the female members of the family, are the base for meals of chicken, fish, and eggs. The chickens come from households, the fish from the river. Beef is rare, and although the villagers own pigs (which roam the streets), they usually sell the meat rather than eating it—with special occasions, such as weddings, being an exception. Many of the best foods are made only for the fiestas; the moles, complex combinations of chiles and seeds, can take up to two days to make. In the fall, grasshoppers—considered a delicacy—are gathered by the children in the fields and toasted or fried at home.[4]

The weather drives a yearly cycle of activities. The fields must be cleared in the winter and spring for the subsequent growing season. The rainy season runs from June through September, during which time families work intensely in the fields, planting crops for the subsequent harvest. The entire area turns green at this time, but by October or November it is dry once again. The crops are gathered in the November harvest. The heat is oppressive year-round but peaks in the spring, before the rains come. Anthropologist Peggy Golde described the heat as "unbearable" and the worst thing about living in the region.[5]

Oapan residents have always faced a continual struggle against the elements, especially lack of adequate rain. The rain is needed to ripen the maize and support the other crops. Without enough rain—of the right timing—the soil becomes too hard to plow easily or the maize plants do not receive enough water to grow. Worry about rain and talk about rain are common in the summer season. Poor regions tend to have very high levels of risk, as they have small buffers of wealth and few opportunities to diversify their investments. Oapan, especially in its early years, has been no exception to this principle.

Until recently the Alto Balsas communities have not been integrated into the broader Mexican economy. Oapan retained a strong indigenous feel and a unique identity. The area fell under nominal Spanish rule in 1521, but it avoided the forced resettlements that the Spaniards undertook throughout the Americas in the sixteenth and seventeenth centuries.[6]

The Oapan of the mid-twentieth century was a world unto itself. In colonial times, depopulation from disease, along with the growth of the hacienda system, encouraged regional isolation in Mexico. Traveling porters, the primary source of mobility in preconquest times, lost their economic importance. The trade and regulatory policies of the colonial state encouraged local self-sufficiency, rather than integration. Mexico thus evolved into a land of isolated regions, often more cut off from each other than they had been before the Spanish conquest. This system benefited small numbers of privileged elites, but it was disastrous for the Mexican population as a whole, largely because market relations were so stunted.[7]

Oapan lies about one hundred miles from Mexico City, but the journey to the village has never been easy (see the accompanying map). The distance to Oapan from Xalitla (a village on the main paved road connecting Mexico City to Acapulco) is only twenty-five kilometers, but making this part of the trip still takes several hours, because most of the road is unpaved, narrow, rocky, and on steep inclines. In the rainy season, the road is sometimes passable only with four-wheel drive. Before this dirt road was opened in 1980, passage was made most commonly by burro, taking six hours or more. Before 1958, no paved highway connected Acapulco and Mexico City, and it was difficult to get close to the area at all.[8]

In the 1950s and 1960s, Oapan had no cars, no electricity, and no modern conveniences. Most families barely had enough to eat, and few fathers could afford to buy a complete set of clothes for all of their children. No one in Oapan spoke Spanish fluently, and many people did not command the elementary rudiments of Spanish. The villagers also had no sense of Nahuatl as a written language, despite its common use in colonial documents.

Sickness and disease were common then. Many young children died from snake and scorpion bites. Given the lack of motorized transportation, it was much harder to visit doctors in Iguala (now a three- or four-hour car or bus trip), so such ailments usually went untreated. Forty years ago, typhoid and cholera were severe problems, claiming the lives of many people, especially children. Meningitis was common as well. Frequent malnutrition, combined with lack of medical care, made the children more susceptible to sicknesses of all kinds. Diarrhea was often fatal.[9]

Anthropologist Peggy Golde, who visited the region in 1959, esti-

Map of Major Places

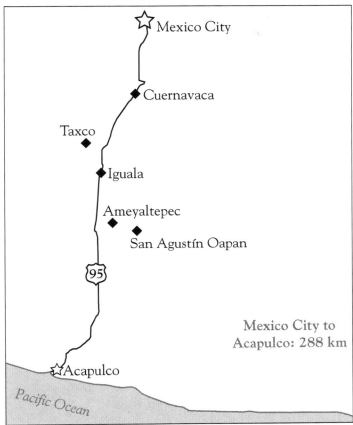

mates that at least half of the men were alcoholics at that time. Villagers made and drank their own mescal, a potent alcoholic drink, using the leaves from the local agave trees (magueys).

In these days, Oapan was tightly knit, but its people were hardly cooperative in every regard. The villagers, by their nature, were suspicious of the outside world and, most of all, of each other. Anthropologist Peggy Golde, who lived in the area (in Ameyaltepec) in 1959, saw the frustrating side of the culture. She refers to "the people's underlying lack of trust and their preparedness to believe the worst, to expect disappointment and loss." She went to study the pottery of the region but continually met the suspicion that she was out to steal the people's pottery-making secrets and make a fortune. Some people thought that she had to come to town to identify the richer residents and thus pave the way for robbers. She felt she was never trusted, and the more she did to help, the worse the problem became. Even after she felt accepted by the community, all relationships were like business relationships. When she did receive help, it was only on the basis of trade or with the expectation of direct reciprocity. Her only encouragement was to find that the villagers experienced these same behavior patterns among themselves. She describes the villagers as selfish and taking no care to disguise their envies.[10] In the language of Robert Putnam (2001), the communities of the region had low levels of social capital.

The Camilo Ayala Family

In the environment of mid-twentieth-century Oapan, the Camilo Ayala family gave birth to eight children, seven of whom survived.[11] The mother, Maria Ayala Ramirez, was a talented ceramics maker in her younger years. The father, Cefarino Camilo, farmed, worked with wood, made furniture, and drank heavily. The father died in the early 1980s, falling on his head in the midst of a drunken brawl, but the mother remains alive in her eighties (note that in Oapan, the older a person is, the less reliable their age estimate is).

Childhood life in Oapan then involved few toys and little in the way of sports. Basketball and soccer had not yet come to the community (the center of town now has a basketball court, and there are several spaces for soccer fields). Juan Camilo recalls playing a great deal of marbles as a boy. Felix Camilo recounts that they had little more than simple balls and wooden sticks to play with. Other forms of recreation included chasing after butterflies, walking around town, playing with the animals, and swimming in the river.[12]

The Camilo children had a regular circle of friends. Their cousins Inocencio and Felix Jimenez, two other painters in this story, lived no more than several houses away, in the Oapan barrio of San Miguel. The family of Roberto and Abraham Mauricio was on the other side of town but still no more than a few minutes walk. All the young boys played together in the river and in the streets of Oapan at a very early age. Marcial cannot recall a time when he did not know these boyhood friends.

The boys nonetheless spent more time at work than at play. Juan Camilo notes that his memories of cutting sugarcane and carrying water from the river go back as far as his memories of playing. The brothers helped the family with chores around the house and in the fields and with gathering food. When the brothers reached their early teen years, they would go out and hunt deer by bow and arrow, returning what they caught to their father.

The Camilo brothers had little formal schooling. Felix Camilo, for instance, recalls going to school from the ages of six to twelve; he says the school did not take older students. Marcial went for four years, learning only some elementary arithmetic, how to write his name, and some very basic Spanish. To this day, the villagers do not make formal education a priority; there is not always a teacher in the school, and the teachers who are there are not very able.[13]

Bill Negron, a photographer who visited the village in 1977, described the village as "heartbreakingly spare." He recalls seeing a single light bulb in the Zócalo, a single Coca-Cola sign, and otherwise little else besides the homes and animals. Of course, the village had been even sparer during the painters' childhood. Negron met the painters and described them as "stoic but gentle and lovely guys."

How Did Amate Paper Come to Oapan?

The Camilo brothers were part of a broader spread of amate painting around the Alto Balsas area. But to see how amate painting came to Oapan, we must step back in time and look at the history of amate paper. Amate provides a classic case of how global trade can resuscitate a much older technology and put it to new uses.

The term *amate* comes from the Nahuatl word *a:matl*, which means both "paper" and "fig tree." Amate paper is now made from a variety of trees from the mulberry family. A machete is used to rip the bark from the tree. The bark is soaked and boiled in a large pot until the fibers can be separated easily. The fibers are then rinsed, pounded with a stone into the shape of paper sheets, and left in the sun to dry until they reach a paper form.[14]

Trade routes have driven the changing fortunes of amate paper. Amate played its largest role in the bureaucratic empires of central

Mexico, especially the Aztec Triple Alliance. It was widely used for decorations, banners, ritualistic ornaments, costumes, awnings, flowers, bags, fans, flags, costume parts, crowns, stoles, hats, imitation hair, vestments, dresses, and bracelets. The Aztec Empire also used amate to make books, now called codices, which contained the basic knowledge of pre-Hispanic Nahuatl civilization. The largest amate library is believed to have been in Texcoco in the Valley of Mexico and contained thousands of manuscripts. These books also served as artworks, as the Nahuas of that time used a pictographic-logographic script and drew no clear distinction between writing and painting. Amate was a centerpiece of bureaucratic administration in one of the world's largest empires. In the time of Montezuma, at least forty-two different locales produced amate, and at least two of these towns were making up to half a million sheets of amate a year. Amate was a central medium for tax payments and trade.[15]

The Spanish conquest brought European paper to the New World. European paper was easier to make and easier to write on than amate paper. Furthermore, the colonial authorities, who controlled the production of documents, were inclined to use regular paper. More generally, the Spanish conquest wiped out most of the indigenous population, largely through disease. By the middle of the twentieth century, the art of making amate paper had been lost almost entirely. Only a few places, most prominently the small village of San Pablito Pahuatlán in the state of Puebla, still made amate. The San Pablito villagers, part of the Otomí people, had preserved amate production for divination and ritual. By the 1930s, however, only several families were continuing to make the paper, mostly to supply local shamans. Even that demand was not fully secure, as many of the Otomí were turning to industrially made paper for their ceremonies.[16]

The growth of tourism revived Otomí paper production. Transportation improvements also brought the Otomí into broader trade networks, and their amate paper found favor in various craft markets. Still, amate production remained on a very small scale.[17]

This story of native crafts now brings us back to the Oapan region but not yet to amate. Prior to the 1960s, pottery was the central medium for pictorial creativity in Oapan and in the neighboring village of Ameyaltepec. Almost every household, including the Camilo brothers' home, had a matriarch who made pottery, both for household use and for outside sale. Most households still have large water vases made by a grandmother or by some other elder family member, usually female. When the tourist boom came to Mexico, Oapan and Ameyaltepec residents realized that they had a marketable asset in the form of their pottery. Pottery production spread rapidly. Women still made the pieces, but men took a greater role in painting and marketing them. This was the primary means for participating in a broader market nexus in Mexico.[18]

While pottery production was profitable, the marketing and transport of the pots remained difficult. Typically, the pots were transported by burro and then by truck to such tourist centers as Taxco, Cuernavaca, and Acapulco. The rate of breakage was very high, given the poor quality of the roads, the length of the trips, and the difficulty of carrying pottery by burro for any length of time.

In essence, amate painting arose to solve the problems of pottery transport. Amates are light and are easily piled or rolled. Glaeser and Kohlhase (2003) have identified falling transportation costs as a central feature of economic growth; the rediscovery of amate paper is one example of this much broader phenomenon.

Max Kerlow and Felipe Ehrenberg of Mexico City, both Mexicans of Eastern European descent, first hit on the amate idea. Kerlow ran a crafts shop in Mexico City (Centro de Arte y Artesanía) and frequently purchased pottery from the Alto Balsas area. He knew the problems with transporting pottery and was looking for another medium to market to his customers. Kerlow and Ehrenberg disagree bitterly as to who deserves the credit, but by 1962 they had three teenage Ameyaltepec pottery artisans—Pablo de Jesús, Pedro de Jesús, and Cristino Flores Medina—painting on amate paper.[19]

Kerlow and Ehrenberg had more contact with Ameyaltepec artisans than with those of Oapan. The former were actively selling their pottery in the Bazar Sábado (Saturday Bazaar), the leading high-quality Mexican crafts market for tourists, located in San Ángel, right next to where Kerlow had his folk art shop. The very origins of amate art reveal the persistent differences between Ameyaltepec and Oapan. Ameyaltepec is closer to the main highway, which makes the Ameyaltepec artisans more mobile and helps make Ameyaltepec a richer community. This kind of economic geography has shaped amate painting from the beginning.

Kerlow was a successful dealer and attracted a high quality of buyer to the amate artists. In addition to the favorable location of his shop, Kerlow was a well-known movie actor. He starred or played in dozens of Mexican movies (his best-known Mexican role was in *Si no te vuelva a ver* (If I Don't See You Again), which won the Mexican equivalent of an Oscar; American viewers might be familiar with his role as Trotsky in *Frida*). Kerlow's clientele thus tended to have cultural stature and a good eye for art. He was also fluent in English, which helped attract North American customers. One of the earliest of his buyers was Mary Price (sister of the movie actor Vincent Price), who assembled a large collection of early amate by buying from Kerlow. Kerlow also had the connections to arrange for some amate exhibitions in Mexico City.[20] In other words, his success in popular culture gave him the connections to promote this new indigenous art form.

The very first Oapan painters borrowed the idea of amate painting from the Ameyaltepec artisans. One early amate painter reports being encouraged by the San Pablito merchants who were selling amate paper. At first, amate paper had been obtained through middlemen, but soon the San Pablito papermakers were traveling to the Alto Balsas region to sell the paper to the painters. The San Pablito merchants had had success selling their paper to the Ameyaltepec painters and thought Oapan would be a lucrative market as well. They brought the paper around and explained to the Oapan residents how they could transfer pottery motifs to it. Felipe Ehrenberg describes the jump of amate painting to Oapan as "practically automatic." Soon, almost everyone in Oapan was trying the art.[21]

Since those origins, amate painting has been clustered tightly by geography. Amate painting spread from Ameyaltepec, but not very far. The villages featuring amate painting are Maxela, Xalitla, Ahue-huepan, Ahuelicán, Ameyaltepec, San Agustín Oapan, San Juan Tetelcingo, Tlamamacan, Analco, and Tula del Rio—all linked to the Alto Balsas Nahua community. Virtually all of the high-quality amates come from four locales: San Agustín Oapan, Ameyaltepec, Xalitla, and Maxela. Once we get past the four main villages, the other Alto Balsas producers of amate paintings focus on generic amate painting for the tourist trade, rather than amate painting as a creative art.[22]

In part, amate painting is geographically clustered so tightly because of how it is taught, through families and social networks. Most amate painters learned the craft through family, relatives, or immediate members of their social network, rather than from outsiders. Families and kinship networks—the fundamental economic, political, and artistic units of the pueblos—served to transmit amate painting among the best Oapan painters. This is partly why the very best amate painters come from such narrow circles, both geographically and socially. Amate painting illustrates the theme of "collaborative circles," small groups of talented individuals who are simultaneously cooperators and competitors.[23]

Many individuals in Oapan and the other amate pueblos decided to pursue their fortunes as painters. No other comparable means of sustenance was available, so in the 1960s and the early 1970s, the return to painting amate, relative to alternative endeavors, reached a peak. The development of the Oapan group is best understood in this context. Labor was plentiful in supply; an effective training network existed, based in families and pottery work; and amate painting was the best available means of earning extra money. Amate art blossomed in the pueblos and has been riding off this initial momentum for nearly forty years. A wide variety of economists, from Alfred Marshall to Paul Krugman, have written about the "learning externalities" that occur when groups of talented individuals share the same space; amate painting—like Silicon Valley, but on a much smaller scale—illustrates this phenomenon.[24]

These origins help explain why the best amate painters are so tightly clustered by age. Around the year 2003, a remarkable percentage of them were between the ages of forty-seven and fifty-seven years old. Some of the older top-rate amate painters who are now dead (e.g., Francisco García Simona and Pablo de Jesús) would be about sixty years old if they were still alive.[25] Arguably the youngest amate painter of renown is Nicolás de Jesús (son of Pablo, the first amate painter), who was forty-two years old in 2003. It is hard to find any notable talent younger than forty years of age, though there are dozens of good painters between the ages of forty and fifty-five.

The ages of these painters make sense if we consider that amate painting started in the early 1960s. If an amate painter is currently fifty, he or she would have been ten or so in the early 1960s. Since the most effective amate training starts at young ages, these individuals were coming of age at just the right time. Interest in amate painting was taking off, and outside markets were opening up.

At the same time, the villages remained immersed in traditional culture, which provided a rich source of themes and inspirations. Unlike today, the fiestas were replete with elaborate ritualistic dances and high-quality wooden and leather masks. Missionaries had yet to make inroads into the native folk religions. The pueblo was a close-knit group, and pueblo culture was the dominant—indeed, virtually the only—influence over Alto Balsas residents. Alto Balsas painters had a unique perspective on the world, which they translated to their amates.

In other words, early amate painting benefited from a favorable mix of trade and isolation. Trade gave artists the necessary raw materials, the idea of amate painting, and a set of wealthier customers. Isolation gave them a unique artistic perspective and a set of aesthetic inspirations to draw upon.

Amate painting came along when Oapan appeared to be in decline. The economic profile of Oapan was already changing by the 1940s—not obviously for the better. New taxes from the 1930s and newer roads lowered the profitability of Oapan porters in the salt trade. For a while, the village was left without a major source of livelihood, and its future looked grim. The reach of Spanish-speaking culture was growing rapidly, and many Mexican villages were being overwhelmed or abandoned. Census data show that the Oapan population was declining throughout the first part of the twentieth century. The population in 1895 was 1,644, which fell to 1,043 by 1930 and 898 by 1940. Amate painting, however, allowed villagers to make a living in their native setting and to express their love for their pueblo and culture. Village population has been growing since the painting of amates began.[26]

Amate in the Camilo Ayala Family

The environment and the core economy of Oapan led the Camilo brothers to art and to painting. Marcial and Juan can recall painting pots before they were ten years old. They learned their painting skills in part from their mother. Felix Camilo started painting pottery later, at fifteen years of age. The making of the ceramics, however, remained in the hands of the women, as it does to this day.

Juan, being the eldest, was the first of the group to paint amates, but

Marcial followed shortly thereafter. Both started in their early to middle teen years, though neither remembers the exact age. In amate, as in pottery, Felix Camilo started later than did his older brothers. Felix was not painting amates until he was eighteen or nineteen years old. Even then, he was painting birds and flowers when his brothers were painting more complex scenes called *historias* (explained shortly).

All the painters in the group report that their parents gave them strong encouragement, if only for financial reasons. The mother of Marcial, Juan, and Felix was extremely pleased when the boys started painting amates. She saw it, first and foremost, as a good way to bring money into the family. She also enjoyed the art itself and could see that her sons enjoyed it as well.

The fourth Camilo brother, Fausto, has never painted amates for a living, but he did try his hand at the craft for a while. He was the black sheep of the family from almost the beginning and never was much attracted to the artistic activities of the others. His mother still describes him as excessively rebellious. In addition to working in the fields, he works with wood, making chairs and furniture, as did his father much earlier.

Three sisters of the family have painted amates. Carmen Camilo Ayala is younger than Felix, the youngest of the painting brothers. She painted amates for many years, with her tutelage coming mainly from Felix, whose style she has to a large extent adopted. She claims that her status as a woman provided no obstacles to becoming an amate painter; during the height of her amate painting career, she painted about fifty amates a year, though none of extremely large size or ambition. Several years ago, however, she gave up painting amates and moved into the more profitable line of pottery production. A second sister, Francisca, the very youngest of the group, also paints amates and pottery, which she sells in the market of Morelia in central Mexico.[27]

An older sister, Amalia, never painted amates, but she painted pottery from the age of twenty-five. She reports learning much from her brothers but claims she never had the materials—paper and paints—to set out on her own as an amate painter. She is respected for the high quality of her pottery, especially her sculpted musicians. The shapes show real motion, and the painting has subtle hues in contrast to the garish colors of most current Oapan ceramics painters.

Painting "Stories"

The first amates of Juan and Marcial were paintings of birds and flowers, a genre from the early days of amate. These pieces took their visual themes from the pottery of the region, which in turn drew on pre-Hispanic styles and motifs. Oapan, of all the Rio Balsas pueblos, has had the longest and closest experience with pottery production. Oapan ceramics, with their relatively simple scenes of animals (deer, rabbits, foxes), birds (eagles, hawks, owls, hummingbirds), and flowers, have a feel that is wispy, charming, and childlike. Juan and Marcial lifted this aesthetic directly into their early amate works.

Marcial was the first Oapan resident to make the breakthrough to painting larger and more ambitious works. He first started painting "stories" (*historias* in Spanish, or *tla:katsintsi:ntih*, which is Nahuatl for "little humans") in his later teen years (Marcial estimates he was eighteen). He was in Acapulco selling the pottery of his mother when he saw numerous high-quality amates from nearby Ameyaltepec. A week later, he attended an amate "tournament" in Mexico City. Both times, the work of Francisco García Simona impressed him the most, virtually entrancing him. García, one of the most renowned amate painters from Ameyaltepec, was one of the first artisans to portray complex pictorial scenes, usually building up combinations of the simpler elements from the earliest amates into grander and more complicated schemes.

The distinctive Ameyaltepec *historia* style fills the paper with detail and stacks various layers of village activity vertically, in the form of bands. One band might show agricultural work, another band might show a wedding, another band might show swimming and fishing in the river, and so on. The bands run unevenly and perhaps fall into each other. Rows of corn sometimes separate the distinct planes within an amate. The sky is sometimes nothing more than a narrow band running along the top of the picture, and the distinction between the horizon and the earth is often not clear. The sky tends to be filled with the sun, moon, and stars all at once—and perhaps with comets as well. Individual figures tend to be less prominent, and colors tend to be spontaneous, almost shocking. Harvests, fieldwork, hunting scenes, weddings, and festival offerings are among the most common themes. The viewer senses from the works that the Ameyaltepec painters live in a crowded, medieval-style town, built into the side of a mountain.

Marcial immediately imagined how he could tell similar "stories" about Oapan. He reports being piqued when he saw that one of García Simona's amates portrayed his beloved Oapan, even though the artist was from the very different Ameyaltepec. Marcial thought he should be the one painting the *historias* of Oapan. Most of all, Marcial recollects having become very bored with painting birds and flowers, noting that sometimes he was painting the same object the same way a thousand times in a row. Marcial later owned a poster portraying a black-and-white amate by García Simona, and he referred to this image for subsequent inspiration.[28]

The role of this poster and the Taxco exhibit illustrate the complexity of cross-cultural exchange and the many kinds of interdependence that are possible. We did not observe the larger Mexican culture wiping out the smaller Nahua culture of Oapan. Instead, we saw that the commerce of the city and the intervention of advanced printing technology helped tie together the artistic traditions of two very close Nahua villages.

Marcial and the other group members drew on the styles of other Ameyaltepec artists in addition to Francisco García. The earliest works of Pablo de Jesús, the very first amate painter, were highly conceptual, with an emotional flavor bordering on the manic. Some portrayed murder, the hunting of animals, and general scenes of chaos. Cristino Flores Medina and others commonly painted just a few central figures, rather than a whole crowd scene. Marcial also recalls having been influenced by Alfonso Lorenzo (who later painted amates using oils, in a pointillist style), Eusebio Díaz (who painted complex scenes of the apocalypse, suffused with millenarian fervor), and Gabriel de la Cruz (who painted field scenes), all from Ameyaltepec.

Marcial's *historias*, however, did not fit the traditional Ameyaltepec model. He drew on Ameyaltepec inspirations while adding more ethnographic detail, a greater concern with fiestas, and a sweeter, more mystical, dreamier mood. He developed a distinct Oapan style of amate, frequently portraying fiestas, masks, Holy Week ceremonies, and other ethnographic themes. In Ameyaltepec, in contrast, fiestas were (and remain) less spectacular, less frequent, and less central to village life. The emphasis on ethnographic themes was in part Marcial portraying what he knew. But it was also a conscious decision to record and commemorate a culture that was changing and vanishing rapidly.

Each painter reports and rues that traditional dances and masks have been disappearing since their childhood.

Typically, there are only a few figures in Marcial's early *historias*, unlike the dozens of smaller figures that might be found in some of the Ameyaltepec *historias*. In Marcial's amates, lines tend to be sharply drawn, planes are angular, and perspective is distorted, with everything appearing excessively flat. The work is detailed, though not to an extreme, as might be found in an Ameyaltepec amate. Colors tend to be sharp yet earthy.

The Rio Balsas provided an especially important theme for Marcial and the other Oapan painters. The river, with a span ranging from ten to fifty meters, plays a central role in the life of the pueblo. In the dry season, the river can be quite shallow; in flood times (typically summer), it can be strong and dangerous. The river also fertilizes and replenishes nearby growing grounds.[29] Villagers go to the river to play and to bathe or simply because other people are there. The Rio Balsas serves as a center for socializing. These river meetings become forums for discussion, gossip, politics, and constructing social alliances. Marcial and the others painted many different aspects of life in or along the river.

Landscapes with figures were another prominent motif and remain so to this day. Early amates of the Oapan group showed people working in the fields, cutting sugarcane, planting or cleaning corn, gathering the harvest, or walking in canyons.

But these portraits were never fully realistic. Instead, they were deliberate works of the imagination, fantasies, an idealized representation of how the world might be or a vision of a hidden paradise. Compared to the reality, the work appeared less hard, the landscape appeared less dry, and the canyons appeared less desolate. Group members frequently use the metaphor of their dreams when describing their work.

Marcial recalls receiving frequent criticism from other pueblo members for painting his *historias*. They told him he was painting "things from another world" [*cosas del otro mundo*] instead of painting reality. At times, they would cut him off and walk in front of his steps on purpose or tell him that his work was no good.[30]

Marcial's amates also reflected Nahua cosmology more explicitly than did the works from Ameyaltepec. Louise M. Burkhart (1988, 48), in her study of sixteenth-century Nahua thought, wrote: "An essential feature of the Nahua cosmos was its animate character. Mountains, bodies of water, the wind, the moon, stars, sun, and heavens, as well as the earth itself, were animate beings. . . . The Nahuas did not set humanity off from the rest of nature like Christianity does. Human beings were a part of the world; the world was not something to be rejected or striven against." Roughly five hundred years later, Marcial reflected such a vision in his amates.

Religious and quasi-religious ceremonies have provided rich material for the amate painters. Oapan residents usually profess an allegiance to Catholicism, but Catholic doctrine has been superimposed on traditional beliefs with strong animist components. The villagers multiply the saints into a complex pantheon of deities and do not place those saints beneath Jesus or the traditional Christian God. In effect, the villagers treat Jesus Christ as simply another saint. Village lore still suggests that the saints can influence and foretell the amount of rain that will come. Villagers therefore court the saints with processions, music, and flowers, especially during the times of fiestas, which is when the people are most worried about the rain.[31]

The year remains crowded with fiestas and sacrificial offerings, few of which are predominantly Catholic. The fiestas in particular provide the closest equivalent to a village religion. As is common in much of the Latin world, Easter (Semana Santa) is the most important holiday and the most important fiesta. The villagers stage a multiday Passion play (representing the death and resurrection of Christ), dating from the Spanish Passion plays of the seventeenth century. The bad guys, such as Judas and the murderers of Christ, are played by live village "actors," whereas Jesus and Mary are inanimate statues (*santos*). These Easter plays provide the major source of what the villagers know about Christianity.

Many villagers also believe in *nahuales*, creatures roughly analogous to "were-animals," or people who temporarily take on animal spirits. These spirits of metamorphosis may be good, bad, or comic. They include foxes, bats, rabbits, cats, burros, jaguars, owls, and lizards. Other *nahuales* take the form of animated dolls. The notion of *nahuales* dates at least as far back as the Aztec Empire, where it served as a central religious concept. Most villagers will profess a belief in *nahuales*, though they will admit they have never seen them. The concept has long been common in Oapan amates.[32]

The Spread of Historia *Painting in Oapan*

Marcial's interest in painting more advanced amates spread quickly. Brother Juan and cousin Inocencio were the first to copy Marcial. Felix Jimenez and the Mauricio brothers followed shortly thereafter, with Felix Camilo coming later. Juan, in addition to being influenced by Marcial, came into direct contact with Francisco García Simona. Juan met Francisco when the two were selling amates in Cuernavaca. Juan saw Francisco's complex *historias* firsthand—including his black-and-white works—and loved the new style as did Marcial. His own works quickly became more complex, and he moved beyond the early simple styles, just as Marcial had. Marcial's influence and strong personality helped develop a cadre of *historia* painters in Oapan, drawn largely from Marcial's friends and relatives. Again, we see talented individuals surrounding themselves with a circle of able collaborators and allies.

The painters Inocencio and Felix Jimenez also came from a traditional Oapan family. Seven of the family's children survived, all boys, another of whom (Marcelino) paints pottery. The family members' early biographies are typical of the region. The father worked in the fields, especially cutting and carrying sugarcane, and the mother painted pottery, in addition to her household duties. Many of the pots were for the local houses, but others were sold in markets in the nearby city of Iguala.

Inocencio started painting amates when he was fifteen years old. He had seen some of the older people in the village painting, took a liking to the task, and was formally introduced to the idea of painting by a friend of the family. The family encouraged him from the start. At first, Inocencio painted on cardboard for practice, but he moved quickly to amates, the standard medium of the time. Like the other painters discussed here, his first amates were of animals and birds. He reports having a great passion for amate painting since the very beginning of his connection with the art.

Inocencio started painting more complex amates *(historias)* through his contact with Marcial. After Marcial started painting *historias*, Inocencio quickly followed his lead. Inocencio, like the other group members, has felt the strong shadow of Marcial. He looks up to Marcial, sees Marcial as a source of authority on virtually all things worldly, and has been much influenced by Marcial in his art.

Felix Jimenez started painting amates a short time after his brother Inocencio did. He started relatively late, at the age of sixteen, moving on to *historias* by the time he was eighteen. For the most part, he was inspired from watching his older brother and, later, through his contact with Marcial. He had little experience painting pottery in his earlier years. This weaker background in pottery and relatively late start in amates may explain why his pictures are often more "painterly" than the works of the others and why he now prefers painting on board to amates.

Roberto Mauricio was born into a family with six surviving children (two sons and four daughters) and recalls his childhood as spent in extreme economic want. He had been painting ceramics since the age of eight and turned to amates by the age of twelve. Roberto first started painting *historias* when he was fifteen years old. He saw the work of Marcial and some posters of *historia* amates in Cuernavaca. Like Marcial, Roberto fell in love with the new style and moved beyond the depictions of birds and flowers that comprised the amates of his youth.

Roberto's older brother, Abraham Mauricio Salazar (forty-eight years old in 2003), also learned to paint *historias*. His career did not follow that of the others, however, as he never painted larger pictures for North American clients. Instead, Abraham Mauricio is best known for illustrating a 1979 Mexican book, *El ciclo magíco de los días*, which features a short amount of text about the customs of Oapan and many reproductions of amates by Abraham. The book, edited by Antonio Saldívar, a bank director (at Banamex) in Cuernavaca, helped expose the educated Mexican public to the amate painters and their locale.

The styles of the group members have diverged over time and continue to do so, but in the early works of all the group members, it is possible to see a consistent Ur-style, rooted in the early *historias* of Marcial. By the very early 1970s, the Camilo brothers, their cousins, and the Mauricio brothers were all painting in this style.[33]

The development of a unique Oapan style was part of a more general development in amate markets. As the amate market grew in the mid-1960s, it became profitable for painters in the differing pueblos to develop new styles. This is a simple illustration of Adam Smith's famous dictum that division of labor is limited by the extent of the market. As the market grew, amate painters from the nearby pueblos, rather than following the early Ameyaltepec model, developed their own signature styles. A quick examination of any quality amate work usually gives away the village of origin, as the viewer can see which style it draws from.

Xalitla painters use a greater amount of open space and emphasize a central figure or scene. In a Xalitla amate, unlike in many Ameyaltepec works, the viewer can easily discern where the ground and the horizon begin and end. Techniques of composition and perspective, while they remain "naive," are more orthodox in Xalitla than elsewhere. In Xalitla pictures, one sees that the painters live in a less crowded town and on flat earth.

Maxela amates are usually long rather than wide. This may reflect the multiple vertical levels of that pueblo, which is built into a steep hill. In contrast with the other amate pueblos, women are the most active painters in Maxela (see chapter 6). In amates from Maxela, the sun is often shown rising or setting behind a mountain, as one might see from the pueblo. Themes tend to be sweeter and are rarely controversial or ambiguous. The colors are softer and use more pastel than would be found in amates of the other pueblos. Weddings, dances, and piñatas are common in the pictures. Flora and fauna are emphasized, and agricultural work is deemphasized, as it plays less of a role in village life in Maxela, even for the men.

Marcial started signing his amates when he was about eighteen years old, essentially once he started painting *historias*. Other group members followed suit. Marcial saw that buyers started asking for amates of particular artists, knowing some of the artists' names, and wanting more from the same person they had bought from previously. Buyers were starting to think of the amates as works of art, not just paper trinkets. By the 1970s, amates were no longer curiosities but, rather, became a well-known genre throughout Mexico, especially in the major tourist centers. Not only were more people buying amates, but regular customers had developed, which encouraged painters to maintain high levels of quality.[34]

As noted earlier, almost all the amate buyers were North Americans or Europeans. The amate painters sold few works to Mexicans. The prices of the *historias* were too high for most Mexicans. Marcial also notes that most Mexicans, especially those with money, thought that his drawings were worth less than European art simply because they came from an indigenous culture. Wealthy Mexicans frequently collect art—arguably more than many other national elites—but their tastes run toward abstract art, Mexican surrealism, modern Latin American art, and European modernism. They do not generally collect Mexican indigenous creations. They generally buy them as decorative folk art, rather than caring about the individual artist.

Mexican society, like many of the other Latin American countries, places a premium on fair skin and European or U.S. cultural habits. Mexican television programs illustrate the maxim that fairer skin means higher status. Mexicans commonly try to cover up or downplay any indigenous roots they might have. Amate paintings, in contrast, remind buyers of the true Mexico—namely, a deeply indigenous and mestizo society only recently emerging from extreme poverty. Not only are the artists and sellers obviously indigenous, but the paintings portray indigenous scenes, such as fieldwork. In contrast to most wealthy Mexicans, many foreign buyers regard amate themes and origins as fascinating or exotic. Amates portray a world that the foreign buyers have never seen, suffered under, or tried to run away from. For these reasons, the amate painters have found much greater acceptance from outsiders.

The going rate for an amate of the *historia* form in the early 1970s was about twenty to forty pesos, roughly between two and four American dollars (the exchange rate was twelve and a half pesos to a dollar until 1976, when it fell by 40 percent overnight). Most of the group members sold at this price. Marcial, however, demanded eighty to one hundred pesos (in the range of six to eight dollars) for his amates. Marcial also refused to bargain or lower his price (he became known for this stubbornness), despite receiving continual advice to bargain with his potential buyers.[35]

The group did not face fully favorable market conditions, as the selling prices for normal street amates had been falling. At the beginning of the 1960s, a good amate might sell for three hundred pesos (about twenty-four dollars at that time); at the end of the 1960s, a comparable amate might sell for only about seventy pesos (five to six dollars). In essence, amate painters flooded the market, causing prices to fall. By the early 1970s, the normal price for a good amate had fallen to about twenty-five pesos, or no more than two dollars. In later times, the good painters earned a living from high-quality amate painting only by cultivating some special niche, such as by developing a network of foreign buyers, which the Oapan group was to do.[36]

In those very early years, the brothers had no trouble justifying the time they spent painting amates. They were teenagers living at home and had not been expected to earn much in the first place. Anything they could bring home was a luxury. Indeed, all the painters in the group brought the money home to their families, to help supply bare essentials for the household. They did not spend it on their own consumption. It was not a question of whether the painters were earning enough to make a living. Now they were earning something rather than nothing at all.[37]

Low prices were not the only problem. Most of all, the group feared the Mexican police. The police demanded bribes, confiscated wares, and generally made life difficult for traveling artisans. They engaged in strategies that economists have described as "rent creation." Many locales require permits from sellers of arts and crafts. In reality, these permits give police a means to extort bribes. A common tactic is for the police to claim that the permit has expired (whether or not it has) and then require an extra payment on the spot. Sometimes the permit will never be made available to the seller in the first place. The especially corrupt police in Acapulco were the reason why the group of painters discussed in this study settled on Cuernavaca as their primary market (there will be more discussion of this locale shortly).[38]

Police problems, while worse in some areas than others, proved to be ubiquitous. Inocencio Chino had one of his first experiences selling amates in Mexico City in one of the town markets when he was a teenager. Inocencio had taken a bus to Mexico City to sell his work, but he had no license to sell in that locale, a common problem for amate painters. He was arrested by a policeman, placed in jail for a few hours, and brought before a judge. The judge pronounced him guilty and then told him not to sell there again. The judge then asked Inocencio how much the amates cost and purchased two from him before letting him go.

Roberto Mauricio, in his early days of amate selling, was hauled before the police in Oaxaca, as they claimed (correctly) that he did not have a permit to sell in Oaxaca State. Roberto made a lengthy speech to the police ("I am not in another country. I am in Mexico. I can sell here . . . to my countrymen . . ."),[39] which he claims required extreme bravery at the time. He then paid the necessary bribe and was released to sell again on the streets.

Felix Jimenez also experienced regular problems with the police, and he offered them periodic bribes to stay in business. He reports receiving five pesos for a bird amate and ten pesos for a *historia* during his earlier years (this translates into about forty and eighty cents, respectively, at that time). Roberto Mauricio concentrated his early selling efforts in Cuernavaca, due to its proximity, population, and wealth. Marcial first tried selling his amates in Acapulco, but police harassment was such a serious problem that he quickly switched to Cuernavaca.

Until recently, Acapulco has remained notorious among amate sellers for its corrupt police. In Acapulco, an amate seller might have to pay off hotel employees, police, inspectors, security guards, and the officials in charge of the beaches.[40] Looking toward more recent times, the greater honesty of the police in Cancún is one reason why sellers are gravitating toward that region.

Markets

The growth in markets allowed Oapan to develop the tradition of the itinerant crafts merchant who paints and sells amates, ceramics, and other craft works. A family will work to build up a sufficient stock of amates and crafts and then will send one family member out to sell the material. The sellers typically stay several weeks outside the pueblo, depending on the time of year and how business is going. They sell in the artisan markets, in the street, on the beach, or wherever buyers can be found. While selling, they live in shared apartments in cheap hotels or boarding houses, where they cook their own food and speak Nahuatl, forming a mini-island of their culture in the larger urban setting. These marketing efforts account for most of the extra income in the village and have driven village growth over the last forty years.[41]

These craft merchants piggybacked on the broader phenomenon of Mexican and North American economic growth. To see who bought amates and supported the painters, let us step back for a minute and look at the general trends in the area.

Throughout the twentieth century, the economy of Oapan and surrounding villages developed closer links with the neighboring urban centers—namely, Iguala, Cuernavaca, Taxco, Acapulco, and, of course, Mexico City. In the twentieth century, Mexico grew at the average rate of about 5 percent a year, extending the reach of large and midsize cities into very remote rural areas.[42]

The Porfirio Diaz regime (1876–1911), which started a long-run trend of improved transportation and infrastructure, drove this growth. In the middle of the nineteenth century, most "roads" were passable only by foot or with beasts of burden, each Mexican state levied its own tariffs, and a traveler could expect to be robbed at least once on any journey of length. All of these conditions were to change. In the early 1870s, Mexican railways were virtually nonexistent, but by 1910 Mexico had over twenty-six thousand miles of railroad track. Transportation improvements allowed regions to trade with each other and made many backwaters into thriving urban centers.[43]

The urban centers of import to Oapan have their economic roots in this era. The first train came to Cuernavaca in 1897, connecting the town to Mexico City. The city grew rapidly, becoming a tourist center, a weekend getaway, and a business and service center for the region. Sugar production in Morelos (the encompassing state) boomed, forming the economic base of the region and allowing Cuernavaca to serve as the major city for the surrounding agricultural communities.[44]

Iguala had not traditionally been the most important city in central Guerrero; Tepecoacuilco had held that role since Aztec times. Nonetheless, in the late nineteenth century, the railroad was built to reach Iguala, causing that city to boom. Migrants streamed into the city, merchant houses were set up, and the town became the service city for the surrounding region, much as Cuernavaca did for Morelos. The economy of Iguala had been based on vegetable oil and soap factories, which were no more than cottage industries, but the railroad enabled the town to grow and diversify.[45]

Taxco, a colonial city in a lovely setting, had been a backwater since its heyday in the seventeenth century. Most of its mines had shut down by the late nineteenth century. Taxco boomed later than did Cuernavaca and Iguala, as it relied on growing tourism in the first part of the twentieth century. In the 1930s, American expatriate William Spratling revitalized its silver crafts and marketed them widely to Americans, often through the medium of department stores. Spratling moved to Taxco in 1929, and by the 1940s, the city was a well-known tourist stop with an American artist colony. Mining was never to regain its former importance there, but the city managed to trade upon its past.[46]

In the early twentieth century, the new road network and the car made it possible to drive from one city to the next. The first car had come to Cuernavaca in 1905. The road linking Taxco to Cuernavaca, which proved essential to the revitalization of Taxco, came in 1931. In 1933 Cuernavaca was connected to Mexico City by federal highway. In 1950 came the Pan-American Highway, linking the United States and Mexico by car; in 1954 another highway linked Nogales, Arizona, to Guadalajara, Mexico's second largest city. Both roads made it much easier for American travelers to reach Mexico or drive around the country.[47]

Acapulco bloomed late. The city became less important after Mexican independence, when large Spanish ships stopped carrying their supplies from Asia to Mexico. After the end of the Second World War, however, the area was revitalized, as the spectacular beaches and mountains drew numerous flights and cruise ships. The Mexican government had built a new airport for the town and promoted it heavily. John Wayne, Errol Flynn, Cary Grant, Rita Hayworth, Frank Sinatra, and Sammy Davis Jr. were among its prominent visitors. Johnny Weissmuller filmed ten Tarzan movies in the immediate area. Elizabeth Taylor had a wedding there, and Jack and Jackie Kennedy took their honeymoon in Acapulco. By 1960, Acapulco was a world-class resort, yet it was cheap enough to attract large numbers of middle-class Americans. Mexico proved to be a convenient neighbor, offering exotic sights close at hand.[48]

In the beginnings of the 1930s, about thirty-three thousand Americans visited Mexico each year. By the 1950s, there were convenient connections by rail, air, and road. The first American commercial flight to Mexico came in 1943, and the routes were opened up to competition in 1957. Greater ease of transport, along with growing prosperity, caused the number of yearly American visitors to rise to about half a million by 1960. By the mid-1970s, this number was close to three million a year. American tourists spent almost two billion dollars a year in Mexico. The Echeverría government (1970–76) took deliberate steps to promote tourism, and by the 1970s, Mexico ranked fourth in the world in terms of gross receipts from tourism, mostly due to visitors from the United States.[49]

Of course, visitors wanted souvenirs and mementos from their trips. Since the 1920s and 1930s, American magazines had been running articles about Mexican folk art, creating the basis for future demand. Dwight Morrow, American ambassador to Mexico, organized a traveling exhibit of Mexican folk art in 1930 (including a stop at the Metropolitan Museum of Art in New York), with the assistance of the Carnegie Corporation. Nelson Rockefeller started collecting Mexican folk art en masse in the 1930s and helped organize a show of Mexican art, including folk art, at the Museum of Modern Art. Spratling's publicity for Taxco has already been noted.[50] All of these developments bore their fruit in the later American tourist boom to Mexico. As Americans flocked to Mexico, the production of masks, woven garments, ceramics, and straw hats rose dramatically. Many of these items might be considered kitschy junk, but in other cases, as with amates, creators used the new market opportunities to make a living with quality work. Rather than destroying Oapan, tourism helped it survive and helped it reach new artistic heights.

The Oapan amate painters sold most of their work in Cuernavaca, largely because of its numerous North American residents and visitors. The sellers sought out North Americans in the streets, in the market, or near the cathedral. Commonly, an amate seller would stand outside restaurants that were popular with foreigners and offer amates to individuals on their way in and out of the door. Marcial recalls carrying fifteen or twenty amates (the work of a month) until all were sold, then going back home to paint more.[51]

When the Oapan painters were to return back home from a sales outing, they would typically be met at Xalitla, the small town on the main road just at the entrance of the high path up to Oapan. Friends or family members came to meet them with burros. Usually, the painters needed help getting back up to the pueblo, since they would be carrying loads and packages. At that time, the village had no phones at all, not even a central village phone (*caseta*). When an individual was to return to the pueblo, he would inform one of the Iguala radio stations of his identity, and the station would announce the coming arrivals to Oapan residents at prespecified times. Individuals in the pueblo would listen to the broadcast and thus know when to meet their compatriots down below with burros. At that time, the entire trip from Cuernavaca back to the pueblo took about ten hours, the last six on burros, often on steep upward inclines.[52]

The Oapan painters (with the exception of Felix Camilo) recall being terrified during their first trips to Cuernavaca. They did not yet know how to speak Spanish, whether they would find a place to sleep, whether they would encounter other pueblo members to help them out, and whether they would have enough money to get back home. A common early fear was that they would be hit by cars, which were largely new to them and appeared to be extremely dangerous.

Nonetheless, the wealth of Cuernavaca made the trip worth the trouble. By the 1970s, Cuernavaca had developed as the most popular residential spot for Americans in Mexico, because of its near perfect climate, lovely flowers and gardens, proximity to Mexico City (about ninety minutes), and good supply of American goods and conveniences. Cuernavaca is relatively rich in medical facilities, movie theaters, and modern shopping malls. By 1970, over 97,000 Americans had retired in Mexico, with Cuernavaca as the leading destination. By 1980, this number had risen to over 150,000 (and by 1990 to 463,000). The American community in Cuernavaca had been long-standing since the early part of the twentieth century, when the railroad made the town accessible. Retirees, however, were driving the new migration. Americans were becoming more adventurous, and longer life spans and greater wealth made retirement a more significant phenomenon. The city first came to the attention of Americans when Dwight Morrow fell in love with the place and spent much of his time there in the 1930s. Once Morrow's daughter married Charles Lindbergh, talk of Cuernavaca spread in the media and in celebrity circles.[53]

As Mexico became wealthier in the postwar era, Cuernavaca became a central destination for Mexican tourists as well. It is estimated that several hundred thousand Mexicans visit the city every weekend, typically from Mexico City. These tourists provided further financial support for the amate revolution.[54]

To sum up, this chapter ends with the painters' lives in parallel. The brothers obtained their first foothold in the marketplace and their first set of clients. All the members of the broader group except for Felix Camilo report having achieved a mature style by this point in time. The Camilo brothers were earning some money from amate painting, though not enough to sustain large families. They were all good friends with the Jimenez and Mauricio brothers, their most important artistic peers in Oapan. The Oapan painters were reaching a critical mass where they taught each other on a regular basis, compared work, and exchanged ideas. Yet they all had little sense of what was to come for themselves or for their community. Oapan was standing on the brink of both greater achievement and cultural dissolution.

3 • *American Discovery*

OUR GROUP OF OAPAN PAINTERS next encountered North American art markets. Rather than selling to tourists, they would sell to art collectors, through the medium of a gallery. The painters, most of all Marcial, acquired a North American patron. Ed Rabkin proved to be a formative influence on the painters' lives. In terms of the theme of liberty versus power, the group suddenly was able to bypass the limitations of the Mexican scene and reach much richer and better-developed markets.

Rabkin's efforts on behalf of the group were heroic. The group, while they remained poor in North American terms, earned a better living than before. They were able to paint on a larger scale and in a variety of media, while enjoying their artistic freedom. Rabkin encouraged them to find their cultural voices rather than simply painting what would sell. The group members had American exhibits, sold works to American museums, became known by American collectors, and were written about in books, catalogs, and magazine articles.

The group was able to leap over many of the constraints they faced in Mexico. They were able to sell more than before, as Rabkin bought large quantities of their work. Dealing with police and facing other local hassles became a much smaller issue in their lives. Rabkin served as the group's protector, even helping them with medical expenses or advising them on how to deal with the outside world. His patronage shows how cross-cultural contact can increase diversity and artistic quality in both the selling country (in this case, Mexico) and the buy-ing country (the United States).

That being said, global art markets did not solve all of the group's problems in the long run. As will be discussed in this chapter, Rabkin could not become wealthy selling the group's pictures, and he could not afford to pay the sums the painters felt they deserved. The artists had their expectations raised, but the long-run reality disappointed them. As each artist broke from Rabkin, he returned to the initial problem of trying to make a living selling in Mexico, without the benefit of international connections. Let us now see how the story of Rabkin and the painters unfolded, with an eye on the benefits of trade.

The Turning Point

In 1972, Marcial, on one of his amate sales trips, encountered Ed Rabkin. Rabkin and his wife, Carolyn, had just moved to Cuernavaca.

Rabkin was born in Montreal but grew up in Coney Island. At the beginning of his career, Rabkin taught emotionally disturbed children and pursued music. He sang in a group called The Tokens with Neil Sedaka and, for a while, was the road manager for The McCoys (who had the hit "Hang on Sloopy"). In 1966, he and a business partner started a Manhattan clothing store that was a leading supplier for many 1960s clothing trends, including unisex styles. The store was sufficiently renowned that it was asked to supply the clothing for the Broadway play *Hair*.

Ed's beautiful wife, Carolyn Mae Lassiter, had been a fashion pho-tography model. African-American by descent, she was one of the first models to successfully cross the "color barrier." She came from a share-cropper family in North Carolina, moved up north, and ended up working as an assistant to a photographer. She and Ed met when he was singing for Columbia Records in 1968 and she did his makeup.

By the early 1970s, the Rabkins were looking for further adventure. They felt that something was missing in American culture. Like many individuals of that time, they sought they own version of "dropping out." Bill Negron, who visited Ed in Cuernavaca, described him as a "flower child" at the time. The Rabkins had sold their clothing bou-tique in New York City and moved to a farm in upstate New York.

Most of all, they wanted new experiences.[1] Upstate New York bored them, and they considered moving abroad. They finally settled on Mexico and Cuernavaca, once they discovered that they could not bring their Great Dane to Afghanistan. They moved to Cuernavaca without any firm plan—simply to see what would happen. The Rabkins were hardly old enough or rich enough to retire (Ed was sixty-five as of 2004), but the American community in Cuernavaca gave them a natural base.[2]

When Rabkin first met Marcial in 1972, he and Carolyn had just arrived in Cuernavaca a few weeks earlier. At the time, Marcial was twenty-one years old. When he ran into Rabkin, Marcial was in the Zócalo (the city center) of Cuernavaca, selling a pile of his amates.

Rabkin was struck by Marcial's charisma, friendly demeanor, and self-confidence. He was impressed that Marcial refused to bargain over price. He ended up buying all of Marcial's amates on that first encounter, but according to Rabkin, it was Marcial's personality that struck him. Rabkin, new to Mexico, was looking to strike up a friendship, and Marcial appeared to be a suitable candidate. At the time, Rabkin had no formal background in the world of art, Mexican folk art, or amate. He realized, however, that Marcial's amates had "more integrity" than the others he had seen around Cuernavaca. Rabkin bought Marcial's entire pile of amates as a gesture of friendship and invited him to visit the house. This kind of openness was new to Marcial.

At the time, Marcial spoke only a little Spanish, and Rabkin spoke even less. Nonetheless, the two struck up a conversation at a very basic level. Marcial told Rabkin a bit about his village and his culture. At the end of the meeting, Rabkin gave Marcial his address with an invitation to return, which Marcial did several months later.[3] The absent-minded Marcial had in fact lost the address that Rabkin gave him. He was walking around Cuernavaca, searching for where he thought he had visited. As a matter of pure chance, Rabkin spotted him while driving in his car.

The relationship between Rabkin and Marcial developed rapidly. Rabkin liked amates but thought Marcial should try painting on board as well. He knew a Mexican painter, Ana Luisa Prida Ramos (discussed further later in this chapter), and he asked her what the next step might be for someone like Marcial. Ana Luisa suggested that board treated with gesso would provide a smooth surface somewhat akin to ceramics. Rabkin then volunteered to provide Marcial with oil and acrylic paints and masonite board if he wished to try more traditional media of painting.

At first, Rabkin asked Marcial to make a simple black-and-white drawing on board, akin to an amate. Afterward, Rabkin asked him to paint something with two colors and then something with three colors. At that point, Marcial simply said, "Now I understand." Rabkin never gave him any more instructions; he simply let Marcial paint as he wished. Suddenly Marcial was pursuing new artistic directions. He showed Rabkin his pictures, and the two talked at length about the direction of Marcial's art.

Rabkin and his wife then invited Marcial to live in their home. It was their basic temperament to pursue things and see where they would lead. Furthermore, unless Marcial had a permanent base in Cuernavaca, the Rabkins would have found it difficult to keep in touch with him, given the difficulties of reaching Oapan. Most of all, they wanted Marcial to have the time to paint and to realize his visions. The Rabkins knew they had discovered something unique, and they stepped into the multiple roles of patrons, supporters, and friends.

Marcial accepted the offer to live with the Rabkins. He is by nature curious, eager to learn, and in search of adventure. He saw this as a chance to pursue his art further, and he had taken a strong liking to the Rabkins. The tradition of traveling merchant and salesman, well established in Oapan, meant that a Cuernavaca residence was already a familiar idea to Marcial. He thought it was possible to live in another locale while maintaining his roots in the village and someday returning there to live. Finally, Marcial knew that if he turned down one lucky break, he could not count on another coming along. However, Marcial had trouble leaving his responsibilities in Oapan. It became possible only when the Rabkins paid for a peon to take Marcial's place in the fields that year.[4]

For the first year, only Marcial was painting in Rabkin's house. These paintings were, at first, for Rabkin's own collection. In addition to supporting him, Rabkin supplied artistic materials, hospitality, inspiration, and stimulating conversations. Marcial recalls that Rabkin explained the difference between artisan work and art and that these discussions were vital to his own ideas about being an artist. The

Rabkins gave Marcial permission to develop his true identity, and they validated the worth of that identity.

In addition to helping Marcial with his art, the Rabkins wanted Marcial to feel as comfortable as possible with the outside world. They also asked Marcial what he would need to be happier, and Marcial mentioned that he missed his younger brother Felix. Shortly thereafter, Marcial brought Felix to the house to paint. Felix had already met Rabkin once briefly in a Cuernavaca restaurant, when he was selling amates to restaurant clientele, as was common practice in Cuernavaca.

Felix came and began to paint, but by a number of accounts, the work was dull and unimaginative. According to Marcial, Felix was very timid at that time. Marcial talked to Felix, and six weeks later, Felix returned with beautiful scenes of village life. Marcial claims he told Felix to paint from the heart and to paint what he feels. Marcial stressed to Felix that there was no contest between the brothers. Recall that Felix had had little prior experience painting *historias*, as most of his amates were still in the simple mode of birds and flowers. Felix Camilo was jumping right into painting with less background than Marcial had. To this day, it is apparent that Felix is a painter on board first and an amate painter second. His amates look like painted pictures on the amate medium, rather than resembling traditional amate styles.[5]

Marcial recommended that Rabkin consider the works of his other friends and family, and Inocencio Jimenez Chino was next to join the group. The artists are fuzzy on the exact chronology of arrivals, but shortly thereafter, a group of six—two groups of brothers and Roberto Mauricio—was painting in Rabkin's house. Rabkin invited each of these individuals, including his spouse (where applicable), to live in Cuernavaca. The artists lived in an adjacent cottage rather than in the house proper.

Marcial notes that when he alone lived with the Rabkins, they ate all kinds of food, which he enjoyed. Once his two brothers arrived, the demand was for food Oapan style, such as rice, beans, tortillas, and chiles.

Like Marcial, the other group members started painting on masonite board. Rabkin's group was the first group of amate artists to experiment systematically with a nonamate medium and stick with it as a preferred means of painting.[6]

Rabkin never intended to be an art dealer, but suddenly he had many pictures. He was not wealthy enough to subsidize the artists indefinitely, so he went into the art business, if only because it seemed like a logical step. He founded Galerie Lara in 1973, named after his daughter, Lara, born in January of that year. The gallery had no separate physical locale but, rather, was part of the complex in Cuernavaca where Rabkin was living with the artists.

Rabkin told the group that he wished to have an exclusive dealing arrangement with them: they were not to sell their paintings to other galleries or other customers without his intermediation. Inocencio and Juan Camilo maintained an independent status, usually by selling amates on the side in Cuernavaca. For the most part, however, Rabkin succeeded in receiving the bulk of the group's output, especially on board.

The group was as much about the fusion of personalities as about art. Rabkin had taken on a set of strong, attractive, and stubborn individuals, and the rest of the story cannot be understood without this context.

Long-time Mexican friend Maria Walsh describes Felix Jimenez as "imaginative and daring." All the group members cite him as the one with the best sense of humor. He has always been organized, alert, and outspoken. He speaks in a serious tone when he is joking and delights in sarcasm. He takes pride in blurting out the truth when no one else will. He has always worn the neatest dress of the group. Today he is the only group member to have a cell phone. Of the group, he has always had the weakest ties to the village, and he has always wished to assimilate into broader Mexican culture.

Inocencio Jimenez Chino is the older and heavier of the two brothers. He is hardworking and known for his many friends. Marcial describes Inocencio as shy and reserved relative to Felix Jimenez. Maria Walsh describes him as more serious and more traditional. Roberto Mauricio says Inocencio is the group member who relaxes the least. But like his brother Felix, Inocencio is pragmatic in temperament.

Roberto Mauricio, who grooms a mustache, is spontaneous, extremely charismatic, and a "sweet talker." He comes across as a dreamer at heart, and his strong personality fits the lay stereotype of an artist. Everyone thinks of him as a "character," and he is much loved by his friends. He says that he only seems crazy but in fact is very respectful of others, a self-description that commands assent from those who know him. He is a left-wing Zapatista, very fond of the Mexican Revolution and Emilio Zapata's willingness to speak up for the Mexican poor. Roberto is likely to see politics in black-and-white terms, as a struggle between good and evil, with himself on the side of good. He will flamboyantly offer opinions and tell lengthy stories at the slightest invitation.

The Rabkins, who had found a group of people and a cause they believed in, took on the dual task of managing these personalities and selling the group's paintings. At the same time, the Rabkins also designed leather goods, including bags, from their house in Cuernavaca, selling their designs to buyers in the United States. The Rabkins thus had their core businesses; life with their daughter, Lara; and life with the Oapan painters, most of all with Marcial and his family. Bill Negron, who visited the house for a week in the mid-1970s, described it as "a wonderful communal situation" and noted that the artists were like "members of the family."

Stylistic Developments

All of the group members praise the artistic freedom that Rabkin granted them. He would sometimes make suggestions as to themes or give them feedback on their output, but he consistently told them to paint their innermost feelings. He also wanted every picture to be different, rather than asking them to repeat the same scene many times. He did not ask them to dumb down their work for the marketplace. In terms of style and quality, Rabkin was close to an ideal patron. He loved the work of the group and wanted to see it develop artistically as much as possible. In essence, by increasing the market for the group's work, he was able to support an increase in its creative diversity.

Marcial's paintings drew on the amate tradition but moved beyond it rapidly. One of his most fully realized early paintings on board was a nocturnal procession. The black background of the night and the radiant sources of light coming from candles and stars would not have been easy to paint on the thinner, amate paper. The varying thicknesses and luminosities of the paint required the sturdier surface of board. Another early painting of Marcial's, dating from 1974, shows villagers knitting and playing together in an outside space. The scene is simple, with animated figures and muted pastel colors distributed into clear and distinct fields. Overall, it is reminiscent of the Cap Haitian school of Haitian pictures. Both of these pictures were much larger than the previous amates of the group.

One commentator described Marcial's style as follows: "Camilo paints in a style art critics call 'primitive' or 'naïve': the colors are bright as Indian calico, the perspective is two-dimensional, often surreal. Camilo paints doll-like portraits, fantastic and minutely detailed landscapes—images of village life as innocent and at the same time as complex as a visual fable."[7]

Marcial explored themes new to the world of amate. In his picture *The Dream*, Marcial placed three dreaming heads at the bottom of the painting and two ethereal spirits on top. The center of the painting, enclosed in an incomplete and irregular oval, showed an idealized version of fieldwork and nearby landscapes. Another picture, a self-portrait, showed Marcial as a proud young man, carrying a stack of amate papers on his back and a small picture he had painted. The background showed a canyon, his house in Oapan, and landscape, while the foreground showed strewn amates and works of pottery, all painted in Oapan style. *What the Sun Sees* portrays a parched and desolate earth, devoid of life. The sun sits in the sky, represented as a small bubble, in which a circle of life still flourishes. Marcial also painted Adam and Eve, Rabkin's daughter with her cat, portraits in a quasi-colonial style, and various surrealistic experiments, some of which verged on the abstract. He remained the conceptual leader of the group.

Felix Jimenez Chino, often considered the second most sophisticated Oapan painter, developed a signature style. Rabkin encouraged him to develop his own ideas, which meant an ability to conceptualize, to delineate character, and to present irony. Felix Jimenez is the only group member who paints the sardonic. When it comes to individual portraiture and capturing emotions within a face, he is arguably the most advanced of the group.

Felix Jimenez experimented just as Marcial did. Selden Rodman (n.d.) wrote of Felix: "[he] is attracted by very complex schema, bringing together segments of his life and dreams enclosed in flowing 'windows.'" These "windows," or paneled pictures, offered multiple perspectives on a single event or character. Felix also painted his dreams, as did Marcial, and injected them with an element of fantasy. His *Aca-pulco Imagined* offers a young man's expectation of what a large city resort might look like. *Lover's Dream* showed the gods offering children to a blissful young couple. *Cabaret* showed the rich dining in a Cuer-navaca restaurant, with the poor coming and begging for alms. One of Felix's best-known paintings, *Cousins*, showed him and Marcial sitting together in a room, playing guitars together.

Each of the artists developed a trademark style. Juan Camilo spe-cialized in landscapes and joyous fiesta scenes. He filled his night skies with sparkling stars. Inocencio is strong with detail and used that tal-ent to portray mystery and depth. He painted large landscapes with a surging Rio Balsas in the center and nighttime scenes filled with urgency or danger. Selden Rodman (1982, 202) noted: "Inocencio's brush drawings in Chinese ink are beautifully adapted to conveying the poetic rhythms of village life. But on occasion Inocencio has painted moonlit landscapes with overtones of violence and magic." Roberto Mauricio painted fiestas, local legends, witches, canyons, and night-time scenes, all with a dreamy feel. As a draftsman he is the only group member who can rival Marcial. He is a natural artist, and his works come across as effortless. Felix Camilo painted flowers, nighttime scenes, self-portraits, and his dreams, among many other themes. He integrated ideas from the others, including Juan's sparkling skies and Felix Jimenez's sense of irony. Usually, his colors were bright and cheerful.

Roberto Mauricio claims that his Catholicism has influenced his painting very much, but in reality the painters relied more heavily on their Nahua religious heritage. When asked for an example of Catholic influence, Roberto cited his numerous amates of the Santa Cruz fiesta, celebrated on the third of May. But this fiesta, which revolves around ensuring a good supply of rain for the summer growing season, does not fit the standard model of a Catholic holiday. Six days before the fiesta begins, designated individuals begin to pray. The day before the fiesta, special dishes are made, including moles and tamales. On May third, the villagers, accompanied by local musicians and dancers, walk up a steep mountain, called Cerro de la Cruz (in Nahuatl, *miswe:weh*, or "big cat"), carrying these food dishes. Upon reaching the top of the mountain, they pray for rain, sometimes to the verge of tears. They also eat the food, and they leave a large turkey in green mole sauce in a ceramic pot as a sacrificial offering. The villagers know that birds (*zopi-lotes* in Nahuatl) will come and eat the offering. The villagers then march back down the mountain, hear the ringing of the church bells, and pray with rosaries. Afterward, those who have climbed the mountain meet in the house of the *fiscál*, the leading church authority of the pueblo, where they eat chicken in red mole sauce and drink until very late at night, while the music continues.[8]

The group members were influenced by the Spanish colonial art they saw in the churches and museums of Cuernavaca. The Diego Rivera mural in the Palacío de Cortés, near the central artisan market of Cuernavaca, made an especially strong impression on all of them. Marcial Camilo and Roberto Mauricio have mentioned Orozco as well as Rivera. The Mexican muralist school gave them a sense of palette, an artistic pride in their indigenous past, a penchant for ambitious works, and ideas of how to portray large historical scenes.

The Palacío exhibited numerous Spanish colonial works as well, which also influenced the painters. Marcial, when he turned to painting on board, produced some portraits very much in the colonial style. Juan Camilo's later pictures of saints owe much to the colonial influence. More generally, Spanish colonial art gave them some sense of the surrealistic and the fantastic.[9]

Politics was not (yet) a theme, but some of the group's pictures developed a notion of the erotic. Both Felix Jimenez and Marcial experimented with the portrayal of androgyny; Felix's favorite painting from his entire career presents Adam and Eve joined together as one creature, a man-woman whose genitals hang beneath him/her. Other panels of the picture contain a dead person, a church scene, a city scene, birds flying, an animal scene, an illustration of the common blood of the races of humankind, a woman making love to the devil, and a more traditional rendition of Adam and Eve.

Marcial's portraits, especially his self-portraits, consistently make the sex of the image ambiguous. His men look like women, and his women look like boys (rather than men), particularly in the facial features. To this day, his self-portraits reflect androgyny, and his features still have a strong feminine boyishness. A Cuernavaca street artist once sketched Marcial's face in the mid-1970s; when I first saw the portrait, I thought it was a picture of a woman.

Splits and Fractures

The artists of the group, especially Marcial, were close with Rabkin, but they complained about prices from almost the beginning. The artists give differing accounts of prices, but they all report the same general range of compensation. First, all were given free materials for painting. In addition, they were paid between 150 and 400 pesos per painting, depending on the size of the picture and its quality, with a typical picture being twenty-four by twenty inches in size. Marcial usually received 500 to 600 pesos, somewhat more than the others. Using the exchange rate in the mid-1970s (before the drastic depreciation of the peso), the compensation ranged from about ten to thirty-five dollars per picture, forty to fifty dollars for Marcial. For purposes of perspective, the daily minimum wage in Mexico ranged in the neighborhood of fifty pesos around 1974. This translates into a little more than four dollars a day, or twenty-eight dollars for a seven-day week.[10]

Rabkin's financial burden was greater than what the painters received, as he incurred many other expenses. He paid transportation, fed them frequently, and often faced emergency expenses, such as when he helped pay the dowry for Marcial's wife, Gloria, or gave the artists money when they were not painting.

Rabkin told the painters that he would help them out if they ever became ill, and this earned him special favor in their eyes. When Felix Camilo needed medical treatments that cost about three thousand pesos, he simply did not have the money. Rabkin stepped in to help, and Felix Camilo was cured. To this day, Rabkin helps Felix with doctor bills, though Felix has not painted for him in a long time.

Roberto Mauricio narrates how Rabkin helped him with his medical bills. When Roberto was about thirty, he suffered from nervous depression for a while and was unable to muster much energy or desire to live. According to Roberto's account, he had severe shakes on a regular basis, his veins hurt him badly, and he was extremely listless after episodes of illness. He stayed in the Rabkin's house and received medical treatments, largely herbal supplements and some acupuncture, again at Rabkin's expense. Roberto recovered within a month's time and still holds this episode as a very fond memory, one of the fondest of his life. Rabkin helped out with an illness of one of Roberto's children as well.

At one point, Felix Jimenez and Inocencio cultivated other American clients in Cuernavaca. In particular, they pursued their relationship with Robert and Maria Walsh, which gave them independent access to North American buyers. Robert was a literature professor at Georgetown; Maria was his Mexican wife. They typically spent July and August of the year in Cuernavaca. In 1973 they met Inocencio while he was selling his amates near the cathedral. They decided they had come across something very special. They bought Inocencio's amates and quickly developed a relationship with Inocencio and his brother Felix (and with Marcial, but to a lesser extent).

Each year, Robert and Maria bought ten to fifteen amates from Inocencio and Felix Jimenez and resold them to their friends in the United States. Typically, such an amate sale would bring about twenty-five dollars, and the couple sent the surplus back to Inocencio and Felix. This allowed them to earn ten times or so per amate than they would have otherwise received. At first, the Walshes bought the amates themselves; later, they relied on intermediaries (first a Señora Guerrero and later Ana Luisa Ramos Prida, who worked with the Rabkins and later dealt in Marcial's art). This way they could receive amates during the course of the year, not just in the summer. Maria Walsh reports that all their friends were delighted with the amates and that she and her husband kept buying and reselling for many years, until they ran out of friends who wanted more amates.[11]

Further outlets failed to develop, however, which sent the group members back to Rabkin. Group members kept on asking for more money, but Rabkin was reluctant to raise their pay by a significant amount. Rabkin never made much money selling the group's works, and he could not run down his capital indefinitely. A quick look at the numbers illustrates the basic predicament. Had there been no disputes, we can imagine each artist painting a picture a week for Rabkin. This would have cost three hundred dollars a week in cash reserves, or about fifteen thousand dollars a year—considering the greater value of money in the 1970s. This sum in no way includes the costs of selling and marketing the work. The Rabkins never turned away or criticized a picture. So they would have had, each year, about fifty pictures by each of the six artists, a difficult quantity to sell even under very favorable circumstances. The Rabkins were generous, but they simply did not have indefinitely deep pockets.

Group members became increasingly frustrated with their situation. As tensions rose, Juan Camilo and Inocencio Chino were the first two to leave the circle. Juan Camilo was unhappy with his pay, but more important, Rabkin was unhappy with the quality of Juan's work. He felt Juan was painting too many generic scenes and repeating the same themes too many times. He also felt Juan was not taking sufficient care with the details. Juan's very early pictures were among the best of the group's works. But he started to paint with increasing speed and decreasing care. His figures became larger, grosser, and less carefully drawn. Repetition replaced the sense of magic. Other group members accused Juan of not having enough patience. Inocencio has criticized Juan's paintings as sloppy, and Felix Jimenez claims that Juan tried to paint "two pictures in a day."[12]

Juan reports that Rabkin never talked with him but, rather, that Marcial simply told Juan one day that Juan would no longer be painting with the group. Juan believes it displeased Rabkin that he was selling his work in other locales. Juan received five hundred pesos from Rabkin as a severance payment and had no further relations with Galerie Lara. Juan still feels very sad about this outcome. He also wonders what role the other group members played in his departure and whether Marcial led a move to oust him.

Inocencio left the house after several months, for strictly pecuniary reasons. He found that Rabkin did not pay him enough to make his time there worthwhile. He went back to working the land in Oapan, while continuing to paint amates in his spare time, as has been the custom since the beginning of amate painting. He also continued to paint pictures for Rabkin, though on a much less regular basis than before. In this regard, his break was less extreme than Juan's. Inocencio tried to sell some of his smaller pictures in Chilpancingo and found that they reaped about four hundred pesos, precisely the amount that Rabkin had been paying him for the much larger landscape pictures. Yet the external market was not always there, and it did not help Inocencio develop much as an artist.

Roberto Mauricio painted about twenty pictures in his first year with Rabkin, working at a consistent pace; Felix Camilo recalls painting as many as forty. These totals declined, however, once the painters became aware they were not going to realize significantly higher prices. Roberto returned to work on the farm and to live in Oapan. He still

painted for Rabkin at times, but he would no longer devote his exclusive energies to the task. Roberto Mauricio estimates that he painted
for Rabkin for about eight years, though the quantity of pictures trailed
off considerably after the first few years. Roberto continued to cultivate
clients for his amate work when he was not painting for Rabkin. He
spent a good deal of time in Cuernavaca, often hanging out in the
Zócalo or in restaurants. He sold works to North Americans whom he
tried to develop into regular clients, with varying degrees of success.
Felix Camilo devoted more of his time to artisan work.

Felix Jimenez stayed with Rabkin for longer than his brother
Inocencio did. In part, Felix liked to paint pictures on board more than
Inocencio did (Inocencio favored amates); in part, Felix wished to stay
away from Oapan. Most important, Felix found it easier to stay in
Rabkin's house because he was still single. Inocencio had married in
1976, but Felix did not marry until the early 1980s. Felix was thus better situated to pursue a career as a full-time painter, at least until his
marriage.

Felix stopped painting for Rabkin almost entirely by 1981. The relationship with Rabkin allowed him to paint in the style of his choice,
but now he needed to support a family. Felix painted only a few pictures for Rabkin after this date, with the very last coming, by his
account, in 1983.

Overall, the group rarely had a good sense of what was happening
with the pictures. Inocencio reports they felt too uninformed to ask
about the price Rabkin was receiving in other markets. They never
knew what kind of American markets Rabkin was cultivating or about
the large collection of their work that the Thompsons were assembling
in Connecticut (these points are discussed further later in this chapter). The group discovered their history in the American market only
recently, when this author told it to them.

Despite the periodic disputes over money, most of the group members have fond memories of their time painting for Rabkin and of their
time in Rabkin's house. Marcial developed the closest connections
with Rabkin and painted the most for him. Marcial ended up living in
the house for over ten years, until Rabkin returned to Santa Fe in the
early 1980s. Marcial reports missing his work in the fields and missing
his pueblo but, nonetheless, enjoying his time in the house very much.

His family and Rabkin's became increasingly close. Maria Walsh describes Marcial as "very devoted to the Rabkins."

Marcial first discovered the outside world through Rabkin. It was in Rabkin's house that Marcial came into contact with art books and learned about Western traditions in art. Marcial also heard classical music there for the first time. He once noted, "When you [Rabkin] first played your records of classical music it was like hearing an echo of my life, something I'd been waiting for." The *Eroica* became his favorite symphony and Beethoven his favorite composer.[13] Marcial still reports having heard "musica celestial" in Beethoven, like the music he had imagined in his own head as a child, many years before. The whole group, in fact, listened to classical music with "intense affection" (to quote Bill Negron), although only Marcial has kept the habit.

Marcial rapidly developed other interests while living in Rabkin's house. He taught himself to play the guitar, and more important, he taught himself Spanish. He studied a Spanish-Nahuatl dictionary and a Spanish-language copy of Carlos Castaneda's *Teachings of Don Juan*, and within a year, he understood Castaneda's entire book and was relatively fluent.

Marcial recalls reading whenever he had spare time from painting and family. His friend Florence Browne describes him as wanting to read "everything and anything." In addition to Castenada, he recalls reading about the Aztecs, reading about the history of Mexico, and reading *National Geographic* magazine to learn about other countries and locales. He recalls starting many more books than he ever finished, being so excited at the beginning of the book but later finding his attention drawn away to yet another one.

Marcial married his wife, Gloria, while he was living in Rabkin's house. In Oapan, marriage follows from a combination of mutual attraction and practical considerations, such as the earning power of the man and the woman's apparent willingness to work hard in the house. Couples rarely know each other well before making the marriage decision, but the parents play little role in choosing a partner. Marcial jokes about the frequency of "love at first sight" in Oapan. Typically, a male will decide it is time to marry and then make several (simultaneous) offers, only later deciding which one to follow through on. Women may court and accept several offers as well, waiting until the last minute to choose the best available option. Most of the men are married by their mid-twenties, most of the women by eighteen or nineteen and possibly as early as fifteen.[14] Gloria, however, was no more than thirteen or fourteen when she married Marcial, and she had not yet started having her period. He met her when the two were carrying water from the Rio Balsas to their homes, the classic Oapan romance story. One day, Marcial simply called up Rabkin from the bus terminal in Cuernavaca and told him he was married. He brought Gloria into the house. Their two daughters, Dahlia and Oliva, were born in Cuernavaca and spent their early years living with the Rabkins. They grew up with Rabkin's daughter, Lara, as if they were sisters.

In addition to his friendship with "Edmundo," Marcial also had a strong connection to Carolyn. They both faced racial and skin color prejudice throughout their lives. Carolyn, in addition to her rural origins, learned to read later in life; these features of her life brought her closer to Marcial.

Marcial was excited by his new life, but other individuals in the pueblo did not understand what was going on. Many thought that Marcial was not being true to the real world. Even Marcial's mother, who had supported his amate painting from the beginning, did not understand. She told him he was losing the customs of his people.

Villagers also noticed that Marcial had changed. Marcial recounts that when he returned to the village and played Beethoven, the other villagers could hear the music from the windows of his house. They regarded him as extremely weird. He recalls receiving both envy and respect.

Rabkin and Selden Rodman

Rabkin was keen to spread his discovery to others. Yet, at first, he had no significant connections in the art world. In the Mexican market, Rabkin sought the assistance of Ana Luisa Ramos Prida, a Mexican surrealist painter who worked in the naive style. Maria Walsh (her close Mexican friend) described Ana Luisa as very mystic and very spiritual and interested in yoga and meditation. Ana Luisa had married an American and thus had strong contacts with the expatriate community in Cuernavaca. She also came from an aristocratic background in Mexico (her father had been the equivalent of attorney general), which gave her many contacts. She helped Rabkin stage some exhibits, sometimes lending her large house, Castillo de la Serena, for this purpose. Ana Luisa also was to play a role in Marcial's later career (as will be explored in chapter 4).

In the American market, Rabkin worked with Selden Rodman, at least initially. Rodman was an author, adventurer, poet, and playwright and was part of the New York intellectual scene for decades. He was friendly with virtually every leading New York intellectual or artist of his day. Rodman was perhaps most renowned for his early support of Haitian art. He oversaw the painting of the Haitian murals in the Port-au-Prince Saint Eglisé Cathedral in the late 1940s. To this day, these murals remain the high point of Haitian artistic achievement. Rodman picked the artists who were to paint, helped them choose themes, found an appropriate venue, and arranged project finance from the United States—by approaching Mrs. Vincent Astor.

Rodman also wrote several early books about Haitian art, which still serve as the most popular introduction to the field and which helped establish Haiti's reputation as a leading center for naive art. He also wrote the first major work on Horace Pippin, the renowned African-American artist. Rodman had longstanding connections with Mexican art, most notably his ties to the Nueva Presencia group of artists in the 1950s and 1960s (in fact, the name of the group came from Rodman's writings). Much earlier, Rodman had interviewed and written about leading Mexican artists, including Rivera, Orozco, and Siquieros. Rodman was a man who discovered and publicized previously neglected artists. He also dealt in Haitian and outsider art from his home in New Jersey, serving a wealthy and influential clientele in the New York metropolitan area.

Rodman's energy was immense, and his artistic eye was highly respected. Once interested in a project, he was extremely generous with his time, energy, and connections. For Rodman, as with Rabkin, the desire to promote greatness came before the desire to earn more money.

One day in 1973, Rabkin simply showed up at Rodman's doorstep in New Jersey with some pictures by Marcial Camilo. This happened before Rabkin started Galerie Lara. An American contact had suggested that Selden was the person they should speak to. Selden's first question was whether the works were for sale. A subsequent letter from

Rabkin described Selden as "very impressed." Two years later, Rabkin reestablished contact and invited Selden to a show of the work in New York City. Rabkin figured, correctly, that Rodman, with his drive, writing skills, reputation, and connections, had the ability to help make things happen. Selden, in fact, gave Rabkin a list of his major clients. Rabkin describes this as the only time he received generous assistance of this nature from anybody in his entire time promoting the group.

In one of Rabkin's early years, he logged fifty-eight thousand miles on his car while driving around the United States during breaks from Cuernavaca. He showed the group's pictures to people, hoping to find buyers—usually making "cold calls" rather than having well-defined leads. He needed someone like Rodman to certify the quality of the group's work.[15]

After receiving Rabkin's visit, Rodman bought some pictures and quickly became committed to the quality of the work. In 1977 Rabkin arranged to take Rodman to the village. Rodman spent one day there and became yet more interested. He met the painters, bought some more pictures, and decided he had found "the next big thing" in the world of outsider art. Marcial painted this visit and Rodman; Rabkin still owns the painting, which he keeps as a memento of the time.

Rabkin and Rodman continued to work together. Rabkin procured the pictures, and Rodman recommended them to his clients. Rodman's most notable customers were Maurice and Linda Thompson of Connecticut—at the time, two well-known Haitian art collectors and outsider art collectors more generally.

The Thompsons remain well-known for the quality of their collection and the quality of their eye. They are perhaps best known for their large, high-quality collection of Hector Hyppolyte pictures. Hyppolyte, typically considered the best Haitian naive painter, produced major works for only about three years (1945–48), until his death. The Thompsons acquired a large number of these works before the paintings rose so much in value. The Thompsons also had been collecting other prominent Haitian and Jamaican painters, all in the naive or outsider traditions. The Thompsons, who lived in Connecticut, had earned their money fixing failing companies and then selling them.

Once the Thompsons had seen some of the paintings at Selden's house, they wanted to buy a large number of them. They commissioned Selden to visit the village and to bring back twenty paintings. They also bought one amate, an early Marcial, painted before Marcial's association with Rabkin. After some communication with Rabkin, the prices were revised to suit the size of the canvas, with a premium being paid for anything by Marcial. The Thompsons paid prices ranging from $250 to $1,250 per picture, the highest amount for the larger canvases by Marcial.

In addition to selling to the Thompsons, Rodman contacted many of his clients for Haitian naive art. Telling them that the Ayalas and company were the next big thing, he persuaded many of them to buy a painting or two. Such collectors as Fahimie Marks and Michael Slosberg bought pictures by the group.

Suddenly the group was "in," and the late 1970s brought a rapid stream of exhibits. One early exhibit, entitled "The Village," was at the Covo de Iongh Gallery in Houston in 1977; works of all the group members were represented. Over the next few years, exhibits followed in the Sindic Gallery (New York City), Wolfe Street Gallery (Washington, D.C.), Sol del Rio Gallery (San Antonio), Delahunte Gallery (Dallas), Horchow Collection (Dallas), and Los Llaves Gallery (Santa Fe). Other exhibits took place in Atlanta, Houston, Los Angeles, and New York (Jay Johnson Gallery) and on the Sanibel and Captiva Islands off the west coast of Florida.[16] In 1979 the group had a show in the Center for the Arts in Scottsdale, Arizona. While none of these galleries had sufficient stature to establish the artists' reputations more permanently, each provided the group's work with valuable exposure to buyers.

Rabkin cites an exhibit at Dade County Community College as the first in the United States. Florence Browne, friend of the Rabkins and Marcial's longtime friend in Cuernavaca, had a brother working at that university. The brother arranged the show, and Marcial flew to Miami (with Rabkin) to see the exhibit and lecture about his art to the students and faculty there. Florence reports how Marcial entranced the audience with his stage presence, even though most of the listeners could not understand his Spanish.

Marcial recounts that his plane trips to the United States have been among the most remarkable of his experiences. The aerial perspective on the world simply stunned him. He says that for him, flying to the United States was as remarkable an achievement as flying to the moon. The Rabkins recollect that Marcial almost backed out of his first plane trip, to Florida, as he arrived at the airport. His fear of flying, however, rapidly turned to a sense of exhilaration.

The most prestigious venue in Mexico was in the Museo Cuauh-nahuac of the Palacío de Cortés in Cuernavaca. This locale is one of the leading tourist attractions in Cuernavaca and is also the leading museum, largely because of the Diego Rivera mural located there. This is the same Diego Rivera work that had inspired the group years earlier, and they were now thrilled to see their pictures exhibited in the same locale. In addition to the other Cuernavaca exhibits in Ana Luisa's Castillo de la Serena, the Racquet Club Gallery of Cuernavaca put on a show as well.

Publicity followed. Ron Arias published the article "Marcial Camilo Ayala" in the fall 1978 issue of *Southwestern Art*. The magazine *Americas*, the official organ of the Organization of American States, wrote up the group's show at the Wolfe Street Gallery in Washington.[17] The subtitle proclaimed, "An Important New Group of Mexican Naïve Painters Enters the International Art Scene." The article praised Marcial, Juan Camilo, and Robert Mauricio in particular, noting the idealized worldview and innovative concepts of their art. This article was no exception, however, to the general paucity of information about the group. Roberto Mauricio, for instance, is called "Roberto Ayala" and is described as the brother of Juan Camilo Ayala.

The MIND Show

The show that received the most attention was the exhibit of 1981 (May 4–31) in the Lockwood-Mathews Mansion Museum in Norwalk, Connecticut. This show represented the group's high watermark within the outsider art world. When American collectors and dealers are asked about the group, this is the show they most commonly cite, by far.

The show was based on the MIND collection, held in the hands of the Thompson family. Selden Rodman also had convinced some of his clients to loan their best pieces for the show, and Rabkin lent out numerous pieces from his inventory. Many of the pieces in the show were reproduced in a small book put out by the MIND foundation, with an introductory essay by Selden Rodman touting the prowess of the group and giving a brief history and background (there will be more discussion on this essay later). The show was widely attended within the outsider art world, and opinions were extremely favorable.

Robert Bishop, director of the American Folk Art Museum in New York City, was entranced by the work of the group. He wrote an introduction to the MIND pamphlet and also vowed to give the group permanent space in the museum once a renovation was completed. Bishop later passed away, however, and the plan never came to fruition.[18]

Further Advances

The Connecticut show was followed by additional successes. Most notably, the International Folk Art Museum in Santa Fe, arguably the leading folk art museum in the world, bought a work by Marcial. This picture, called *History of Mexico*, dated from 1973 and was about eight feet long and four feet high. Marsha Bol, curator for Latin American folk art at the time, describes the work as a "really good inclusion" that was popular with the museum staff. She notes that the museum was interested in the historical perspective of the work, the scale, and the indigenous background of the artist. She viewed the work as an important link between the amate tradition and "the newly-arisen easel painting style." In a letter to Rabkin, she noted particular interest in Marcial's recorded explanation of the narrative of the painting. The museum first asked Rabkin to donate the painting, but he refused. The museum then bought the work for six thousand dollars when several private individuals made the funds available for this purchase. This was the largest sum of money any of the group's paintings had yielded at the time. Rabkin invited Marcial to the museum in Santa Fe, where an inauguration ceremony for the picture was held in 1982 (June 18). The picture hung in the lobby for four years and is now held in storage.[19]

The early 1980s saw the publication of a children's book, *El Maiz*, illustrated by Marcial, who also helped with the text. The book showed the importance of corn—from its planting to its harvest to its consumption—in a "typical" Mexican indigenous village. The basic material was drawn from Marcial's upbringing in Oapan. The genesis of the book came from Christina Urrutia of Cuernavaca, who asked Rabkin if Marcial might be interested in doing a book with her. Marcial painted about twenty small pictures on board for the book. He received royalty rights and claims he has earned about twenty-six thousand pesos from the endeavor. In 1984 the book received a second printing of ten thousand copies, so the enterprise appears to have been a success. For a while, there was talk of doing a version in English, but this never came to pass.[20]

Rodman continued to publicize the group. Simon and Schuster, a leading American trade house, published his *Popular Artists in Tune with the World* in 1982. This was the same written material from the MIND catalog, although Rodman chose a somewhat different selection of photos of the art. The focus again was Marcial.

Rodman's written treatment was enthusiastic and colorful. He promoted Marcial as a genius, able to imagine, conceptualize, and execute at the highest levels of artistic ability. He gave each member of the group a distinct personality and style, typically with little restraint. For instance, he described Marcial as follows: "broadfaced, high-cheekboned, with eyes as 'Oriental' as an Indonesian's, [he] comes out to greet us. He has a lovely smile, the kind that masks no secrets."

Although it was readable and enthusiastic, Rodman's treatment was not scholarly in nature. Rodman makes Marcial sound like an untutored art naïf who suddenly received a paintbrush and began to paint his innermost feelings with great brilliance. In fact, Marcial was working hard on his art since he was a teenager. Far from being an "untrained" artist, he worked through extremely intensive forms of training. Rodman discusses the amate tradition of Oapan and the surrounding region, but it is hardly central to the narrative. For this reason, many or most of the North American buyers of the group knew little or nothing of amates.

In fact, Rodman, who spoke virtually no Spanish, had only passing acquaintance with San Agustín. He had spent only a single day in the village, at Rabkin's invitation. Felix Camilo described Rodman's visit as "arriving at eight o'clock in the morning, leaving by five in the afternoon." Rodman had visited Guerrero before, but he had no background concerning the Alto Balsas Nahua. Written literature on the Balsas communities remains scarce, but at the time, there was virtually nothing to read.[21]

Rodman was a dealer and, most of all, an art lover, publicist, and promoter. He had an eye for the story before anything else. While he had written several dozen books, most with an intellectual slant, none were academic. Instead, he brought various countries and art movements to life for his readers. He adopted the same tack with Marcial and the group. When Rabkin told Rodman an appealing story, Rodman put it down on paper, sometimes adding his own twists.

For the MIND catalog, Robert Bishop, then director of the Museum of American Folk Art, wrote a preface in which he compared the Alto Balsas artisans favorably to the Haitian naive painters. Bishop described the paintings as "major works of art" and as "historical and social documents that are impossible to deny." The contemporary reader winces, however, when Bishop refers to the "primitive lives" of the artists. He also writes, "why they started to paint, only they will know," never considering that money might have been a motive, that painting had been the primary occupation in the village at that time, or that the artists might have motives of creative self-expression.

Some of the stories in the Rodman treatment fail to receive confirmation from the artists. For instance, Rodman wrote of Marcial, "he is amused by his father who used to chide him for wasting his time painting but who now, with unprecedented wealth rolling in, adjures him to 'Paint faster, son! Paint faster!'" Today, Marcial, the other brothers, and their mother recount a very different story. They recall initial encouragement from the boys' father. They did not see themselves as receiving "unprecedented wealth" or think that any other family member possibly might have had this impression.

In the late 1970s and early 1980s, a number of other outsider art dealers began to promote the group. Dealer Ute Stebich, when asked to give a blurb for the artists, offered the following: "Most astonishing among this variety of themes are those which reveal their private thoughts and personal philosophy. Not only are such themes difficult to realize, but they require self-assurance, maturity of mind, and most important, trust in the spectator. Credit for building this trust in people, neglected and exploited for centuries goes to Mr. and Mrs. Ed Rabkin, who discovered these artists. Free of any prejudice, they gave moral and material support, thus enriching the world of art with this important contribution."[22]

Leading folk art collector Larry Kent bought two pictures from Rodman, both of which had been in the Connecticut show: Marcial's *What the Sun Sees* and Felix Jimenez's *The Lovers*. Kent describes these pictures as fitting into his larger collection of folk art and his collection of Mexican folk art in particular. He praises the works of the group. Kent notes: "Artworks I have by Marcial and Felix are refreshing and keep me questioning what's going on in each painting. There seem to be no definitive answers."[23]

Fahimie Marks was another Haitian art collector who was interested in the group. She bought several pictures from Rodman, a number of which were represented in the 1982 Connecticut show. She once gave the following endorsement: "The transcendent quality of these artists is their continuing growth. Many artists of the naïve school achieve early pre-eminence but most strive to maintain the superiority of their creations by reason of the insatiable pressures of patrons and collectors. The Aztec family seems to be an exception to the rule."[24]

It is no accident that the Haitian naive art dealers and collectors took such a special interest in the group. First, the group style resembled Haitian art in several respects, such as perspective and use of color. Not surprisingly, Marcial subsequently became a big fan of Haitian art, after seeing some color plates in Rodman's books. Buyers of Haitian art therefore turned out to be natural candidates to collect Marcial and the group. Second, art dealers need to have something to promote. Most of the best naive Haitian painters, however, were either dead, incapacitated, or in serious decline by the mid-1970s. It became increasingly hard to buy from the artist at cheap prices and sell to sophisticated collectors at much higher prices. Haitian dealers have thus looked around for other works to sell, including Cuban art, Jamaican art, Nicaraguan art, and Mexican art.

During this era, dealers promoted Marcial's pictures at the prices that very good Haitian works would command—namely, in the range of one to five thousand dollars. While sales in the upper end of this range were infrequent, no one laughed at the prices being asked. In the outsider art world of the late 1970s and early 1980s, these prices were extremely respectable, as they predated the recent boom in the outsider art market. For purposes of comparison, only a few leading Haitian artists sold above this range in the time period under consideration. In these years, Philome Obin sold in the range of five to ten thousand dollars, and even first-rate works by Hector Hyppolite sold for only slightly above ten thousand dollars.[25]

The Santa Fe Gallery

Rabkin left Cuernavaca to return to the United States, reopening Galerie Lara in June 1982.[26] The new Galerie Lara was in downtown Santa Fe, at 227 Don Gaspar, Santa Fe, New Mexico, near many of the other downtown galleries. Rabkin brought an extensive collection of ceremonial masks from Guerrero, many of which he had purchased in the nearby pueblo of San Francisco Ozomatlán. He sold African masks as well.[27] Nonetheless, the works of the group formed the centerpiece of his gallery.

The Rabkins cite the devaluation and economic collapse of Mexico as their main reason for leaving. The painters offer differing, but broadly consistent, accounts on why Rabkin left Mexico. Inocencio asserts that Rabkin left Mexico once things there became "too expensive." Felix Camilo reports that Rabkin told him it was too hard to find clients in Mexico. Felix Jimenez mentions that Rabkin simply did not like it in Mexico anymore.

Rabkin did have good economic reasons to leave. The years 1981–82 marked a watershed time in Mexico's major economic crisis, which had been brewing for years. Growth turned sharply negative, and inflation rose into the triple digits, exceeding 100 percent in 1982. Mexico showed itself unable to make its debt payments, and the peso plummeted in foreign exchange markets. The exchange rate went from 22.5 pesos to the dollar in 1982 to 1,500 pesos to the dollar by 1987. Real wages fell by 50 percent over this same time frame. Mexico appeared less desirable as a place to live, and the Rabkins were realizing that Mexican collectors were not about to start buying the group in large numbers. The Rabkins, who were not making any money in the first place, were broke by the time they arrived in Santa Fe.[28]

Procuring the supply of pictures was now a greater problem than before. Typically, Rabkin met Marcial in Cíudad Juarez along the Mexican-American border. Marcial brought pictures from the group, typically about twenty each trip, and would hand them over to Rabkin in Mexico. Rabkin would drive the pictures across the border in his car and bring them back to Santa Fe.

Marcial recalls these trips as great hardships, mainly because it was thirty-three hours from Oapan to Juarez by bus. Marcial claims he has never been able to sleep well in buses. Marcial also complained that Rabkin once promised to pay his entire expenses for the trip and then later only paid half, telling him he would pay the entire tab next time around. He presented this misunderstanding as typical of the kind of disputes the group had over money. Nonetheless, Marcial continued to go to Juarez to bring the pictures to Rabkin.

By this time, however, the flow of paintings had slowed. Inocencio sent very few paintings to Rabkin through Ciudad Juarez. Juan Camilo had stopped painting for Rabkin. Felix Jimenez had not yet stopped but was about to. Roberto had not been a regular source of supply for a few years. For most of the Santa Fe years, Marcial and Felix Camilo were the only reliable sources of paintings.

Even this arrangement fell apart after a few years. It became harder to sustain the Santa Fe gallery. Santa Fe was becoming increasingly expensive, its art market was becoming increasingly competitive, and the American market for the group had been slowing down. The Rabkins had to endure the long hours of running a walk-in gallery seven days a week. Furthermore, Santa Fe was changing; the town had originally been a place for people seeking "something different," but it was moving increasingly into the mainstream of tourism. By 1989 the Rabkins closed the walk-in gallery and retreated to selling the pictures from their home.

The painters became ever more frustrated with the financial arrangements. Marcial made his last trip to Ciudad Juarez in the early 1990s. At this time, he told Rabkin that he would paint no more. Rabkin no longer had a means of receiving fresh supply, and he and his wife were in any case burned out from their extensive efforts.

Why Failure?

By the 1990s, the rest of the outsider art world had lost much of its interest in the group, which had reached its reputational peak in the early 1980s. Four group members—Felix Jimenez, Inocencio, Juan Camilo, and Roberto Mauricio—had stopped painting for Rabkin or were on the verge of stopping. The outside world was demanding quality work, but supply was irregular, and Rabkin was reluctant to sell many of his best pictures.

The market for the group also suffered from a lack of natural buyers. The outsider art movement and art markets in general are marked by national preferences; Brazilians buy Brazilian art, Americans buy American art, Canadians buy Canadian art, and so on. Many artistic eras offer a kind of "gold standard," a single national tradition that attracts buyers of all sorts and is extremely liquid in the marketplace. In nineteenth-century art, the French provide this standard, and arguably the Americans (e.g., Jasper Johns and Andy Warhol) provide the standard for contemporary art today. Outsider art, however, has not developed such a standard, which leaves the market segmented.

The tradition of "street amates" also makes it harder for high-quality amates to gain acceptance in the art world. When Mexicans think of amates, they typically think of the cheap copies sold in the streets of Taxco and in the bazaars of Mexico City. All art forms have low-end imitations, but most Mexicans do not know that high-quality amate works exist. Even sophisticated folk art collectors often identify amates with the cheap street product—commonly seen in Texas, the Southwest, and California—rather than with quality work or original art. They simply have not seen the higher-quality works.

The Alto Balsas arts also failed to achieve a critical mass in terms of size and scope. For an area to become established as an artistic genre, it needs a basic minimum of activity. Haitian art, for instance, is a known genre with a well-established set of collectors. A quick perusal of the Internet will show that there are at least fifty or so Haitian painters with established reputations, and there are arguably up to a hundred, albeit of varying quality. One can collect Haitian art and follow something with a very definite identity. While most art collectors do not buy Haitian pictures, it stands as a well-defined area of specialization, attracting enough partisans to keep it going.

Haitian art is something easy to identify and classify. All educated people have heard of the country of Haiti. The art also has the well-known theme of voodoo, to set it apart from other artistic genres. In contrast, Alto Balsas art has never had the same clarity of definition. The Alto Balsas Nahuas are one of many dozens of subcultures in Mexico. Hardly anyone has heard of them, and they never make the American news. Most Mexican-Americans do not identify with them. They have no single cultural point of identification analogous to the role of voodoo in Haitian art.

The initial solution to this problem was to have the Alto Balsas painters "free ride" on the infrastructure that had been developed for Haitian art. This succeeded to some extent and gave the artists a needed boost in their early years, but it ultimately proved inadequate. Too many Haitian buyers wanted Haitian art only, which relegated the Alto Balsas painters to a secondary or side role.

Other Mexican naive painters have met similar fates, largely for similar reasons. Fernando Castillo (1882–1940), for instance, is one the most talented Mexican naive painters, but he has never developed a strong following, either in the United States or in Mexico. He belongs to no easily identifiable group, and he has only a small natural constituency of buyers. While the quality of his work is high, his name is not widely known, even among outsider art partisans.[29]

No active resale market for Alto Balsas art developed. Buyers who wanted to unload one of their Alto Balsas paintings had few opportunities to do so. The early buyers, cultivated by Rodman, already had some works by the group. No new set of buyers was coming along to support the liquidity of the market. Rodman's difficulties in selling the work did not help, as they meant that Rodman promoted the group less. Rodman's age (he was over seventy by the beginning of the 1980s) also made it harder to him to replenish his supply of buyer contacts.

Most generally, the Rabkins faced a difficult task. They poured a great amount of time, money, effort, and love into a project that had strong quixotic elements. If we consider the Cuernavaca years, very few Mexican galleries made money in those years. Mexico was on the verge of economic collapse. The Rabkins nonetheless kept some version of the gallery going for about twenty years, a remarkably long time in the art world. The Rabkins's other business successes also show that they had a good sense of how to make money. Florence Browne, their friend from Cuernavaca, believes that both their leather business and their art gallery were undercapitalized. She thought that both were promising commercial ventures and that the Rabkins were talented, but ultimately the Rabkins did not have deep enough pockets to continue indefinitely.

For an art market to succeed, a good deal of complementary infrastructure is required, on both the supply side and the demand or marketing side. On the supply side, Alto Balsas art required a training network and an intense native ethos. On the marketing side, success required a thick market of sophisticated, well-placed buyers and an active set of dealers and secondary institutions. The works of six Mexican outsider art painters alone, no matter how interesting, could not provide enough capital to sustain the needed infrastructure on the demand side. Painters do best when they can market their work in strong and plentiful clusters, not when they approach the world as a very small group.

No galleries have managed to succeed by selling the works of six outsider painters only. The Phyllis Kind Gallery in New York City is commonly considered the most commercially successful of all the outsider art galleries. That enterprise prospered by identifying and marketing the leading American outsider artists at a time when their work rose rapidly in value. Phyllis Kind herself is seen as a "living legend" in the outsider art world. This gallery has carried hundreds of artists, rather than just six. Galerie St. Etienne, also of New York, has dealt outsider art with some success but also has relied on its leading position in German expressionist art. This gallery, too, deals in large numbers of artists, not just a few.

More generally, most outsider galleries do not meet with significant commercial success. Often, outsider art is dealt from homes. The dealers might have some accumulated wealth or a small inheritance. They enjoy being art dealers for a living and so continue with the endeavor. If they are lucky or especially skillful, they will be able to cover their costs and expenses. Carrying a high quality of art does not typically make their task easier. In fact, it usually makes it harder. A purely commercial orientation will encourage galleries to carry many decorative pieces and sell them relatively cheaply. The higher the quality of the work they carry is, the harder it is to find appropriate buyers, and the greater is the amount of upfront investment needed. If a gallery sells cheaper, more commercial items on the side, that gallery is no longer a trusted certifier of artistic quality.

Today, Rabkin continues to sell his stock of pictures from the house and sometimes on eBay, but they do not provide a significant source of income. His house is full of beautiful paintings by the group, but he is reluctant to allow buyers to cherry-pick and take home his favorites.

After Rabkin stopped promoting the pictures so actively, the remaining markets for the group became weaker. Some galleries sold off their pictures for whatever they could get and cut their losses. In 2001

I received an email from one individual who saw two Inocencio Chino paintings in an antique store. He wrote to ask whether the asking price of seventy-five dollars was reasonable.

Ralph White of Texas came across the group's work but had little sense of their identity. He bought eight works when a Dallas art gallery went out of business. He could not find any information on the artists, but he liked the paintings. In the late 1990s, he exhibited them at the Collin County Historical Museum in Texas, where he reports they were "very highly appreciated." He later placed them in an art show at a local gallery, though they were not for sale. White is not a dedicated art collector but has since spoken of perhaps turning some of the artists' works into giclee prints.[30]

Nancy Bloom has four paintings from the group, which her (now deceased) husband bought from the gallery on the Sanibel and Captive Islands, Florida. She loves the paintings but has had no idea what they are or how much they are worth (one is by Felix Camilo, two by Felix Jimenez, and one by Marcial). She is afraid that when she passes away, the pictures "could end up getting in a garage sale." Her helper, Janie Burke, wrote me an email to ask what kind of market could be found for the paintings now, but I was unable to refer her to any gallery that made a market in the works of the artists.[31]

When I first started asking art dealers and buyers about the Oapan group, no one had much information. A few told me to ask Rabkin. Others were not sure if the painters were still alive or still painting. Ute Stebich, a leading outsider art dealer who once promoted the group, responded: "Marcial Camilo Ayala. I haven't heard that name in a *long* time."

Summary Remarks

International markets and the patronage of Ed Rabkin gave a significant boost to the cultural voices of the Oapan group. Group members experienced a cross-cultural odyssey and a rise in their living standards and fame. In these regards, the forces of trade helped the group overcome the limitations of power and the deprivations of Mexico. Globalization, whatever its real-world imperfections, proved to be a kind of personal and artistic savior in the story at hand.

More generally, Rabkin served as a classic instance of a beneficial cultural entrepreneur. He combined a personal, cultural, humanitarian, and commercial interest in the group. His lengthy efforts brought a significant upswing in the fortunes of the group and put them on the artistic map in the United States. He also enabled the painters to draw ideas from a greater number of cross-cultural and international sources. We saw amate painting evolve into differing and more diverse media. The painters kept their initial inspirations but were able to realize their visions and voices on a larger and better-publicized scale than before.

But global markets were not strong enough to support the group at all points in time. Each of the painters returned to his Mexican milieu and tried to reestablish his artistic voice through other means. In several cases, the painters have tried to build on the foundations from their years with Rabkin. Let us now turn to how their stories have proceeded, with a continuing eye on the theme of how trading opportunities shape the arts.

4 • The Lives Today

AFTER THE DEALINGS WITH RABKIN DISSOLVED, the Oapan group was left to sell in Mexican markets for paintings and amates. The size and reach of their markets shrunk considerably, and they lost their connection to international art markets. To the extent the painters had stayed with Rabkin, they had been insulated from the need to market their work. The painters, especially Juan Camilo, had sold smaller works on the side, but always to casual buyers or to tourists rather than to serious collectors. The absence of marketing connections and skills now came back to haunt the group, most of all Marcial. The Rabkins had done an enormous amount to expose him to the world, but he did not have many independent contacts with North American customers or dealers.

This market collapse had grave consequences for the scale and scope of projects that the artists were able to undertake. Only Marcial was able to keep painting on a large scale, and even he could not do so with much success. As we will see, the lack of access to international markets changed the painters' lives and works dramatically.

The subsequent life stories, however, show rebuilding rather than permanent collapse. The painters acquired important skills, both artistic and cultural, during the Rabkin years, and they continued to build on these foundations. As time passed, they found new ways of painting to support their families and new ways of expressing their artistic creativity.

All the group members, with the possible exception of Felix Camilo, have enjoyed rising standards of living. General economic growth has made Oapan larger and wealthier than ever before. The number of animals is multiplying, as families invest their money from arts and crafts in mules, burros, and pigs, all frequent sights in town streets. There are many more houses than before and many houses that are larger and of higher quality. Many families have upgraded their homes by adding extra rooms or wings. When the 1960s started, all house roofs were of palm leaves. Today, almost all of them are concrete or laminated.

The true standard of living is difficult to estimate, given how much of the income is taken in kind and through self-employed agriculture. Most families grow enough food to meet their dietary needs. Their homes are already built and offer plenty of space. Clean water, while not plentiful, is readily available from wells. Electricity came to the village in 1979 and is now taken for granted.[1]

On top of this base, families will earn an income from amate, pottery, and craft sales. The most successful of these families will hold small "craft empires" and earn up to twenty or thirty thousand dollars yearly, but these cases are rare. More commonly, these earnings will fall in the range of one to three thousand dollars yearly for a family of five to ten people. If the town government wishes to attract a municipal assistant (topiles), it must offer about fifteen hundred dollars for the year. Hiring a day's labor for fieldwork costs about five to six dollars. A day's work from a carpenter costs about ten dollars. On top of these sums, some families will receive remittances from sons working in the United States, ranging up to several thousand dollars a year, although Oapan sons have been slower to leave than their peers in neighboring pueblos.[2]

It is difficult to compare these figures to the past. Before the amate trade of the 1960s and 1970s, for instance, a family was lucky to earn any outside income at all. Oapan was literally on the verge of subsistence, and starvation was a possible fate. Since there was so little to buy, it is hard to judge how much the money was worth at that time, despite lower prices. Arguably, in real terms, the money today is worth more than before, if only because of the road and the Iguala Wal-Mart several hours away. That being said, let us assume (generously) that a family in 1960 had an outside income worth five hundred dollars in real terms. If a comparable family might earn two thousand dollars today, this translates into an average growth rate approaching 3.28 percent a year over those forty-three years. This figure does not begin to include the in-kind benefits that the villagers now enjoy. If we think of one-third of the improvement in living standards as coming from in-kind benefits, the rate of growth is a healthy 4.92 percent a year. If the in-kind benefits account for half of the improvements, the rate of growth is an impressive 6.5 percent a year.

These in-kind improvements are significant. For instance, electricity expands the amount and flexibility of available time. The higher-quality road gives much greater access to goods and services. Day trips for shopping are now common, whereas overnight visits were required before. A child can now be brought to a doctor in Iguala in only several hours time; in the 1970s, the trip had to be undertaken by burro.

Oapan residents are now remarkably mobile. They regularly travel three to four hours to Iguala (pop. 60,000) to go shopping, buy artisan materials, or sell wares—or simply for something to do. Taxco (pop. 52,000), Cuernavaca (pop. 346,000), and Acapulco (pop. 640,000) are further away but receive regular visits as well—largely for economic reasons, but also for a change of pace. It is common for villagers to get up at four o'clock in the morning to make one of these trips with a pickup truck, by bus, or in a *combi* (casual vehicle) leaving town. Many of the artisans strike out for longer trips to more distant locales, such as Puerto Vallarta, Guadalajara, Oaxaca, Tijuana, and Cancún.

San Agustín has developed increasing electronic ties to the outside world. The town has a central phone, or *caseta*. The *caseta* is manned by a villager, usually a woman, from morning hours to about eight at night. The woman responds to callers with a short "Bueno," and the caller requests the name of the party he or she wishes to speak to. The woman then announces a length of time, usually ranging between five and fifteen minutes, based on experience with how long it takes that person to get to the phone. The caller is to hang up and call back in that amount of time. The person's name is then called out through a loudspeaker, and that person (ostensibly) comes running to the phone, ready to speak once the return call comes. A number of households now have private phones, though this is a recent development.[3]

Many homes have small televisions, although due to the surrounding mountain, they receive only two channels—offering largely soap operas, sports, and news. A few of the richer families have a "sky antenna," or satellite dish, which might supply up to thirty channels and more programs. The first of these devices came several years ago. Radio is common but by no means universal, and difficulty of reception remains a problem.

Overall, Oapan residents have a fair amount of free time to spend with family and friends. While they work hard at agriculture and crafts, there is a considerable amount of downtime, often imposed by the constraints of fieldwork itself, and they will rest between household tasks. Painting, housework, talking, and watching the children are all crammed into a typical daily hour, often with a background of Mexican music. Craft labor allows individuals to set their own schedules and to spend a good deal of time with family.

In this chapter, I will look first at the painters that stayed in Oapan and then at the group members that struck out for other locales. This contrast will illustrate the double-edged nature of cultural globalization. Amates and the paintings on board never would have existed without foreign support. In this regard, the net influence of globalization is strongly positive. Nonetheless, foreign influences also have proved corrupting in certain ways. We will see how economic geography has shaped each of the lives and how the greater wealth of the area has presented new choices. The painters who left the village have had better opportunities to find clients and continue to paint for a living. Those same painters, however, also have been forced to make greater compromises with the marketplace and sometimes to abandon the uniqueness and originality of their Oapan style. Insofar as they have met with creative success, it has been through particular patrons and specialized support, rather than in the more general and anonymous art marketplace.

The logic behind such trade-offs is general. At the final margin of choice, the artist's personally preferred style would, if the artist moved in that direction, involve lower pay (Cowen and Tabarrok 2000). To the extent that creative rewards and monetary rewards lie in the same direction, the artist already will have exploited those moves. So the available margins typically involve some trade-off between creativity and pay. Artists therefore typically feel that the marketplace is frustrating their desires; and at the margin, it is—even if the market enables their projects in the first place. Each of the lives has responded to creative trade-offs in different ways, and to the extent an individual left Oapan, he has faced such trade-offs in especially stark form.

Those That Stayed Behind

Juan Camilo Ayala • After ceasing to paint for Rabkin, Juan Camilo sought artisan work in Mexico City as a painter. Most commonly, he decorated parts of homes, especially ceilings. In the mid-1980s, however, Juan was painting a ceiling and fell from his ladder two stories to the ground, landing on his head. He was knocked unconscious and almost died. To this day, he is still missing part of his skull, and he experiences recurring (though infrequent) pains where the injury occurred. This episode discouraged Juan from pursuing ceiling painting, and he returned to amates and pictures.

Juan then tried to market his amates in Cuernavaca, as he had done previously. Florence Browne, an American resident of Cuernavaca, recounts meeting Juan frequently in the Cuernavaca market during those years. She says that Juan brought excellent work to town but that it was very difficult to sell it for decent prices, given how many amates were circulating. Most customers did not know the difference between lesser and better works. Sometimes Florence had to give Juan a little extra money so he had enough to get back home. She says that Juan became extremely discouraged over time and eventually stopped coming to the town market. Juan then tried selling in Acapulco, with somewhat better results. Yet he did not make much money there either and experienced recurring problems with the police.

Juan was hit by yet more bad luck. His oldest son died at the age of twelve, after being bitten by a scorpion near the Rio Balsas. The next oldest son died as well, this time of a fever that went untreated for too long. Juan reports that after each death, he was sad for a very long while and could not look at pictures of his deceased sons without breaking into tears.

Juan's relations with his brother Marcial became particularly strained in the 1980s. By Marcial's account, his father had promised him some of the family land. After the father died, the mother reallocated that portion to Juan. Since that time, relations between Juan and

Marcial worsened. This same family fight led just about everyone to break with Fausto, the fourth brother. Even Felix Camilo, who remains on good terms with just about everybody, is distant from Fausto. At the same time, Juan's lack of market success made it harder for him to deal with Marcial's broader reputation. Since this time, more than twenty years ago, the brothers have barely spoken to each other. The break between them has been exacerbated by political differences (Juan is the more conservative of the two) and by an intense dislike between their wives. More generally, Marcial has always been closer to their father, Juan to their mother. Juan responded to the alcoholism of his father differently than did Marcial. Juan has eschewed alcohol altogether, which he regards as holding no virtues, an unusual attitude in his community. He refers to the example of his father in convincing him of the evils of alcohol and disapproves of Marcial's drinking. Yet despite all these bitter differences between the two brothers, each is eager to hear reports about the other, at least if it can seem he is not listening too eagerly.

Feuds of this kind are common in the region. Anthropologist Peggy Golde, writing about the Nahuas, notes that when trust is broken, as it is frequently, it is imperative to avoid confrontations and challenges, which spiral out of control and lead to perpetual enmities. Golde describes the villagers as having "limited alternatives available to them to handle, rationalize, channel, and cope with their feelings." She continues, "If the people appeared to have less tolerance for real and imagined slights and were insecure about life in general, they had few means to strengthen themselves or enhance their opportunities—so why shouldn't they be defensive, self-protective, and hypervigilant?"[4]

Although Juan lagged behind the artistic successes of Marcial, his commercial fortunes finally improved. In the late 1990s, Juan started selling his work in Oaxaca and Puerto Escondido, two rising tourist locales. He notes that these cities are less saturated by amates than are many other places; he claims that he is the only good amate painter selling *historias* in either locale and attributes his success to this fact. Typically, he will spend two months a year selling in Oaxaca State, in winter and early spring. During the summer and fall months, he works in the fields and prepares the harvest. His two oldest surviving children help with painting ceramics, usually selling these works to tourist shops in Cancún. The combined income from these activities has been enough to make ends meet.

To his new customers, Juan has been selling both amates and small (twelve-by-twelve-inch) pictures on board. The amates have been both generic scenes of birds and flora, which went for five to ten dollars, and *historias*, which went for much more, depending on their size and quality. The board pictures were usually landscapes or river scenes. Juan claims that river scenes tend to be the most popular with tourists. Juan has brought his twenty-two-year-old (ca. 2003) daughter, Alcividiades, to Puerto Escondido to sell as well. She paints on board in the style of her father, favoring a romantic, dreamy look and scenes of weddings.

Juan recounts proudly that one of the Canadian tourists in Puerto Escondido recognized his name and his work when he saw Juan selling in the street. The tourist told Juan he had seen his work in a museum. The tourist and his group then invited Juan out for dinner and bought many of the works he was carrying. Juan and his daughter report other requests for paintings by Juan Camilo Ayala, though this is more likely the result of his reputation among other picture-buying tourists than the result of individuals knowing about his prior reputation through American exhibits or museums.

For many years, Juan did not attempt any large-scale works. The small size of his board paintings was a matter of economic necessity. Tourists will buy only what they can carry home easily. These small board paintings are colorful and appealing, but they were not comparable in ambition to Juan's earlier works for Rabkin.

My own role in Juan's life dates from 1997. In that year, I visited the home of Selden Rodman in Oakland, New Jersey. I typically went to Selden's to buy Haitian naive art, but on this visit, I noticed several Mexican paintings in Selden's living room—pictures by the Oapan group members. I asked Selden if he would sell the paintings, and he said no. I finally asked Selden how I could get a hold of other paintings by these artists. He was not sure, but he said an old friend of his, Ed Rabkin, might still have some. So I contacted Rabkin and bought some pictures by Marcial, Felix, and Juan Camilo.

I liked the pictures enough that I set off to Mexico to track down the artists. After arriving in Oapan, I asked for the artists and was led to

Juan's house (neither Marcial nor Felix were in the village at that time). I asked a very surprised Juan if he had any paintings to sell. He said no, instead offering me some very small amates for a few dollars apiece. I liked the amates but said I also wanted a much larger work, painted on board. I left him some money and my address, which his son wrote on a ceiling beam of the house. Juan's wife asked me numerous times if I was a friend of Edmundo's (Rabkin).[5]

The second time I came, Juan had mobilized his eldest son and daughter to paint for me as well. They offered me a selection of more than twenty full-size paintings, in the belief that the chance of selling to me was the most profitable use of their time. I bought the lot and gave away many to friends. Before my third visit, I specified that I wanted only a few paintings, but when I visited, I was again confronted with a selection of over twenty works, many by the eldest son and daughter. This time I bought only the larger (forty-nine-by-thirty-two-inch) canvases by Juan. Since that time, I have asked for more amates than paintings, as I no longer have room for more large paintings.

Using me as a contact, numerous North Americans have ordered works from Juan, usually paintings rather than amates. A dealer named Martin Kroll (discussed later in this chapter) has ordered and exhibited several works by Juan. Gloria Frank, a leading Haitian art dealer in New York, ordered and exhibited a work by Juan as well. The Mercatus Center, a research institution at George Mason University, ordered some black-and-white amates from Juan, which it uses as gifts to its donors.[6]

The family now runs a modest mail-order business based mostly on the works of Juan. Juan's son Leonardo has learned how to take orders and how to send the works out using a mailing service in Iguala with connections to Federal Express. The family now has one of the few private telephones in Oapan, largely to handle these orders. During the rainy season, Juan still works in the fields, but for the rest of the year, he is busy painting. In 2002 he finished two very large black-and-white amates for me, each about eight feet by four feet. Juan considers these to be his two best works.

Much of Juan's work is still radiant and life-affirming, but he has made a distinct move to darker moods and styles, including the portrayal of death and sadness. Several years ago, Juan started to paint santos, a new development in his art. These works show a marked Spanish colonial influence, which Juan picked up from a magazine reproduction of an image from a museum. Each time I visit, Juan asks me if I can bring color plates of other paintings, so that he may develop new ideas for his art; I obliged by bringing a book of plates by Leonardo da Vinci, after whom Juan had named his eldest surviving son.

Other group members have expressed surprise at seeing the quality of Juan's recent work. Previously, they thought of him as talented but not having the patience to paint well. Both Inocencio and Marcial, however, have revised their opinion after seeing photos and examples of Juan's recent work. These reactions, which I reported to Juan, pleased him greatly.

Since the deaths of his first two sons, Juan and his family have had generally good health and no major crises. They have enjoyed good fortune and now own a CD player and a television in addition to their telephone. Juan is obsessed with investing in the education of his children. He sent even his daughter away for schooling in Iguala, once she reached nine years of age. This practice is unusual in Oapan, where many children, especially daughters, receive no real education at all.

The family is now spread across two (nearby) houses, Juan's house and the house of Juan's mother-in-law. They consider this expansion to be a mark of status. It also gives Juan the ability to paint in one courtyard undisturbed while the children play or talk in the other locale. Juan's family has been upgrading their houses for several years, adding new spaces and furniture. The homes are typical, having a large open courtyard in the center, connecting to a backyard. This open space provides room for painting, cooking, eating, and socializing, in addition to the family animals, which include mules, burros, chickens, roosters, and dogs. On each side of the courtyard is a building, with rooms for sleeping and storage, but family members often sleep outside in hammocks. Oapan residents basically live outside, using the house for storage and for protection against the sun and rain.

When they have extra money, the family rents a "sky antenna" connection by the month, which gives them access to a wide range of Spanish-language channels, including pornographic movies. They watch the news as well, and since 9/11, they frequently ask about the dangers of terrorism in the United States.[7]

The eldest son, Leonardo, twenty-six as of 2003, has given up his plans to emigrate to the United States. He studied in Iguala and became fully literate and fluent in Spanish. Nonetheless, he will stay in Oapan and take Juan's place as the head of the family ceramics business. He also hopes to be a leader in village politics. He has had numerous marriage engagements fall through, which is common in Oapan. He now claims he would prefer to save up his money to expand the family business, rather than spend it on a family of his own. Sometimes it appears that Leonardo enjoys the back-and-forth of broken engagements. Such a pattern of behavior has historical roots. Referring to her 1959 stay in Ameyaltepec, Peggy Golde wrote, "It seemed to me that courtship behavior, whether actual or vicarious, provided an important form of recreation in the village: it offered suspense, a challenge to the ingenuity, the deliberate creation of tension associated with the danger of exposure, and ultimately, with enough perseverance and cleverness, satisfaction and triumph."[8]

The eldest daughter, Alcividiades, has despaired for her future, fearing she is an old maid. Until she marries, she is expected to do a large part of the household chores and help raise the younger children. She used to talk of moving to Houston to clean houses. The second youngest son, Perfecto, is twenty (ca. 2003) and expresses a strong desire to leave for the United States. He stands outside the family circle and has no interest in art or amates.

Juan's children, like most Oapan residents, evince a great interest in the love lives of others, especially foreigners; I frequently receive queries about the marriages and relationships of the other foreigners who have visited. If any single foreigner visits Oapan, the villagers quickly decide whom in Oapan that person ought to marry. Peggy Golde, in her visits forty years ago, noted that area residents believe that American women boss around their husbands and run the household.[9] Leonardo and Alcividiades have a rough sense of the American notion of "girlfriend" and ask frequently—and only half in jest—whether my girlfriends have hit me very much.

Idle chatter and gossip, typically coming during or around mealtimes, occupy much of the family's time. Juan's wife, mother-in-law, and eldest daughter share in the cooking chores. The others come in and out to eat, depending on their schedules and when they are hungry. Almost always, somebody is at some stage in the cooking process, although the whole family never eats together. The family is harmonious but has few close outside friends and is known for its insularity.

Juan has said that he has never wanted to leave Oapan, since that is where he has his family and animals and where he works in the fields. His dream is to improve his house and have more animals. He views Leonardo as his heir apparent in the family and hopes Leonard will be able to extend the family's amate and crafts business.

Felix Camilo Ayala • Like Juan, Felix retreated to life in the village after Rabkin and sold on a very small scale. His family, including seven children, earns its living by painting on ceramic, typically making decorative works for sale in urban markets, such as Cuernavaca. For a while, Felix was painting plates and laminated crosses. Felix's wife passed away several years ago, and he is therefore extremely busy with the immediate affairs of the family. Several of the children have not yet entered their teen years. Felix spends little time working in the fields, which he does not enjoy and which takes him away from the household.

The laminated crosses have proven especially popular, but they mean less to Felix than his pictures of Oapan. None of the three Camilo brothers are very religious in the formal sense. They will self-identify as Catholics and profess a belief in a God, but only Marcial has a doctrinal sense of what Christianity or Catholicism means.

In a typical year, Felix will paint about one hundred amates and forty pictures on board, usually of small size (twelve by twelve inches or slightly larger). He does not expect to sell all of these but, rather, paints many of them for his own enjoyment. He sells some of the amates in Cuernavaca and is hoping to work out an arrangement to sell some of them in Cancún, though he is not pursuing this aggressively. Lately he has received several foreign commissions for amates from dealer Martin Kroll.

In the last few years, he has not been able to fulfill these commissions promptly, due to the illness of his young son, who suffers periodic fainting spells. Doctors have told Felix that his son has epilepsy. Sometimes his son requires regular and close attention, but more generally, Felix says that he himself does not have the concentration to paint well at the moment. Felix does not know what to do about this situation.

Both Marcial and Juan are on friendly terms with Felix, though with some distance. At neither house is he a regular visitor. In terms of art, both Marcial and Juan regard Felix's best works as excellent, but neither gives him much artistic respect. Felix was always the "younger brother" of the three, looking up to the others. Nonetheless, Felix is a valued voice among his friends. He is one of the few individuals in Oapan about whom I have never heard other people speak negatively.

Felix sees little change in his style over time, though he thinks his current paintings are simpler than before. He would like to paint larger and more ambitious works once again, though he does not regard this as likely. In 2001 I commissioned several larger works on masonite board from Felix, though I had not yet received them as of 2004.

Felix's eldest daughter, Sinforosa, who is now twenty-three, does much of the work to raise the children, cook the meals, and take care of the house. Her existence is generally regarded as very burdensome, given the absence of the mother.

Marcial notes that Felix stands a very good chance of marrying again, if he so wishes. But according to Marcial, Felix is unlikely to remarry as long as he has the daughters to cook and run the household. Once they are married off, Felix might remarry to have someone to cook for the younger sons. Marcial notes there are enough widows and abandoned women in the village for Felix to choose from.

The Felix Camilo household differs greatly from Juan's home. Felix's household is typically very quiet, almost somber. Everyone appears sad and lethargic. The elder children paint pottery when they have time, to support the family, but no one has a plan for how the family might advance its prospects. When asked about politics, Felix will defer to Marcial, saying he must speak to his older brother. Felix's dream is to finish construction of his house, purchase more animals, and raise his children successfully. His immediate task, however, is simply to make ends meet and hold the family together for the next day.

Roberto Mauricio • Of all the painters, Roberto has been tied to the land most closely. He always stopped painting to harvest the yearly crop, returning to art only once the fieldwork was taken care of. He has set up his home and land (on the edge of town) as a ranch with horses and cattle. Everyone thinks of Roberto as a cowboy. He lives in Oapan all the time, is married, has eight children, and has an especially large piece of land.

Roberto pursued a part-time career as a musician. For eight years, he has played guitar and sang in an Oapan group called Organizacíon

Musical. The group plays in the other local pueblos. In a given year, Roberto is likely to play fifteen or twenty dates, with an evening's work consisting of about five hours of music. A night's work typically yields six hundred pesos—about sixty-five dollars at the 2004 exchange rate. Roberto greatly enjoys making music (just as he enjoys his art), and he practices guitar on a regular basis.

By his own admission, Roberto "drinks too much" [*tomo demasiado*]. Nonetheless, he is likely to be sober in the summer months, when his work is needed in the fields. He claims his eyes are very bad and getting worse all the time. He fears going blind and now wears glasses to paint his amates. His arms hurt him very badly sometimes, and he frequently has nightmares about his death. According to his wife, however, he refuses to go see a doctor or to take vitamins.

Roberto paints amates on an irregular basis. He sells some of his lower-quality amates through his sister, typically in Oaxaca or on the beach at Puerto Escondido. The amates sell for roughly twenty dollars apiece. Roberto receives half of this sum, with the other half going to his sister. At times, Roberto sells other amates at the Sunday market at Tepotzlán, a well-known tourist town less than an hour from Cuernavaca. His niece handles these items, again splitting the proceeds with Roberto. Some of these amates show very fine work, while many others are more perfunctory.

He sells his highest-quality works to visiting collectors for much higher prices. He keeps these at home rather than offering them in the market. It seems that Roberto painted these for his own satisfaction, rather than for profit, but will sell them to justify the expenditure of time or depending on his mood that day. He makes no active effort to market these works or to produce more of them, even when he is offered a superior price. He simply is not oriented toward trying to succeed as an artist.

Thomas Bird, a German living in New York, sometimes comes to visit Roberto and purchase amates. Bird has been visiting the region for over two decades and comes periodically, especially when his work takes him to Cuernavaca, which it does regularly. In addition to myself, this is Roberto's only foreign buyer at the moment.

A number of other people, including art dealers, have expressed interest in obtaining some high-quality amates by Roberto, but the supply has not been forthcoming. Sometimes Roberto pleads that he must work in the fields or play guitar with his group. At other times, he says that his body hurts, his eyes are failing him, he cannot concentrate, or he is simply exhausted. For a while he claimed that he no longer has enough energy to paint on board, although in 2003 he did paint a few works in this medium. When Roberto paints amates for me, he gives them to Leonardo, Juan's son, who ships them to me with works by Juan. Unlike the other group members, he has no compunction about breaking a previous agreement to paint; he might, for instance, claim that he was drunk when he agreed to a previous price, then ask for—and expect—a better one.

Roberto's household appears to be happy. His own family considers him to be eccentric, but they defer to him as leader. Unlike in Juan's house, the family eats meals together at the same time, and they have a sufficiently long table to do so.

The family is relatively prosperous by Oapan standards, but in the past, they have relied on remittances from two of Roberto's sons working in Los Angeles. These sons, in their early twenties, sent money back home on a regular basis. Nonetheless, both became disillusioned with their time in the United States and returned to Oapan in 2001. Most of all, they complain about their treatment at the hands of other Mexicans in the United States. They worked in the fields picking strawberries and felt they were badly treated and underpaid, relative to what they had expected. Both had painted amates, in the style of their father, but found that the avocation did not pay much.

Roberto believes that his best current amates represent the artistic peaks of his career. He says he now has more experience "with the fight" [con la lucha], a common phrase in Oapan. His professed dream is to arrange the house and ranch in satisfactory condition and to resume painting on a larger scale. He recently wrote to me: "Fifty years we will continue painting, although the vision is fading. I already use eyeglasses to be able to paint, and I will continue the fight, and we will die making the fight."[10]

Segmentation in Current Amate Markets

To understand the economic fates of these painters, we must look more closely at how amate markets have developed over the last twenty years. In the very early years of amate, the distinction between quality amates and street amates was not well defined. Clearly some amates were better—some much better—than others, but all the painters were aiming at the same narrow segment of audience, namely, those people who bought from a few select craft shops. Later, in the Cuernavaca years of the 1970s, both very good and very bad amates were offered for sale in the same street. It could be the case that both the very best and the very worst amate painters would sell their amates in the same locale for fifteen to twenty-five pesos (with an exchange rate of 12.5 pesos to one American dollar at that time).

Over time, a split developed between "high" and "low" amate culture. As the market developed, painters were segmented into tiers of quality. Some painters aimed at wealthy and relatively informed buyers. These individuals were either folk art collectors or simply individuals with a good enough eye to tell the difference between cheap and carefully done works. Other painters directed their wares at tourists looking for a quick souvenir with bright colors. The low-quality painters took over the street, whereas the high-quality painters sold through private connections and pursued differing forms of quality certification.

Growing price dispersion reflects this growing segmentation. In 1970, the price range for amates was between ten and one hundred pesos, with most amates being sold in the street. Now prices range from thirty pesos for cheap street sales to several thousand pesos for the best works at the upper end of the market, which are usually purchased directly from the artist (these later figures refer to an exchange rate of nine to eleven pesos for an American dollar around 2001–4).

If a painter does not have connections to wealthy and informed buyers, he or she is doomed to sell in cheaper markets, even if the objective quality of the work is high. This is in essence what happened to Juan Camilo, Felix Camilo, and Roberto Mauricio. As market segmentation proceeded throughout the 1980s and 1990s, the economic situation of these individuals failed to show any prospects of improvement. For reasons of geography and their limited capital, these painters could not access buyers who had any inkling of their previous reputations.

In more general terms, the price of an amate does not correspond in any simple way to what an art critic might consider to be "quality." The pricing of amates depends also on the location and reputation of the painter and on the pricing strategy of the seller, which in turn follows from the economic situation of the producing family. Think of families as choosing a pricing strategy in advance, depending on the role that amates play in the family income and on their opportunities to sell, which in turn depends on location. Buying is sufficiently irregular and dispersed that there is no central market for amates and thus no set of uniform prices. For this reason, it is hard to construct any simple story correlating amates' "artistic quality" and their price.

As amate painters have greater contact with foreign buyers (or, more generally, with wealthy buyers), they move to a dual pricing strategy. They will sell cheaper, lesser (though still good) works at very low prices and better works at substantially higher prices. Once they understand that the buyer can judge quality, they know that the cheaper, lower-quality works will not cannibalize the demand for their higher-quality, finer creations.

Oapan artists have earned higher prices only by leaving the pueblo and cultivating wealthier buyers in other locales. It is in this context that the varying economic fates of the group members must be seen.

Those That Left

Inocencio Jimenez Chino • Inocencio and Felix Jimenez Chino, both pragmatic by nature, landed with their feet on the ground following the end of the Oapan painters' relationship with Rabkin. Now they both live in San Miguél Allende, a popular tourist destination in the state of Guanajuato, approximately three hours from Mexico City. One American writer described San Miguél as "a kind of Mexican Williamsburg" (Cohan 2000, 13). San Miguél also has a large and growing retirement community of Americans—now numbering about five thousand—and is becoming more popular than Cuernavaca among new retirees.[11]

In San Miguél, these artists sell largely to tourists and command prices much higher than back home in Oapan. Their full-size amates sell for about two hundred dollars, and their full-size paintings on board and canvas sell for more, ranging from three to five hundred dollars depending on the size of the work, with smaller works selling for correspondingly less. While neither brother is wealthy, each possesses a certain degree of lower middle-class comfort.

Both their paths to San Miguél were circuitous. After leaving
Rabkin's house in Cuernavaca, Inocencio returned to working the
fields in Oapan. He eventually felt restless in this environment, how-
ever, and sought more opportunities to paint. In 1988 he moved to
Guadalajara with his wife, Florencia, to sell amates in the *portales*—an
unofficial, covered kind of crafts market in the street, near the center of
town. He stayed in Guadalajara three years, then moved to San Miguél
Allende in the early 1990s to seek more customers. Inocencio found
San Miguél a more profitable and more pleasant environment than
Guadalajara and has remained there until this day. In a typical year,
Inocencio splits his time between San Miguél Allende, Oapan, and
Iguala, though spending most of the time in San Miguél.

Inocencio currently spends virtually no time working in the field.
Last year, he worked with the corn crop for a short while, but amate
painting consumes most of his work time. He visits Oapan frequently
but regards his trips there as time to rest and visit friends, though he
will work on amates when there.

Inocencio also spends a good deal of time painting in his cousin's
house in Iguala. He takes a spare room in the house and has much free
time to paint. At the same time, he can visit friends in nearby Oapan
when he so desires. He does not sell his work in Iguala, which is visited
by few tourists; rather, he brings the amates he finishes there back to
San Miguél.

Inocencio sells amates—and, to a lesser extent, paintings—from a
variety of outlets. Most significantly, he has a connection with a San
Miguél Allende crafts shop, Sabía, which serves as his primary means
of finding customers. The shop sells high-quality folk art from a variety
of Mexican states, including Guerrero, Oaxaca, and Michoacán. Along
with Inocencio's work, they also carry lithographs by Nicolás de Jesús,
an amate painter from Ameyaltepec (who will be discussed in more
detail later in this chapter). This same store also has a branch in Oaxaca, and they ship some of Inocencio's amates down there to be sold.
At any one point in time, the store might hold six of Inocencio's
amates. Inocencio also sells some of his work through Galerie San
Miguél and through the ceramics table that his wife runs near the central square. His wife sells most of her painted ceramic work through this
table, but some of her works are available in Puerto Vallarta as well. In
a typical year, Inocencio will sell twenty-five amates and four paintings

on fiberboard. The amates will range in price from fifty to two hundred dollars, depending on their size.

Inocencio has contact with some North American buyers. He sometimes paints amates for Martin Kroll, a retired schoolteacher who holds periodic exhibits of Inocencio's work, typically in Arizona or San Antonio. Kroll deals naive art from his house, including works from Mexico, Yugoslavia, and sometimes Haiti. He originally established contact with Inocencio through Ana Luisa Ramos Prida. Maria and Robert Walsh (discussed in chapter 3), introduced Kroll to the idea of selling amates. The Walshes had read an article by Kroll on naive art and contacted him with information about Inocencio. Inocencio also sells to a buyer near San Francisco, through his affiliation with a San Miguél gallery. The buyer has bought several large amates from Inocencio, with themes relating to the conquest and village politics.[12]

Inocencio's current amate sales bring in money, but he cannot sell very many amates for very high prices. His wife's work as a ceramics painter therefore contributes more to the regular income of the family (Inocencio and Florencia recently adopted a child but have no biological children of their own). Florencia receives ceramic molds from Iguala, as do many of the households in Oapan, and paints them various blues and bright colors for sale in the marketplace. The resulting ceramics include suns, sun and moon combinations, cats, turtles, and a variety of other animals. While a typical piece brings in only five to ten dollars, the sale of ceramics is much steadier than that of amates.[13]

Inocencio also has served as a language consultant to anthropologist Jonathan Amith. Amith is working, with the assistance of Department of Education funding, to compile a dictionary of the dialect of Nahuatl spoken in the pueblo. In two recent summers, Jonathan has had Inocencio and Florencia flown up to Yale to help study the vocabulary and grammar of Nahuatl. Florencia's pay for this effort has helped Inocencio continue his work painting amates.[14]

Inocencio's amates now use bright, almost fluorescent colors. He has abandoned the natural colors he used in his youth, in favor of eye-catching colors, to attract tourists in the markets and stores of San Miguél Allende. This is particularly ironic because of Inocencio's history as a painter. Inocencio's first exposure to nonamate art came when he visited the Diego Rivera murals in Cuernavaca as a teenager. He was struck by their soft and earthy colors and vowed to paint in a similar manner, which he did for a long time, at least until the last ten years or so.

Inocencio reports two major regrets as a painter, both of which he hopes to remedy. First, he has always had to sell his entire output to maintain the household and thus has not been able to keep some of his best work for himself. (Marcial expresses a similar regret.) Second, he has wanted to explore more different and interesting themes than his tourist clientele in San Miguél Allende has allowed him to do. In particular, he wishes to learn how to paint "dreams and apocalypses" and has said that he may try some of these themes in the future. In this regard, his wishes reflect the influence of Marcial, and when speaking to Inocencio, the listener still very much feels the strength of Marcial's shadow whenever his name comes up.

Felix Jimenez Chino • Shortly after Felix Jimenez stopped painting for Rabkin, he realized he needed to find other customers. In 1983 he started selling his work in Jardin San Jacinto, which is part of the Bazar Sábado, the same folk art center where Max Kerlow, Felipe Ehrenberg, and the Ameyaltepec painters originally founded amate painting. Felix's "post" is in an outdoor garden, where many other painters sell their wares. Felix usually shows up every other Saturday, taking the three- to four-hour bus ride from San Miguél. The current price for this post is forty pesos a month. On Sundays, Felix sells in another weekly crafts market, held behind the Monument de la Madre in Mexico City. Most of Felix's sales come from these outlets or from contacts he makes at these stands.

At times, Felix has sold in the Galeria Berica in San Miguél, but currently he has no works there. They insisted that he agree to an exclusive dealing arrangement with them, at least within the confines of San Miguél. Felix reports not being very happy with this gallery, largely because they sell many differing things, not just art. He would rather sell his work in a gallery that carries paintings only, which carries higher status in the art world, but so far he has not managed to achieve this feat.

Typically, Felix paints five pictures in a month, of varying sizes, and sells most of them. The largest go for about five hundred dollars (more when they feature hand-painted frames), but he more commonly sells smaller sizes for about three hundred dollars.

Seven years ago, Felix Jimenez moved to San Miguél. He had wanted to move earlier, but he waited until his son finished school in Oapan. A cousin of his wife recommended San Miguél, and after visiting, he decided he liked the idea of living there. San Miguél was also much closer to Felix's Mexico City outlet (a bus ride of three to four hours, rather than ten, from Oapan). Felix's wife paints ceramics, of the mass-produced colorful kind, which are then typically sold in the nearby town of Guanajuato. She spends most of her time there, which is about ninety minutes from San Miguél.

Felix's business does not rely on his residence in San Miguél, which is where the family decided to live. Felix has not worked much in the fields for many years and has the weakest ties to Oapan of the group considered in this study. Unlike the other group members, for instance, he does not stay in Oapan for most major fiestas. He is the only one who has very deliberately tried to assimilate into broader Mexican culture.

Virtually all of Felix's clients are foreigners, even though he markets his work only in Mexico City. Typically, his customers come from the United States, Spain, or France. They praise his work for its "naive" style, which Felix believes is much less popular among the Mexican upper classes. Felix now paints self-consciously within this style. Felix also concentrates on painting pictures more than amates. His foreign clientele typically knows little of amates and enjoys colorful paintings of village life. Amates might also fail to capture the attention of the buyers in the rather crowded and noisy park, full of other artists with large and brightly colored canvases. In a typical year, Felix might sell twenty pictures on board and another ten on canvas, of varying sizes. He also will sell a few amates in a given year, typically at the Bazar Sábado.[15]

Like Inocencio, Felix uses brighter colors than before, so that he may attract the attention of potential buyers in the park. He also tends to repeat the same kind of scene over and over again, such as a river scene or a fireworks scene. He does not want to keep multiple versions of the same picture in his inventory at the same time, but once he sells a painting of a given kind, he tends to paint another of a similar nature. He finds that brilliant portrayals of stars and fireworks sell especially well. Felix's pictures also have become more "pretty." He has been told that his flower scenes, replete with bright colors, are especially popular, so he paints more of those.

Felix admits that these developments are not positive for his art. When Felix is asked what his favorite pictures are, he cites works in his previous style, when he painted for Rabkin. (His very favorite picture is the androgynous paneled piece I described in chapter 3.) Felix also claims, however, that he has become a far superior painter of detail than before, due to continued practice.

Felix and his brother Inocencio are not unfriendly to each other, but they keep a certain distance. They do not generally share customers, refer customers, or market their work together. They sell to different customers and through different outlets, using separate and disconnected markets. Despite their proximity and their mutual distance from Oapan, they do not visit each other's homes on a very regular basis.

Marcial Camilo Ayala • Marcial now lives in Cuernavaca, while maintaining his traditional house in the pueblo. Marcial has a wife, two daughters, and two sons. The two daughters are now grown and have married. Oliva, the younger daughter, paints very actively—on amate paper, board, and ceramics. She married in December 2002 and had her first child late in 2003.

After Rabkin, Marcial found several new patrons, though without consistent commercial success. The first was Ana Luisa Prida Ramos (already mentioned in chapter 3), who had already been selling Marcial's works through Rabkin. When Rabkin left, she took Marcial under her wing more directly. Ana Luisa had been a relatively well-known painter herself, largely of a naive and surrealist bent. The pictures Marcial painted for her drew from her influence.

First, she encouraged Marcial to switch the material he was working on. Rather than painting on board or even canvas, he now was to paint on the fibrous kwaxtli material (*cuaxtle* in Spanish), as she had done for many years. Kwaxtli comes from right outside of Oapan (from the neighboring "enemy" pueblo of San Miguél), where it is sewn together and used as a seat for riding burros and mules.

Three-dimensionality distinguishes kwaxtli as a painting material. The "canvas" is literally fibrous and is puffed up into dimensions. The painting not only looks but is three-dimensional. Marcial, who started off painting with very flat perspective, now produced works that explored an opposing sense of dimensionality. The dimensionality allowed Marcial to produce many intriguing effects. But at the same time, the material was very difficult to paint on—precisely because of the dimensionality. Many works look striking from a distance, but up close, the viewer sees that the paint often smears or is applied in what appears to be a sloppy manner.

Marcial's themes changed as well. Marcial now painted animals much more frequently than before. Many of his prior pictures had con-tained animals (indeed, a realistic scene of San Agustín can hardly avoid them), but rarely were animals the center of attention in the pic-ture. From now on, at least half of his scenes were to concern animals almost exclusively, as one might find in a jungle painting by Henri Rousseau. The colors became much brighter as well, in some instances florid. Purple became common as a central color. The canvas became more crowded, and the mood became more surrealistic. All of these qualities can be seen in the work of Ana Luisa Ramos Prida as well, except for the crowded nature of the canvas.

Felix Jimenez opines that Marcial's work in the 1990s never reached its previous quality. With the protection of Rabkin gone, Marcial had to paint for the market to earn a living. Felix believes that Marcial had to hurry his work much more and that he paid less attention to detail. Another of Marcial's later dealers, Alberto Wuggetzer, while a fan of the work, admits that many would-be clients found it to be too kitschy. Marcial himself, however, will admit no inferiority of this work; he claims it simply represents another stage of his development as an artist.

Ana Luisa helped arrange several exhibits of Marcial, some in Mex-ico City and others in Cuernavaca. Marcial estimates that he painted up to twenty pictures for her on coconut fiber and about ten or twelve on board. The coconut fiber pictures sold best.

For a while, Ana Luisa had an exclusive dealing arrangement with Marcial. She complained, however, that the artist did not paint enough for her. More significantly, she complained that the artist would offer pictures to her friends, thereby undercutting her attempt to make a market for him. Later, Ana Luisa fell ill, and by the middle of the 1990s, her activities were seriously curtailed. She required a hip replacement and finally died in 1999.[16]

By the middle of the 1990s, the Bio-Arte gallery of Cuernavaca stepped in as Marcial's new promoter. Bio-Arte is run by a Bavarian named Alberto Wuggetzer, who moved to Mexico in 1955 to pursue a career in bee husbandry. In 1980 Wuggetzer started Bio-Arte as a very fancy, very high-quality store for furniture and furnishings, located near the center of Cuernavaca. Later, Wuggetzer bought Ana Luisa's stock of Marcial paintings and ordered another thirty or thirty-five more. He had already been familiar with the work, as Ana Luisa had held a successful exhibit of Marcial's work in Bio-Arte in the early 1990s. Wuggetzer is first and foremost a businessman, but he also loved Marcial's art and wished to promote it.

Like Ana Luisa, Wuggetzer encouraged Marcial to paint on coconut fiber. He wanted pictures that were strongly dimensional, were very colorful, and portrayed many animals. He prefers the multidimensional works, which he believes show far more life than the flatter pictures on board or canvas.

Wuggetzer had great success selling Marcial's work in the first half of the 1990s, when he sold over thirty pictures. More recently, the pictures have not been selling. Wuggetzer claims that lack of security and numerous kidnappings have driven many Americans out of Cuernavaca. He also blames the growing presence of superstores (e.g., Wal-Mart), prominent in Cuernavaca, for a more general decline in his business. Finally, Bio-Arte was probably not well suited to promote Marcial in the first place. It reaches a broad clientele but is essentially a high-class crafts and furniture shop rather than an art gallery. By its nature, the store cannot credibly present itself as a place where one would buy a serious painting for a high price.

Bio-Arte sold Marcial's pictures primarily to Americans, typically residents of Cuernavaca or nearby environs. Like so many people involved with the work, Wuggetzer believes that most Mexicans undervalue their indigenous artists. So much of Marcial's work portrays poor people or work in the fields, and Wuggetzer believes that at this point in time, Mexicans would sooner put these themes behind them.

Mrs. France Chancellor of Cuernavaca is a good example of how Marcial's new customers differed from his previous ones. His earlier customers typically collected Haitian and naive art and were well versed in art markets, and they often had some connection to Rabkin or Selden Rodman. Mrs. Chancellor has an extensive art collection but with no particular links to naive painting. After her husband died, she pursued a greater interest in things spiritual, partly through the arts.

Her very upscale house, just outside of Cuernavaca, is full of works representing different aspects of spirituality. These include not only Mexican paintings—usually of a religious-surrealist bent—but also Tibetan Buddhist items and portraits of Christ. Some of her surrealist pictures portray rather voluptuous naked women. She bought most of her seven pictures by Marcial from Bio-Arte, but her favorite was commissioned from him directly. It represents Marcial's conception of God and portrays a blazing ball of light, surrounded by stars. When asked why she was first attracted to his art, France said she does not know of any painter anywhere who so strongly sees and portrays the life forces present in animals and plants.

Marcial found his most regular patron, Miguel Valentine Watanabe Uchida ("Señor Watanabe" to Marcial), through his cousin Felix Jimenez. Felix was marketing his pictures in the Bazar Sábado when he caught the attention of Watanabe. Felix sold a picture to Watanabe and later gave Watanabe's address to Marcial. Watanabe and Marcial established contact in Cuernavaca, and Watanabe fell in love with Marcial's work.

Watanabe is a Mexican of Japanese origin. He owns a network of camera shops in Mexico, and his very large house, on top of a high hill in an expensive neighborhood, suggests extreme wealth. Since having met Marcial, Watanabe has ordered at least thirty-five paintings and numerous amates, some of very large size. Watanabe favors bright and florid colors, jungle scenes, a certain sentimentality of feeling, and the bumpy kwaxtli base. Marcial notes that Watanabe likes pictures that are "full of life" [llena de vida]. Watanabe also has an extensive collection of masks (not just Mexican) and buys a few other Latin American artists in concentrated fashion, typically favoring works that are large, bright, and full of detail.

Rabkin stayed in touch with Marcial. But until recently, his other earlier promoters, such as Selden Rodman, did not know that he was still painting or even if he was still alive.

In 1994 Marcial moved to Taxco. His daughters were getting older and starting to paint. Taxco offered many opportunities to sell. Marcial's family runs a pottery and trinket stand in the town square, usually manned by his wife or daughter. Marcial's son Israel suffered from a skin disease, and Marcial believed that the cooler climate of Taxco would be good for him, which it proved to be. Most of all, Marcial expressed frustration with life in Oapan and the lack of things to do there. Taxco has an active town square, many shops and restaurants, and a general sense of life and vitality.

Nicolás de Jesús, an amate painter and graphic artist from Ameyal-tepec and a close friend of Marcial's, claims that Marcial's 1993 stint as *comisario* also pushed him to leave the pueblo. As *comisario*, Marcial was responsible for resolving pueblo disputes (see chapter 5 for more on this episode), and Nicolás believes this caused Marcial to lose patience with the pueblo and its inhabitants.

The 1990s brought only a single trip to the United States by Marcial. In 1993 he flew to Los Angeles for three days. A documentary featuring Kevin Costner about the indigenous tribes in the Americas was being filmed. Through the intermediation of Cathy Good, an anthropologist and longtime friend, Marcial was chosen as the spokesperson for the Nahuas. During his time in Los Angeles, he received numerous interviews and questions about his culture and the customs of his pueblo. A television program called *Five Hundred Nations* was made from the material and later shown on the Discovery Channel. The final cut contained Marcial's remarks about the large pyramids just outside of Mexico City: Marcial remarked that at first he was impressed by their beauty and that he then realized he was viewing the equivalent of a dead father.

Marcial's greatest catastrophe came in 1995, when his wife, Gloria, hemorrhaged during the birth of Miguel Angel, their last son. Gloria almost died, as she gave birth in Oapan with only a midwife, rather than seeing her pregnancy to an end in Taxco.[17] From this birth, Gloria also developed severe complications from a hormonal misbalance, which Cuernavaca doctors could not diagnose for a long time. She was sick for several years. Marcial spent much time looking after her and the children. His ability to paint and market his art reached an all-time low during this period. Gloria has since recovered fully and resumed her successful ceramics stand in Taxco. Florence Browne describes her as a very good business manager, "the practical one in the family," and the one whose commercial sense made it possible for Marcial to continue his career as an artist.

Marcial tried to do the best work possible while still making a living, but times were difficult for most of the 1990s. Marcial's wife insisted repeatedly that they "try selling something else," other than art, but

Marcial refused to budge. He simply could not imagine life without painting, and he assumed that someday his prospects would improve.

I first met Marcial when I went to Mexico in 1998 to track him down. I found him by questioning the amate sellers in the central square of Taxco. They led me to his daughter, Oliva, who was manning the family ceramic stand. Oliva took me to a dark room off the central square, where I encountered Marcial squinting and painting a piece of pottery. Two young children, a son and a grandson, were running around the room and screaming, occasionally jumping into his lap.

Since that time, I have ordered paintings and amates from Marcial regularly. The amates include a sixteen-amate series on the history of the Nahua people and an eight-by-four-foot amate of Oapan superimposed on the horizon of the world. At first, I requested particular themes for paintings, such as when I asked for the painting of Dante's *Divine Comedy*, but now I usually leave the choice of subject matter up to him. That being said, Marcial often prefers to be given an idea to work with; he considers it a challenge, an inspiration, and a valuable piece of feedback from his customers. With this in mind, I recently requested a biblical painting from him, based on the story of Jacob's ladder from Genesis.

Sometimes Marcial enjoys receiving very exact instructions from a client. He will ask what colors he should use, what figures he should paint, and what kind of look each part of the painting should have. He likes the idea of pleasing the customer and also enjoys the challenge of nonetheless sneaking in his own creativity, even with virtually every aspect of the picture specified. At other times, he will simply ignore the instructions and paint what he wants.

When I brought Marcial a copy of Dante's *Divine Comedy*, I told him it reminded me of his work. I said it was dreamy, full of symbols, and Christian on the surface but pagan underneath. He smiled and laughed, then read the book twice, claiming he did not understand it the first time. The resulting painting shows a remarkable understanding of the work, from the opening lone walk along a path, to the differing levels of hell and purgatory, to the ascent into paradise. On the right side of the picture, Virgil is taking Dante by the hand. The overall style is reminiscent of nineteenth-century Victorian fairy art. Marcial relates that Dante's portrayal of the levels of heaven and hell reminds him of Nahua mythology and that he found the book so interesting for this reason. He particularly enjoyed the "passages about crossing the river" and Dante's entire idea of the "liberation of the soul."[18]

Some of Marcial's works are planned out in great detail. The sixteen-amate series on the Nahua people, for instance, induced him to read several books on the history of the Spanish conquest of Mexico. I had intended the series to be about Oapan and the Alto Balsas region, but Marcial wished to go back further. He responded with a detailed outline to paint the struggle between Cortés and Montezuma. The first few of these amates concern Nahua cosmology, but the series then rapidly moves into the history of the conquest, specifically the march of Cortés and his siege of Tenochtitlan (now Mexico City). After he did some reading, Marcial wrote out detailed notes about each amate, and he is painting an amate in the series every few months.

Gloria Frank, a leading New York Haitian and Outsider art dealer, decided to order several paintings and several amates from Marcial, which she has marketed successfully in her New York shows. Gloria attended the original Connecticut show in the early 1980s and still recalls how impressed she was by the work. She owns a copy of the MIND catalog and remarked, "I love the work of all of those guys." Until very recently, however, she had not known that any of them were still painting or still alive.

Marcial now earns much more per picture than he did when painting for Rabkin. He paints fewer pictures but devotes more attention to detail. Outsider art collectors and dealers have lavished high praise on these works. Laurie Carmody, one such dealer, compared them to the works of the very best Haitian painters. Friend and cousin Felix Jimenez, never one to hold back criticism, also believes that Marcial's work is now much better. He notes that Marcial "paints with calm" once again.

Marcial has started marketing his amates to other venues in Cuernavaca, which he had not done since starting with Rabkin. A Cuernavaca gallery named Qué Milagro! now carries his amate work, along with that of Nicolás de Jesús of Ameyaltepec. Qué Milagro! is located directly across the street from Las Maniñitas, probably the most expensive and fanciest hotel in Cuernavaca.

Marcial does business differently than does Juan Camilo. Juan works regularly, but Marcial works in spurts. He appears to go months without working seriously, though in this "downtime," he is preparing the canvas or board and thinking out ideas. He will then put in huge bursts of effort for a month or two and produce many works at once. For a definite exhibition, the painting will always be ready on time. Otherwise, if there is any latitude in the initial agreement whatsoever, the buyer is never sure when the painting will be ready. The only certainty is that the painting will be late. Marcial is a perfectionist and will not send a painting or amate unless he is fully happy with it. Often, the buyer is asked to pay half up front and then receives repeated requests for more money over time, before the work is finished. Sometimes a buyer will order one work and Marcial will do two of the same, allowing the buyer to pick his or her favorite. Or Marcial will do several different pictures for the buyer, hoping he or she will want to buy all of them. He also will start many (noncommissioned) paintings and never finish them. Right now Marcial has more commissions than he is able to handle.[19]

Sometimes Marcial is late with commissions for more dangerous reasons. He occasionally goes on drinking binges, especially when he is in Oapan or when old friends come to visit. The alcohol makes his diabetes worse, and he has spells of not being able to work at all. He has had temporary periods of dizziness, deafness, double vision, and incapacitation, though none of these problems has lasted for long to date. He faces a longer-run danger of liver and kidney failure. Marcial has taken care to see doctors in recent times, but he has not always been so careful. He admits that he is afraid of doctors and that he would rather ignore his medical problems than deal with them.

His amate commission from the Smithsonian, Marcial's most significant recent success, came in the summer of 2001. The opening exhibit for this museum is to concern the major indigenous groups in the United States and Mexico, and the Alto Balsas Nahua were defined as one of those groups. The curators decided to give that culture a space in the opening exhibit. A Smithsonian employee and assistant curator, Alexander Benitez, was told to research the Alto Balsas arts, and naturally his attention was drawn to amate. An Internet search put him in touch with a Cuernavaca dealer, Lilia Quiroz, who has sold high-quality amates and pottery from Oapan and the surrounding pueblos. Quiroz referred him to me (I had previously bought ceramics from her and corresponded with her by email). Benitez visited my house, took numerous photos, and brought the results back to the senior curators. The decision was made to commission two joint amates, painted by Marcial and Nicolás de Jesús. A further decision was made that the amates should concern two significant recent struggles in the region: (1) a protest against a dam and (2) a land dispute between San Agustín and the neighboring community of San Miguél (see chapter 5 on these struggles). In 2002 the Smithsonian flew Marcial to Washington for a week, to consult about the nature of the exhibit.

Despite these recent successes, Marcial's economic position remains fragile, given how many pictures he must sell each year to make a good living and how much time he is putting into each work. He is always short of money. In part, it costs him money to maintain residences in Oapan, Taxco, and Cuernavaca. Marcial also finds himself drawn into other people's causes. When a relative gets into trouble or has to pay for a funeral, Marcial is there to help. He is willing to run down his savings, believing that he is invincible in a fashion and that more money will always be coming in sooner or later, through some means or another.

Marcial has largely abandoned the florid style he used during most of the 1990s, though it still surfaces occasionally. His current works are a hybrid of many styles, with closer attention to detail than before. His perspective has become less flat and more cubist. He is more versatile in his use of color and draws on a broader range of artistic styles. Marcial claims that he learned much from Ana Luisa, including how to mix colors better and how to prepare a board or canvas for the application of subsequent paint. His current work is superior technically to his earlier work, without having lost his sincerity, imagination, dreaminess, or fundamentally naive style.

Very recently, Marcial has reestablished a more active friendship with Rabkin, who came in January 2001 to visit Marcial in Taxco. He and Rabkin have made plans to exhibit some art painted by Marcial's daughter Oliva. Rabkin has also talked of flying Oliva to New York.

Marcial's family life differs greatly from that of his brothers. He and Gloria now live apart, although they see each other frequently and are loyal to each other as a couple. Recently, Marcial moved to Cuernavaca to set up a small studio and pursue superior opportunities there. His wife and family still live in Taxco. Marcial found it impossible to paint rapidly in the Taxco apartment, given its poor light and limited space and the carousing of his young son and grandson. His patron Watanabe offered him free apartment space in a building Watanabe owns in the center of Cuernavaca, and Marcial accepted the offer. He now has four good-sized rooms, one very large for painting. The apartment is otherwise bare, containing only painting materials, a single bed, and some of Gloria's ceramics for sale in Cuernavaca.

Marcial's family also has more dispersion in age than does Juan's family. Marcial has two young boys and two grown girls, with no child in the middle. Of all the children, Oliva is the closest to Marcial. She looks like him, looks to him for approval, and is following in his footsteps as a naive painter. While Dahlia remains close to the family, she pursues her own directions to a greater extent. Juan's family remains all gathered in Oapan. Marcial's family relations, though emotionally close, are more like a series of temporary bilateral connections.

Nicolás de Jesús • It sheds light on Marcial's career to contrast it with that of Nicolás de Jesús of Ameyaltepec, the Alto Balsas artist with the greatest commercial success. Nicolás has pursued commercial strategies distinct from those of his peers and, in fact, is no longer considered an amate painter at all.

It is difficult to estimate Nicolás's exact income, but his standard of living far exceeds that of the other amate painters. Though by no means a millionaire, he has modern electrical appliances in every room of his Ameyaltepec house and maintains alternative residences in Acapulco and Chilpancingo. An owner of a nice new white car, he plans to send his three daughters to English-language schools.

Nicolás started off like most other amate painters of the region, painting pottery and simple bird amates. He was the son of Pablo de Jesús, arguably the first amate painter and still one of the most highly regarded. Pablo trained Nicolás from a very young age. When Pablo was murdered making a sales trip to Iguala, Nicolás took over the family amate business.[20]

Whereas the Oapan painters tended to focus their sales in Cuernavaca, Nicolás and his family were more entrepreneurial from the beginning. Relying on Ameyaltepec social networks, they sold as far afield as Tijuana, Guadalajara, Cancún, Cozumel, and numerous other locales.[21]

By the early 1980s, Nicolás was widely recognized by the other amate painters as one of the best in the region. Nonetheless, Nicolás realized he had few opportunities for advancement as a standard amate painter. In 1982 Nicolás traveled to Mexico City, where he came in contact with a print shop called Artegrafías Limitadas. He participated in the making of a print portfolio and learned how to make his work into aquatints. Felipe Ehrenberg, who had first worked with Max Kerlow in Mexico City to introduce amate paper to the village artisans, had maintained contact with Nicolás. Twenty years later, in the early 1980s, Felipe taught Nicolás the basic techniques of etching, graphic work, and lithography. Nicolás learned how to turn amates into "multiples" of various kinds.

In 1988 Nicolás seized yet another opportunity and set out for the United States to earn a better living. He spent time in San Francisco and Los Angeles before finally setting in Chicago for six years with his wife. At first, he had no visa, but he later obtained a legal visa through his art exhibitions. His three daughters were all born in the United States and thus are American citizens. In Chicago, Nicolás joined an artists' workshop, where he learned more about graphic techniques. He recalls working at night and sleeping during the day so that he could obtain scarce studio space. While he admits to drinking very heavily during this time, he also worked very hard and focused his efforts toward marketplace success.[22]

Nicolás then decided to buy his own equipment and go into business as an independent artist. He rented space in Oak Park, Illinois, and found numerous American buyers interested in his work. Commonly he would make a print run of 150 to 250 for a single amate and then sell these works on his own, without relying on gallery intermediation. The works were a big success, and Nicolás exhibited his material in numerous places around the United States, including the Mexican Fine Arts Center in Chicago, various universities, and the Chicago Public Library. Many of his reviews were very favorable, and his presence coincided with a time of increasing American interest in Mexico. Along with Marcial, Nicolás received the Smithsonian commission for amate painting in 2001.

In addition to selling works, Nicolás received a variety of other opportunities to earn money. In the early 1990s, for instance, he was commissioned to draw the illustrations for a cookbook of dishes from rural parts of Mexico, *Cuisines of Hidden Mexico: A Culinary Journey to Guerrero and Michoacan.*[23]

Nicolás returned to Mexico in the early 1990s, largely so his daughters could grow up in the pueblo rather than in Chicago. Since that time, his American success has given him entrée into Mexican markets. Indeed, Nicolás claims that without his years in America, his commercial success in Mexico would not have been possible.

Now Nicolás has turned his Ameyaltepec house into a studio and has trained his wife and daughters in the techniques of printmaking. He and his family make all of the works themselves and need not hire any outside parties. He sells these works to a variety of galleries throughout Mexico, including in Mexico City, Oaxaca, San Miguél Allende, and Cuernavaca. In a typical year, he might make ten prints, each with a run of at least 150. Of course, not all of these works sell, but if we think of a typical print as selling for $150, with Nicolás receiving half of that, we can see that his yearly income far exceeds that of the traditional amate painters. If he sells half of these works in a given year, that amounts to about $56,250, which goes a long way in rural Mexico.

Nicolás notes that his American market connections have dried up since he left the United States, though he has recently moved to reestablish them. He now sells to Steven Clark (Quetzal Gallery, Kingston, New York) and to Fourth World Artisans in Chicago. In any case, Nicolás earns a good living selling through Mexican galleries, and his clientele remains almost exclusively American, albeit in a Mexican locale. Since working at lithography, Nicolás has spent little time doing traditional amates, though he still paints a few large murals on amate paper, which he exhibits and sells to private customers.

Unlike many of the amate painters, including the Oapan group, Nicolás was never much influenced by Diego Rivera or the other Mexican painters. Instead, Nicolás cites Posada, a Mexican printmaker from the early twentieth century, as his dominant influence. To this day, the work of Nicolás reveals a strong Posada influence with regard to both themes and techniques.

Nicolás's access to foreign buyers allowed him—indeed, required him—to expand beyond the traditional themes of amate painting. He takes a special interest in Day of the Dead scenes, which he paints as more strictly Mexican than as Nahua or Alto Balsas in the narrower sense. Nicolás also paints political works of general interest. Many of the amate painters have painted political works, but these have tended to involve local disputes (see chapter 5). Nicolás's political works aim at larger audiences and thus have more general themes. He commonly portrays the struggles of the people against various oppressive dictatorships in a more general Latin American context, not necessarily in a Mexican setting.[24] Nicolás also makes multiples—based on amates—showing explicit sex (either intercourse or oral sex), typically within an Ameyaltepec dwelling. Nicolás notes that he deliberately set out to break all the old taboos of amate painting.[25]

Despite these successes, many amate painters in the Ameyaltepec (though not the Oapan group of this study) grouse at the work of Nicolás. His pieces are seen as too slick and not sufficiently traditional. Most of all, the other Ameyaltepec painters complain because he sells copies rather than original works. They do not think or talk of him as an amate painter.

Nicolás is a great admirer of the art of Marcial, whom he believes to be an artist of the first rank. The two are close friends and talk frequently about art and politics. Nicolás believes that Marcial has not met more success for several reasons. Most important, he believes that Marcial's work is not held widely enough. This makes it hard for Marcial's reputation to spread. He has encouraged Marcial to make lithographs to remedy this deficiency. He also thinks it is a problem that Marcial works relatively slowly. He praises the careful attention that Marcial gives to each work, as well as the resulting quality. Nonetheless, he feels that Marcial never has enough finished paintings on hand to mount a finished exhibit if a gallery should again be interested.

A visit to Nicolás and Marcial quickly reveals further differences of importance. Nicolás, for instance, has an entire press kit ready to hand out to visitors, with photocopies of reviews and press coverage, both in English and in Spanish. Marcial does not even have on hand a resume or a complete list of his previous exhibits. Nicolás also comes across as a consummate businessman. Marcial does not.

I asked Marcial and Felix Jimenez whether they wished to make lithographs. Marcial described his continuing attachment to the idea of an original work of art. In economic terms, he believes that simply making lithographs would not be enough to succeed and that Nicolás's achievement is how he constructed a distribution network. Marcial also worries that selling copies would lower the value of his original works; he notes that none of his customers have asked for copies. Furthermore, switching to multiples cannot be done overnight but would require a substantial investment of time and effort in learning new techniques. When asked about Nicolás, Felix Jimenez smiled and said "to each his own path" [cada quien su propio sendero]. He indicated that all successful people think that others should follow in their footsteps, and he seconded Marcial's comments. That being said, in recent times, Marcial has flirted with the idea of making multiples and has had some exploratory conversations with Nicolás in this direction.

Rabkin and Rodman • Ed Rabkin and his wife, Carolyn, still live in Santa Fe, New Mexico. Their daughter, Lara, lives in New York City, where she is working as a singer. Carolyn has pursued a career as a sculptor. She describes Marcial as her teacher. One of her greatest successes has been having a work exhibited in the High Museum in Atlanta. In 2002 she was interviewed by the Discovery Channel for a television program on her sculpture.

Since having discontinued the storefront version of Galerie Lara, Ed Rabkin has expanded his connection to amate markets. He now sells numerous amate products, including the raw paper, books with quality amate covers, lampshades, decorations, and amate wall hangings. He sells through mail order and through eBay.[26]

Rabkin has dealt in amate paper to some extent for a long time. In 1978 he asked Marcial to visit (twice) the Otomí village of San Pablito, where the paper is made. Marcial helped Rabkin set up business connections and procure supply. Marcial recalls his shock when visiting the pueblo and seeing that all the men carried machetes for martial display, rather than for work in the fields. The Otomí have had a reputation of being warlike since pre-Hispanic times and have continued martial traditions to the present day. Marcial was able to help Rabkin get the paper. Today, Rabkin has expanded these connections and turned them into a profitable business.

In 1999 Rabkin and Selden Rodman held a weekend exhibit of the group's work in Selden's New Jersey house. He accepted some pictures from Rabkin on consignment and publicized a show in his home. The results, however, were less than auspicious. Carole Rodman, Selden's wife, claims that the exhibit failed because the quality of the work was not high enough. Rabkin did not let his best paintings go to Carla Rodman (Selden's daughter, who picked out the pieces for the show) when she visited his home. Carole Rodman also remarked that the clientele on the mailing list for the show consisted mostly of Haitian buyers. These individuals wanted Haitian works, not Mexican ones. The only picture sold was a music scene by Felix Jimenez, which was sold when a photo of the piece was put on a postcard and mailed to a client in Texas.

Since that time, Rodman showed no further interest in marketing the group's works. He passed away at the age of ninety-three in November 2002, when he slipped while walking to his mailbox. He fell on the back of his head, went into a coma, and died shortly thereafter at a local hospital. Historian Gary Fountain of Ithaca, New York, is now in the process of writing a biography of Selden. Before his death, Rodman frequently proclaimed that the Oapan group was underrated and was due to make a comeback someday.

Juan Camilo Ayala, *Amate Painting,* approximately 1980, 15″ x 22.5″. This early amate of Juan's originally sold to FONART and is now in the collection of the author.

Juan Camilo Ayala, *Patron Saint of Guadalajara,* on amate paper, 15″ x 22.5″. Collection of the author.

St. John Carmelzman San Agustin Oapan Mex.

Roberto Mauricio

Roberto Mauricio, *Self-Portrait*, black-and-white amate, 15″ x 22.5″.
Collection of the author.

(*above left*) Juan Camilo Ayala, *Offering and Fiesta*, on amate paper,
15″ x 22.5″. Collection of the author.

(*below left*) Roberto Mauricio, *Women Eating Watermelon*, on amate paper,
15″ x 22.5″. Collection of the author.

Inocencio Jimenez Chino 1998

Inocencio Jimenez Chino 1997

Inocencio Jimenez Chino, segment of an amate mural on the conquest of the
Aztecs, 2000, 15.5″ x 67″. Collection of Alec Giaimo.

(*above left*) Inocencio Jimenez Chino, *Fieldwork*, 1998, on amate paper, 7.25″ x
11.25″. Collection of Alec Giaimo.

(*below left*) Inocencio Jimenez Chino, *Rio Balsas*, 1997, black-and-white amate,
7.25″ x 11.25″. Collection of Alec Giaimo.

Marcial Camilo Ayala, *Oapan*, 2003, on amate paper, 15″ x 22.5″. Collection of Vernon and Candace Smith.

(*above left*) Felix Jimenez Chino, *Cousins Playing Guitar*, 2002, on board, 27″ x 35″. Felix is on the left in this self-portrait; the cousin on the right is Marcial. Collection of the author.

(*below left*) Marcial Camilo Ayala, *Fireworks*, 2003, on amate paper, 15″ x 22.5″. Private collection.

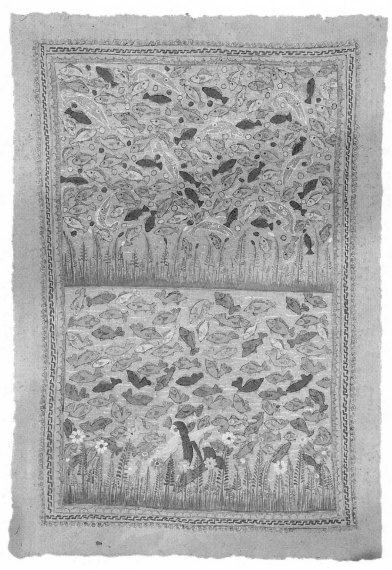

Alcividiades Camilo Altamirano, *Mermaid*, on amate paper, 22.5″ x 15″.
Collection of the author.

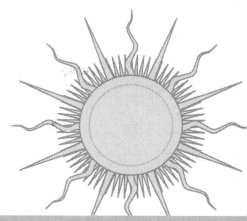

5 • How the Outside World Shapes Politics

PUBLIC CHOICE AND LOCAL GOVERNMENT

I NOW RETURN MORE EXPLICITLY to the theme of liberty versus power. We have seen the history of the painters in markets both within Mexico and abroad. The question remains how politics and power relations have shaped their lives. In Oapan and in Mexico more generally, we observe a largely dysfunctional politics. This has limited the progress of the painters and has threatened to undo Oapan's material progress. Much of Mexican politics has been about extracting wealth from productive individuals, rather than supplying public goods to rural communities. Let us look at this political side of life more closely. Throughout the narrative, we will see the contrast between productive marketplace exchange and "parasitic" relations through state power, referring back to the distinction of Stanislav Andreski (1966), mentioned in chapter 1 of this study.

Rural Mexican municipal government as found in Oapan and numerous other pueblos presents some special features of interest.

—Local governmental structures are extremely weak, relative to the outside forces they confront.

—Corruption is a paramount danger.

—Under the cargo system (explained further in this chapter), local office holding is a cost rather than a benefit.

—Local democracy is participatory.

—The political spectrum is usually defined along issues of preservation versus change, rather than along traditional left- and
right-wing ideologies.

—The lines between politics, religion, and kinship are blurred;
personal quarrels dominate politics.

These features, taken together, have created a political environment
that discourages the production and accumulation of wealth. This
chapter will look at the central political issues of the last fifteen years,
how they have influenced the lives and careers of our artists, and the
burdens they have created. But first let us see in more detail how local
politics operates in Oapan and what kind of incentives it creates.

The Cargo System

The system of town government in rural Mexico is derived from both
pre-Hispanic and colonial influences. Town politics are participatory
and democratic. Political decisions consume significant resources and
time, in part because further lobbying remains possible right up until a
decision is implemented. A decision to involve oneself in politics
therefore places one's time and money at the mercy of community
demands. Furthermore, the community is sufficiently small that a personal relationship or enmity usually precedes a political one. In effect,
weak systems of local government are superimposed on social and kin-
ship-based quarrels. Politics, religion, and personal relationships cannot be separated from each other but, rather, form an interwoven
whole.

Unpaid volunteer labor, under the threat of community pressure, is
the core form of political service. The *comisarios*, the *mayordomo*, and
the *fiscal* are the most important political posts. In addition to these
major offices, volunteers are used to record village transactions (the
secretario), serve in the village band, perform songs and prayers, and
help the major officeholders prepare for fiestas. This activity includes
sewing, making candles, baking bread, repairing public buildings,
cleaning wells, and carpentry, among other tasks.[1]

Fiscal affairs in rural Mexican communities differ from North American municipal systems. Public expenditures often come directly from the pocket of the officeholder, rather than from the general till or from tax revenues. Holding political office is more of a cost or a form of coerced contribution than a means of enrichment. Officeholders, for instance, pay for most of the town fiestas, one of the most prominent public goods. This practice, common to many Mexican and Central American pueblos, is known as the *cargo system*.

Most duties in the cargo system are organized around local public goods. The *comisario* is the political leader, akin to a mayor. The *comisario* is responsible for acting as town ambassador to the outside world, making sure town affairs run smoothly, organizing the fiestas, enforcing the laws, deciding when a tribunal *(juzgado)* should be called, preventing disorderly behavior, and, most of all, resolving disputes among the townspeople.[2]

A *mayordomo* takes care of the chapel of his barrio, opens and closes the doors of the church at the appropriate times, and contributes expenses toward the fiestas. He buys fireworks, skyrockets *(cohetes)*, flowers, chicken, beef, corn, and beer for ceremonial events. In these tasks, a *mayordomo* is assisted by his *padrino*, whom he chooses each year. The most significant obligations are for carnival in the winter and for the fiestas of Santiago (patron saint of the village) held in both May and July. The most regular obligation occurs every Sunday, when the *mayordomo* and his *padrino* must make sure that the church rosary ceremony is supplied with flowers. When the town "authorities" (discussed shortly) pick a new *mayordomo*, they show up at his house with beer and cigarettes. Accepting the offering signals a willingness to do the job.[3]

The *fiscal* organizes some religious festivals and takes care of the church. He is responsible for opening and closing the church every day, caring for offerings, keeping the church clean, taking care of the church "saints" (santos, or statues, used in some fiestas), coordinating the activities of the church singers, and receiving offerings to the saints.

The powers of these officeholders are tightly circumscribed, and we can think of Oapan government as constrained and responsive to public opinion. Individuals serve a one-year term, which typically is not repeated. Major officeholders must meet the informal approval of those whom pueblo members call "the authorities" (*las autoridades*). These are respected individuals, typically older, who have held important pueblo posts in the past. They are the ultimate court of opinion through which all political decisions must pass if those decisions are to command long-run support within the community.[4]

The cargo system appears strange to the American observer, but it is not without economic and political sense. In lieu of using tax revenue, the community conscripts labor and forces a few individuals each year to pay an especially large part of the total tax bill through "donations" of their time and money. This system, due to its implicitly coercive elements, gets the better candidates at relatively low expense. Furthermore, in the long run, most families would rather donate more of their labor than more of their money, given their limited earning opportunities. Jonathan Amith estimates that the current yearly tax burden at the village level runs about eighty dollars a family; at this margin, most villagers would rather work more than pay more. Furthermore, assessing higher taxes could be problematic given how much of village income is paid in kind or produced within the household.[5]

The cargo system eases monitoring costs. The authorities assess the lifetime contribution of each family head and then decide which subsequent burdens would be appropriate. Most of the cargo expenditures take the form of highly visible outputs, such as fireworks, beer, candles, and flowers. During a fiesta, all villagers can see how good a job the officeholder has done. Monitoring the labor contribution in the form of the cargos is not much harder than monitoring additional tax contributions.[6]

The cargo system also makes it easier for the community to implement discretionary taxation. The injured, the sick, the alcoholic, and the totally destitute are not typically expected to execute major cargos. No one wants these people to hold major offices, so the decision to excuse them is noncontroversial and "incentive-compatible," to use a phrase from economics. It would be harder, however, for authorities to use discretion to adjust the tax burden of each family each year. Everyone might agree that an alcoholic should not hold a major cargo, but not everyone will agree what, if anything, alcoholism should imply for a pecuniary tax burden. The cargo system thus helps an inevitably discretionary system to economize on decision-making costs.

We should avoid trying to find a "functional" reason for every village practice, the cargo system included. The cargo system appears to have evolved for complex historical reasons, having to do with the combination of earlier Hispanic and pre-Hispanic systems of local government (see Carrasco 1961). In this sense, the particulars of history, rather than any theory, account for the practice. Functional explanations, however, play some role in explaining the persistence of institutions, rather than their origins. Cargo systems change and evolve all the time (see Smith 1977), and a system that did not benefit anybody probably would not last. So we should think of these explanations as showing why there are some benefits to the system, not why the system is an optimum or best possible practice.

Some anthropologists writing about other Mexican villages have treated the cargo system as a means of purchasing social status and rising in the hierarchy of the village. This hypothesis, however, overrates the value of the status returns in Oapan relative to the expenditures and the hassles.[7]

The operation of the cargo system resembles a university department in some regards. High-status individuals are seen as eligible for cargos, much as an academic department might pressure successful members to become department chair for several years. Senior members of the department think about who has not yet been chair and who might serve as a plausible candidate. (Given that power seekers are dangerous, the individuals who most want the job are not necessarily most wanted by others.) They then try to recruit this individual with a mix of pressure and persuasion, most of all appealing to guilt and a sense of community service.

Being chair offers some kinds of status but not others. Saying no when one is a due to be chair or is an eligible candidate involves a negative stigma. Furthermore, there is status in being asked, even though the job itself brings little status. Nonetheless, being a good chair is not the primary means to status in academia, just as being *comisario* is not the primary means to status in the pueblo. In Oapan social networks, wealth, articulate speaking, and effective politicking produce more prestige than does office holding. Whether as a department chair or as a *comisario*, it is easier to lose prestige through one's service than to gain it. Both jobs are more of a burden than a blessing. In both cases, individuals almost immediately look forward to the end of their term.

Most individuals accept the cargos simply because they have to. They could leave the village altogether, as many people do (see chapters 4 and 6), but otherwise an eligible candidate is expected to take the job. Failure to take the job would result in a loss of all personal standing within the village. While the job is costly, until lately many individuals have not expected to accumulate much wealth in any case. In other words, the feeling was that a person could either lose his wealth through a cargo or lose it in some other fashion.

Performing a major cargo duty does, of course, bring some rents. A *comisario*, for instance, has considerable influence for his year in office and some influence beyond that, at least if he has been successful in building coalitions. People come to him to ask for favors, much as they might go to a department chair. There is little doubt that many *comisarios* take pleasure in being a center of attention in this fashion. We should not, however, think of the office as a vehicle for personal enrichment; as we will see, it is more likely a road to bankruptcy.

For better or worse, a cargo system is hard to get rid of once in place. Most of the minor cargo burdens fall on the young, individuals between twenty and thirty years of age. The major cargos fall on individuals who are somewhat older but still relatively young, in the range of thirty to fifty years old. The elderly typically have served their major cargos at some time in the past. This demographic distribution of the tax burden makes the system very stable. The elderly already have paid their taxes for life and are receiving a steady stream of benefits from the labor of others. Thus, they tend to oppose change, for the same reasons that the elderly in Western democracies oppose changing social security systems. Reformers have found age-linked social security systems to be among the most difficult institutions to change or improve, and the cargo system is "sticky" for similar reasons. Marcial, for instance, having served as *comisario*, is now off the hook for life if he wishes. (He was asked to serve again in 2003 but declined, citing his previous service.) At this point in his life, he would not fare better if the community relied more heavily on direct taxation and assessments, which he would not be able to escape.

Marcial as Comisarío

Marcial is the only group member to have served as *comisario*, as he was primary *comisario* in 1993. In this year, he was the political leader of the pueblo, and he combined functions of a mayor, police force, and cultural preservation agency.

It is widely agreed that serving as *comisario* is more than a full-time job. Everyone in the village brings their complaints to the *comisario*. Marcial reiterates that he received no pay for hearing these opinions and resolving disputes. In theory, the *comisario* receives payment from the fines he collects, but very little of this income actually ends up in his hands. When individuals are censured for disorderly conduct, they are to pay a fine, at the discretion of the *comisario*, but no more than one or two hundred pesos (ten to twenty dollars). This does not represent corruption, as it is widely understood and accepted that officeholders capture the fines. But Marcial, like most *comisarios*, saw little of this money. The helpers of the *comisario*, the *comisionados*, ask that the money be spent on them. For instance, if they bring someone to jail, they will ask that the *comisario* give them soft drinks or something to eat. The more wrongdoings they uncover, the more they will get paid, thus giving them an incentive to work. Usually there is little or nothing left over for the *comisario* from the fines, and half of what is left goes to the *segundo*, the *comisario* next in command beneath the primary *comisario*.[8]

Social pressures also discourage the *comisario* from levying excessive fines. If a *comisario* appears to be collecting too much money, residents start talking about how the *comisario* is intent on building up his house, rather than governing the town.

Accepting the *comisario* office is therefore a very costly decision. Marcial notes that 1993, the year he held office, was a disastrous year for his art. He did not have time to finish a single picture, and he also had no opportunities to travel to sell his work or obtain future commissions. In addition to these opportunity costs, Marcial estimates that the cargo cost him direct expenditures of at least ten thousand pesos (in this year, the exchange rate ranged from three to four pesos per dollar), just about all the resources he held at that time. He describes the decision to accept the post as a great compromise.

Marcial believes that his selection as *comisario* involved more than just his leadership abilities. At the time, Oapan residents thought he had enough money to do it, considering what they thought he had earned from his art. Given his international reputation, "the authorities" thought he was much richer than he in fact was.[9]

Neither Juan Camilo nor Felix Camilo has held a major post in the pueblo. Sometime between fifteen and twenty years ago, Juan was one of the *regidores* helping the *comisario*. Much earlier, when he had just reached maturity, he was a *topile*, assisting with the fiestas. Felix Camilo has never served as *comisario* or *mayordomo*, but he was a *topile* six years ago. He spent a good deal of his time as *topile* helping to build the school and to build the basketball court in the center of town. He says the cargo cost him a good bit of time but not very much money. For the foreseeable future, the passing of his spouse and his associated home responsibilities give him plausible excuse from major duties.

Juan claims there has been talk of his becoming *comisario*, but it is not clear when, if ever, this will happen. Juan has mixed feelings about the prospect, but his family is opposed to the idea. They do not want the expenses and aggravation that such a post would bring. Roberto Mauricio, in contrast, expresses no reservations about wanting to be *comisario*, and this is in part why he probably will never be suitable for the job. When asked why he wants to do the job, he responded, "Because I like justice."[10]

Inocencio Chino once served as *mayordomo*, which he estimates cost him about twenty thousand pesos (about two thousand dollars) in direct expenses, not counting the opportunity cost of his time.[11] The *mayordomo*'s family and social network will help him bear these costs to some extent, but the *mayordomo* must repay these favors with future reciprocal assistance. Inocencio's work as *mayordomo* also altered his lifestyle and work practices for the year of his term. His duties kept him tied to Oapan virtually all of that year; rather than living in San Miguél Allende and visiting Oapan occasionally, he lived in Oapan and visited San Miguél Allende only occasionally.

Felix Jimenez has had less involvement in the cargo system and in village politics. Twenty years ago, Felix served as an assistant to the fiscal. Eight years ago, Felix served as assistant to a village *mayordomo*. Another time, in the early 1980s, just after his marriage, he served as a *topile*. Felix recognizes that his burden has been relatively light. He says, "They haven't touched me yet" [*Todavía no me tocan*]. He notes that he stands ready to serve if called on, but he evinces no great enthusiasm for the possibility.

Marcial understands Felix's attitude very well. While Marcial loves politics, he did not love being *comisario*. He enjoys speaking out, organizing, and exercising informal influence, but he hates office holding, the associated busywork, and the need to hear everyone's complaint. From his point of view, the *comisario* office brought all the worst aspects of politics into his life. In 1995 Marcial was tentatively assigned another burdensome cargo (leader of the Comisariado de los Bienes Comunales, dealing with land rights), but he refused the post, claiming he knew his rights and that he had served the community enough.

Church Disputes

Marcial's tenure as *comisario* came at an especially tumultuous and contentious moment. Issues of religion, politics, development, and external relations were all reaching crisis points during this time.

The most vitriolic internal dispute concerned the nature of church service. In Oapan, there has been a modern priest (a charismatic) and a traditional priest (a Lefebvrist), both of whom visit the pueblo. The villagers have fought over whether the ways of the modern priest or the traditional priest should reign, and the disagreement came to a head in 1993. Today, this still represents the most significant fracture within the Oapan community.[12]

Relative to the tastes of many Oapan residents, the modern priest has an extremely charismatic sense of the Catholic religion. In particular, he is known for playing the guitar during church services, for encouraging dancing, for encouraging clapping, and for holding Mass in Spanish rather than in Latin. Many townspeople, especially the elderly, consider these practices to be distasteful and irreverent. They can recall being told that these same practices were the mark of the devil. Marcial notes that these people cannot change their ideas overnight. They were brought up to oppose these practices and do not want to see them in their church. The opponents of the modern priest sought to limit his presence in Oapan as much as possible.

The dispute reached a head in 1993 when the local church official (the fiscal) from Oapan would not let the modern priest into the town church to give Mass. Most townspeople chose sides, and feelings exploded rapidly. The dispute manifested itself by public arguments, shouting, episodes of pushing and fighting, and many hard feelings, often among close friends. Some of the combatants had to serve short (one-day) stints in the pueblo jail. A town assembly was held to discuss the issue, with Marcial presiding as *comisario*. It was decreed that music and dancing would no longer take place in the church.

Marcial notes that he personally favors guitar playing in the church, having enjoyed guitar music since he learned the instrument at Rabkin's house in his early twenties. Nonetheless, Marcial feels that it is unfair to subject the elderly residents of Oapan to guitar music, given that many of them feel it is a tool of the devil. He maintains that if the church service can be done only one way or another, it should be done without the charismatic flourishes. Marcial objected that the charismatic faction gathered in small groups and behaved in conspiratorial fashion. Rather than taking their case to the pueblo, they first went around and tried to organize as much private support for their case as possible. Marcial regards this as unhelpful factionalism. Marcial's ideal solution would be a compromise to allow both sides to have their way at different times or in different chapels. The villagers were willing to accept such a compromise, but the bishop of the modern priest vetoed the agreement. According to Marcial, the bishop has close ties to the government, is very inflexible, and wields considerable power.

The church disputes simmered for years, then heated up again in September 1999, when the modern priest showed up to perform a wedding service, even though he was not scheduled to appear. The traditional priest was saying Mass for the wedding when the modern priest climbed up on stage to give Mass as well. The modern priest then tried to push the traditional priest off the pulpit, but he failed in this endeavor. (Oapan residents refer to this episode as "la lucha de los altares" [the struggle, or fight, of the altars].) Village members, including many supporters of the modern priest, then scolded the modern priest for acting in such an impolitic manner. A modest melee ensued, during which the modern priest hid in a car to avoid being hit; some mariachi musicians had to hide in a car as well. The next day, the modern priest showed up to celebrate a modern mass, in Spanish rather than Latin. Many villagers then entered the church and pulled the priest out by force, ending the mass.

For a while, it was decreed that no priest would come to Oapan, and the church effectively was closed. Later, a temporary compromise was reached. Currently, traditional Mass, in Latin, is held in one of the capillas (chapels), but not in the central church. The mass in Spanish has been canceled altogether, and no mass is held in the central church. Marcial doubts, however, whether this solution will last long.

All of the brothers and the other leading amate painters regard these disputes as ridiculous. They wish for unity of the village and resolution of the dispute, without caring greatly about whether the guitar is played or what language is used for Mass. Given the villagers' almost complete lack of knowledge about Christian doctrine, it is unlikely that disparate theological visions lie at the heart of the church disputes. Felix and Juan Camilo both cite the silliness of the argument and reiterate that "people simply like to fight," especially because they are bored. This is the core theory of politics that the amate painters hold about other village members and sometimes about each other.

Marcial sees the dispute in terms of a modernization faction and an antimodernization faction. In essence, the two sides are arguing over the future of the pueblo and its relation to the outside world. It is a common pattern in Latin America for the more charismatic or Protestant religions to support commerce, a strong work ethic, and modernization, while turning their back on many indigenous customs, including costly fiestas. In the Alto Balsas region, the charismatic factions are much stronger in the more modernized pueblos of Ameyaltepec and Xalitla and in the larger cities. The pro-charismatics of Oapan reiterate that other locales have the priest play the guitar and perform Mass in Spanish, and they ask why Oapan cannot do the same. The anticharismatic faction understands these associations with modernization and resents them. So even if the villagers do not have well worked-out theologies, the church has become a symbolic forum for disputes over how Oapan should develop.

Felix Jimenez, ever the skeptic, offers a more cynical explanation. He sees the disputes as rooted fundamentally in envies among different group leaders, each vying for leadership in the town. He believes they have used the issues to manipulate the public and to enhance their own power, without necessarily caring much about the matter at hand.

Many villagers worry more about the fact of dispute per se than over which side is right. These "believers" (*creyentes*, as Marcial calls them) think that the disgrace of the fight gets put on the entire pueblo. They worry that this will lead to a lack of good rain and other harmful consequences. In essence, they have pagan reasons for worrying about Catholic disputes.

Throughout the 1990s, these religious disputes have mapped into party disputes, causing the village to split into competing factions. The village has two main parties, Partido Revolucionario Institucional

(PRI) and Partido de la Revolucion Democratica (PRD), correspond-
ing to the two major parties on the Mexican national scene (President
Fox's party, Partido Acción Nacional [PAN], is just starting to have
members in Oapan). On the national scene, PRI has the image of the
establishment party that ruled in the past, while PRD is more left-wing.
The role of these parties in the village does not map tightly to their ide-
ological reputations at the national level, but the divide is nonetheless
real. The choice of party signals a stance on internal village politics.
Interestingly, in Nahuatl, the word *partido*, Spanish for "political
party," also means "split" or "schism."[13]

Marcial, Inocencio, Roberto Mauricio, and Felix Jimenez all belong
to PRD. At the village level, PRD should be thought of as favoring
indigenous rights and opposed to the Mexican national establishment.
The Oapan branch of PRI is less confrontational toward the national
establishment. While PRI is generally a conservative party, its relatively pro-establishment stance often puts PRI members on the side of
modernization rather than preservation of older ways, given that the
national party establishment favors the economic development of
Guerrero. The village branch of PRI is also less aggressive, compared to
PRD, in speaking up for indigenous rights. In this regard, it corresponds
to the national party.

Ironically, the opponents of the modern priest tend to come from
the left-wing PRD party, and his supporters tend to come from PRI.
This makes some sense, since PRD supporters tend to attach greater
importance to preserving indigenous cultures. That said, most individuals of the pueblo do not have a good idea what either party is about at
the national level, so party membership should not be considered an
explanatory variable in these disputes. If anything, party membership
results from a position in the disputes, rather than vice versa.

The split in the pueblo has grown more extreme over the last
decade. Currently, the PRD forces control village politics, as they have
a solid majority within the village, including among the elders. They
hold most of the major political offices. The PRI followers are reluctant
to accept village posts, on the grounds that they would have to work
with the other party. Inocencio fears that the PRI followers no longer
regard town governance as legitimate, on the grounds that they do not
have adequate representation.

The political fracture has influenced the fiestas of the pueblo and split their audience. The PRI followers are now seeking to stage their own fiestas, typically to be held after the fiestas of the PRD followers. They want to have a different *castillo* (fireworks structure) and different bullfights. So far, the PRD forces have resisted this potential split in the fiestas. When the PRI supporters tried to bring in their own bulls for their own bullfight, the PRD forces blocked the road and would not allow it. Disputes over the *castillos*, the bullfights, and the fiestas have exacerbated the underlying tensions in the pueblo.

Marcial is in the PRD camp largely because of his dislike of PRI and its role in the dam crisis in the 1990s (discussed shortly). Marcial feels that PRI pays less heed to indigenous rights than does PRD; thus, he is a (reluctant) member of the latter. During my interviews with him, Marcial insisted that I write that he is unhappy with both parties and does not like politics, although the latter proposition does not command assent from his friends and does not fit his behavior. Inocencio also belongs to PRD, but he stresses that neither party offers a consistent ideology, political program, or vision for the future of San Agustín. Felix Jimenez holds a cynical attitude as well, though again ending up on the PRD side of the ledger.

Felix Camilo claims to value peace and unity above any partisan struggle. He looks back to earlier times when the village was more united. He belongs to PRI rather than PRD, though he claims he is not a strong partisan of the former. He says that the politics of PRD bother him—that despite party claims to stand for "the people" and for indigenous rights, many of the party members are rich and "drive cars" rather than fighting for the people. He believes that PRD is based on a lie and hypocrisy, for which reasons he will not join it. He blames "the teachers" of Oapan for stirring up the recent troubles.

Roberto Mauricio takes the most aggressively left-wing stance of the group. He proudly identifies himself as a Zapatista, and he describes himself as fighting for "justice" *[justicia]* and "right" *[derecho]* against the forces of evil. He belongs to PRD and hates PRI, which he identifies with previous and corrupt Mexican governments. When pressed, he will reiterate clichés rather than give substantive answers to political questions. Within the village, he has the reputation of enjoying a fight for its own sake.

Both Inocencio and Felix Jimenez believe that the fracturing of local government derives, in part, from the recent democratization of Mexico and the arrival of parties in the village. Democratization means that voting now matters, unlike in the past when PRI held a virtual monopoly. In earlier times, outside politicians never visited the village, as they had no need to. Today, political candidates come to the village to obtain votes and support. This tends to politicize the village, create factions, and split opinion. The outsiders are perceived as having access to resources that the villagers cannot access, if only the ability to pave the road down the mountain.[14]

Inocencio Chino partly attributes the political disputes to the women of the village (he is not the only Oapan male to hold this opinion). Inocencio claims, for instance, that the women on each side of the dispute get more politically agitated than do the men. He narrated how the women on each side make fun of each other, brag and boast to each other, and engage in a kind of "trash talking" over the political disputes. One woman was even taken away to the state jail in Chilpancingo, primarily for her extreme insults, although she was released within the day.

The greater wealth of the village might be another reason why politics has heated up, although the villagers do not themselves cite this factor. In earlier times, there was much less of a surplus to fight over, as residents were living much closer to subsistence. In contemporary times, the fiestas involve more material resources, the land is worth more, the church has more money, and there are more public projects to be funded and thus more charges to be assessed. At the same time, the increasing wealth of the village has created more free time, including free time to pursue politics. Villagers need not spend all their spare time working the fields to hold off starvation; they now enjoy a surplus, albeit a modest one.[15]

We can think of the village as having a set of social networks and a set of conventions for how those networks operate. Those conventions evolved over many decades when Oapan was a much poorer and much more isolated place. The conventions may have produced stability in an earlier time, but in the more modern environment of greater wealth, more free time, more contact with the outside world, and more democracy, they have led to quarrels and disunity.

More generally, the Oapan experience suggests a modification to extant theories of cooperation. A wide variety of writings in the social sciences argue that cooperation is possible when interactions are repeated, anonymity is absent, and the number of participants is relatively small.[16] These same conditions, however, are precisely what have damaged cooperative behavior in Oapan, at least once people could find the time and energy to fight. When individuals are driven by envy and the desire for status, their behavior will not fit models of material self-interest. They will seek to feel good about themselves and to hold a feeling of self-righteousness, rather than striking a quick and simple bargain or compromise. In part, the various parties are locked into ongoing bargaining games and are always looking to maximize their share of the surplus. Simple favor trading no longer suffices, as everyone cares about his or her bargaining position for the future. In part, the participants simply do not like the idea of giving up their historic grudges and enabling their enemies to benefit as well. Excess familiarity becomes the root of conflict rather than the solution. Since neither party will find a cooperative solution to be fair or acceptable in terms of local prestige, repeated interactions only escalate the emotional import of conflict.[17] For these reasons, the so-called Coase theorem does not apply to village politics. Disputants cannot eliminate their problems simply by sitting down at the bargaining table and cutting a deal. The principle of identity—a person's sense of who he or she is and what he or she stands for—often interferes with the principle of mutual benefit through trade.

Although the costs of political chaos in the village are high, Oapan residents sometimes benefit from having a weak and disunified government. Limiting the power of the pueblo officials makes it both harder and less worthwhile for outside parties to purchase the loyalties of those individuals. The pueblo faces periodic confrontations with the outside world, during which time the entire future of the pueblo may be at stake. Material interests from the outside world, such as the Mexican federal government or General Motors (in episodes discussed in this chapter), are immense relative to the resources of the pueblo. To the extent that individuals in power are corruptible, the pueblo will never have the resources to purchase their loyalties. By checking their political power so tightly, the pueblo ensures or tries to ensure that corruption cannot be used against them. During normal times, this may lead to ineffective government with weak powers, but during critical periods, the system may pay off by allowing the loyalties of the leaders to stay connected with the interests of the pueblo. The village has little unity and weak leaders, but these same features also help the village to survive.[18] With this background in mind, let us look at two of the major political crises that Oapan politics has faced.

The Fight against the Dam

The possible construction of a dam was the most important political event in the region in the 1990s. The dam would have been built at San Juan Tetelcingo (a Nahua pueblo between Oapan and Ameyalte-pec), to meet the growing national demand for electricity. It was hoped that the World Bank would come through with a loan for the project. The proposed dam would have inundated the Rio Balsas, flooding most of the local Nahua communities and requiring their relocation. Oapan residents would have lost their homes, their growing fields, their ances-tral graves, and their cultural identity. They would have been lumped together with displaced individuals from other villages—including their historic enemy San Miguel Tecuiciapan (discussed later in this chapter)—on a nearby piece of unpromising mountainous land with no water. Marcial has described the proposed relocation repeatedly as "murdering us." As the best known amate artist of Oapan and as *comis-ario* for part of the protest period, Marcial was a leader in the fight against the dam.[19]

Oapan residents likely would have received little compensation for a resettlement. Earlier in the 1980s, the giant Caracol hydrodam had been built on the Rio Balsas, some forty kilometers downstream from the proposed site. Several other pueblos were inundated permanently, and their residents were relocated. The leaders of those pueblos, who agreed to the relocations, received a mix of bribes, compensation, and government jobs. Most of the displaced villagers received little or nothing, and some of the communities disappeared entirely, as the inhabitants left for Mexico City slums or the United States.[20]

The dam idea first became known in the village in 1990, though the Mexican government had been making plans since 1959. The Mexican government had not wished to reveal its hand, for fear of exciting opposition, but the villagers finally found out when plans for the dam fell into their hands (the carrier of this information does not wish to be identified). Opposition then grew rapidly, especially once the region learned of the previous histories of other dams and other communities. In Oapan, for instance, the villagers refused to cooperate with visiting engineers, the town signed a formal act of noncompliance, the townswomen started a religious vigil against the dam, and the village sent out citizens' committees to speak to other pueblos.

Marcial was a leader throughout all these events, but Juan and Felix Camilo did not participate in these activities. Juan believed that Oapan residents should not resist too stridently; he claimed, "the government can kill us." Although Marcial lives outside of town, he directs his attention back to Oapan frequently, most of all for politics—especially for matters related to the dam.

In response to the dam crisis, the Alto Balsas Nahua formed the Consejo de Pueblos Nahuas del Alto Balsas (CPNAB) in October 1990. In English, the name of the organization would translate roughly as the "Council of Nahua Communities of the Upper Balsas." The group consisted of numerous town *comisarios*, other local leaders of note, including Marcial, and some sympathetic members of outside support groups. The purpose of the council was to speak against the dam with a unified public voice. The villagers believed that the municipal government was corruptible and controlled by PRI loyalists. They feared it might give away the pueblos while acting in the name of the people. The Nahua council, they thought, would help prevent such an outcome. From this point onward, the region, led by the council, displayed a political unity unparalleled in its history. At least temporarily, the usual squabbling was replaced by a concerted and successful attempt at collective action. The community drew on its social capital to work together toward a common end.

In addition to organizing demonstrations, roadblocks, and protests, the council drew up a petition to Carlos Salinas, then president of Mexico, asking him to cancel the dam. The petition referred explicitly to amates and crafts.

Mr. President, our towns are very well known, not just in the Mexican Republic but also in many foreign countries around the world, for our bark paintings and our artisanship in producing pottery, wooden masks, handwoven hammocks, and other craft items. We have given much to our country, to the point that one of our bark paintings now appears on television with the words,

"Mexico se pinta solo," showing that our art is considered part of the patrimony of all Mexicans. How is it possible that Mexico, and the government over which you preside, should celebrate the Quincentenary of the discovery of America with a project that would destroy a region of the most authentic Mexican culture?[21]

Opinion began to turn in the favor of the pueblos. The council organized several roadblocks of the Mexico City–Acapulco highway, and these roadblocks won press attention, generated support from environmentalists, and caused some members of the opposition party (PRD) to take the side of the villagers. A march to Mexico City garnered further attention.

Ongoing road accidents made the villagers yet more upset. The government was building a large bridge (now Puente Mezcala) to the eastern side of Oapan to create a new highway between Cuernavaca and Acapulco. In addition, Pemex was drilling in the region. Suddenly large vehicles were passing through Oapan pueblo streets frequently. They ran over numerous pigs—valuable investment assets for the villagers—without showing remorse or offering compensation. One day, they ran over a fifteen-year-old girl, which, according to Roberto Mauricio, was the turning point in mobilizing the sentiments of the pueblo. In the eyes of the villagers, the bridge project and the dam were part of a broader pattern of outside interference in the Alto Balsas communities.

In January 1992, Oapan residents organized a town roadblock for nineteen days. The roadblock hindered construction of the bridge and also the Pemex drilling activity, given that vehicles could no longer pass to the east. Rather than responding with force, the state government decided to negotiate. The governor of Guerrero canceled the dam, at least for the duration of his term (one more year), and the immediate pressure was removed. The federal government subsequently ratified this decision.

The real action took place behind the scenes, when the World Bank indicated it would not lend money to finance the dam. The World Bank had been receiving sustained criticism for its environmental policies and for requiring the forcible resettlement of indigenous peoples through large-scale hydroelectric projects. Once it became apparent that the dam was to be a public relations disaster, the bank declined to pursue it. From the very beginning, the bank appears to have had doubts about the project. Scott Guggenheim, who worked for the World Bank on the potential project, notes that the bank never thought the dam a good idea in cost-benefit terms and became even more worried once social problems arose.[22] He notes that the bank never let the project get to the appraisal phase. Thus, the project was doomed at the outset for lack of financing, though Marcial mentions rumors that private capital, perhaps from Japan, may someday step in to pay for the dam.

Guerrero is considered one of the more violent states in Mexico, and it has a history of terrorism, but Oapan residents remained peaceful throughout all of these disputes. When asked about violence, Oapan residents unanimously proclaim their pacific nature and take pride in this element of their culture. Even at the time of the Mexican Revolution, the region was relatively peaceful, despite widespread turmoil in Guerrero and Morelos.[23]

Marcial and Jonathan Amith

Marcial's role in the struggle against the dam involved a project to produce and publicize protest amates. For the first time in the history of the genre, amates were used as a form of political protest. Working with anthropologist Jonathan Amith, Marcial helped bring together the leading amate painters, persuaded them to produce anti-dam amates, distributed photocopies of the protest amates, and contributed to an amate calendar. These amates later appeared with others in a major exhibit at the Mexican Fine Arts Center Museum in Chicago.

Jonathan Amith directed much of this work. As Rabkin was fading from the scene, Amith was the next American to devote part of his life to helping the amate painters. Amith, now in his late forties, has lived in Oapan for about a year and a quarter and in the neighboring village of Ameyaltepec for over two years. He has made it his life's mission to study and preserve the culture of the region, typically working long hours on his numerous Oapan-related projects.

Amith's fundamental interests are in the Nahuatl language and in the Alto Balsas region as an object of anthropological study. The pre-Hispanic civilizations of Mexico captured his imagination, and Amith wanted to learn Nahuatl to study Aztec poetry. He first went to Mexico in 1975, when he stayed in Cuernavaca and took a class in classical Nahuatl. (He saw and enjoyed amates there at that time but did not think of studying them.) He later enrolled in graduate study in anthropology in Yale, again furthering his study of classical Nahuatl.

Amith decided that if he was to study Nahuatl, he needed to know modern versions of the language. To his mind, knowing only classical Nahuatl is like being a Shakespeare scholar but speaking no modern English. Amith thus set out to expand his horizons. He is by nature thorough and willing to cross intellectual boundaries to satisfy his curiosity. Although he is not a linguist by training, he studied linguistics intensely. For practice, he worked as a bricklayer in the outskirts of Mexico City (for about a dollar a day) once he discovered that many of the other bricklayers spoke Nahuatl.

Through his earlier contacts in Cuernavaca, Amith was put in touch with some residents of Ameyaltepec who had been selling in the central market there. He spent four days in Ameyaltepec and loved it, most of all because Nahuatl was spoken there on a consistent basis. He soon returned for a longer stay to continue his study. His interest in Nahuatl remained, but he also wondered why Ameyaltepec was relatively wealthy compared to other Mexican pueblos and what kinds of relationships it had with its neighbors, including Oapan. These topics led him to investigate artisan work, amates, and the land tenure of the region.

Throughout this time, Amith lived off of graduate fellowships, two Fulbright grants, and a grant form the Organization of American States grant. Later, he secured a research position in Guadalajara, which supported him during the time of the dam protests and the organization of the amate exhibit.

Amith is now compiling a dictionary to preserve the Nahuatl language and teach it to the villagers. He estimates that this project will require at least another ten years of labor, as much of the work consists of very slow transcription of taped recordings of Nahuatl speech. Villagers claim he speaks the language as well as they do; some say he speaks it better, since he learns old and obscure words from the elderly. Although trained as an anthropologist, Amith underwent intense self-training in linguistics to proceed with the dictionary project. He now teaches Alto Balsas Nahuatl every summer at a language institute at Yale University.

Amith's devotion to the village and its culture knows few bounds. He is currently running a botany project to catalog the flowers and plants of the Oapan area. Another of Amith's projects concerns out-migration from Oapan to the United States. He spent several months in the village in the fall of 2001 interviewing the villagers about their migration experiences or those of their children. He is using these same tapes to generate Nahuatl texts for use in his campaign to record and preserve the language. He sees all his projects as having a methodolog-ical unity, based on village involvement, the generation of knowledge about the culture, and investment in teaching the villagers to be more literate about their culture and more interested in its preservation. Through Amith's work, we again see outside forces from North Amer-ica helping to preserve the culture of the pueblo.

Amith took almost fifteen years to produce his Yale doctoral disser-tation, entitled "The Möbius Strip." The dissertation studies the colo-nial economic history of central Guerrero, seen through the lens of economic geography. Amith studied patterns of trade, landownership, migration, and the construction of markets, mostly in the neighbor-hood of Taxco and Iguala—though he often ventured into the Alto Balsas region. The final product reflected several years in the archives and weighed in at over eight hundred pages of basic text and much more in terms of appendixes, references, maps, and so on.

To this day, Amith lives from grants, an unreliable source of support, and has his wife's salary as a backup (she teaches anthropology in Ore-gon). Amith has never held a tenure-track job in an anthropology department; he prefers to *do* anthropology rather than work to please his peers or to follow the latest academic fad. Amith is disillusioned with academia, and it hurts him to see many anthropologists far less committed than he is receive regular academic jobs. Now he has built a house in Oapan so he can live there for five months a year and pursue his work.[24]

Marcial reports that he first met Amith in Ameyaltepec, through the intermediation of anthropologist Cathy Good (who was working in the region at the same time). Marcial and Amith became close, how-ever, only when the threat of the dam came along. When Amith heard about the threat of the dam, he had the idea to make amate leaflets as a form of protest. With the assistance of Marcial and some other artists, he recruited the leading amate painters to produce anti-dam amates. Amith wrote a number of texts and then asked the artists to illustrate those texts. When the amates were finished, everyone was amazed at their high quality. All the major Oapan amate painters contributed except Juan Camilo, who remained on the outs with Marcial (some painters from the other villages contributed as well). The resulting amates were then reproduced and distributed at meetings, roadblocks, and protests. The amates served as publicity and as a fund-raising device. Amith, who is entrepreneurial and driven by nature, also came up with the idea of doing an amate calendar based on those works. He patched together funding from a number of sources and relied on some pro bono work. The resulting calendar was shown at the International Book Fair in Guadalajara in 1992 (November 28–December 7) and received many favorable comments.[25]

Marcial's protest amate shows Santiago, the patron saint of Oapan, taking to his horse to fight the dam. At the same time, the dam is bursting, and the waters are sweeping away the villagers, their town, and their animals. The amate invokes the spirit of apocalypse. Felix Jimenez portrayed the dam as a giant serpent, spewing poison and wreckage. On each side of the amate, the viewer can see the exodus of residents from the area. A swath of water, cutting through the middle of the picture, comprises the serpent's body and is inundating the churches of the region. Another Felix Jimenez amate is divided into two panels, each with a classroom scene. In one half, a group of students are voting on whether the Spanish arrival in the New World should be called a conquest, invasion, or encounter. In the other half, an anthropologist points to a picture of a "good Indian" (in traditional garb) and a "bad Indian," the latter shown protesting against the dam. Inocencio painted the villagers carrying anti-dam signs and taking a bus to go protest. Roberto Mauricio showed a fiesta march entering the church while lawyers and politicians debate the fate of the community in a series of upper panels. Felix Camilo depicted Nahuas being forced to carry stones to build a church for their Spanish masters, taking apart a pyramid in the process.[26]

In the end, the dam struggle sparked publicity for amate art. The amates gave rise to an exhibit held at the Mexican Fine Arts Center

Museum in Chicago (January 27–May 27, 1995). Amith relates how he flew to Chicago and showed the amates to the museum's director, who decided on the spot to mount a major exhibit. The museum people had known of amates, as a kind of tourist art, but they never knew that amates could reach such high artistic quality. Amith was commissioned to serve as exhibit curator, a significant undertaking, for which he received no more than six thousand dollars plus expenses. In addition to the protest amates, he sought out the best amates from other collections and urged their owners to lend them. Toward this end, he took at least one thousand photographs of amates, which he retains on file.

Amith also arranged for Marcial, Inocencio Chino, Roberto Mauricio, and several painters from the other villages to travel to Chicago, see the exhibit, and show the world how they make their art. Marcial, of course, had traveled before, but the other painters found many surprises. Roberto Mauricio cited snow (which he saw for the first time), the view from the Sears Tower, flying in the airplane, seeing the clouds close up, the quality of the hotel (he specifically mentioned the presence of a heater in the room), and the respect with which he was treated. After his eight days in Chicago, however, Roberto concluded that the United States was not a land of "justice and right" any more than Mexico was.

Roberto also recalls the contrast between being feted in Chicago and life back in the pueblo. The victory against the dam had been won, but upon returning, Roberto faced some of the toughest economic times of his life. He reports spending every day doing hard work in the fields and then sometimes painting amates through the night for extra money. It was very difficult to make ends meet, and sometimes he did not have time to sleep during the night or did not sleep for more than a few hours.

The Amate Tradition

The Amith project and exhibit gave rise to a book called *The Amate Tradition,* published with English text on one side of each page and Spanish on the other. This book, with sixty-two high-quality color plates of amates and many other plates of ceramics, remains the definitive amate catalog. It represents the history of amate painting from its beginnings in Ameyaltepec to the amates protesting the dam. Nearly all of the major amate painters are represented. The back of the book contains extensive anthropological and archaeological information, including numerous black-and-white photos of the dam protests, Oapan, and its residents.

The book was published by the Mexican Fine Arts Center Museum in conjunction with a Mexican publisher La Casa de las Imágenes and marketed by the University of New Mexico Press. The print run was three thousand, divided evenly between the two countries. The book was funded by a grant of twenty-five thousand dollars from a cultural fund, Fideicomiso para la Cultura Mexico/USA, which drew from both the Rockefeller Foundation and Mexican government sources. The book was very well received in Mexico and sold out quickly there, but it attracted less attention in the United States. One review, in the *American Anthropologist* (Leibsohn 1997), praised how Amith portrayed the dynamism of the Rio Balsas communities, but the reviewer complained that Amith used none of the artists' own words. The reviewer noted that she "learned much" from the book and would use some of the amate images for teaching, but she appears determined to find objections, wishing that the book somehow had been done differently.

Amith's text differed greatly from that of Selden Rodman. Rodman was the marketer, Amith the scholar. Amith spent years in the region and talked to everybody he could. In addition to knowing all the painters, he tracked down Max Kerlow in Mexico City, among many others from the early history of amate. He has tried to track down Mary Price, the early amate collector—so far unsuccessfully. Rodman wrote in colorful prose, Amith in scholarly prose.

Amith's treatment, while meeting high standards of scholarship, did little to boost the market for amates. His book focused on history and anthropology. It gave the reader little sense of the personalities involved. Amith had no links to any gallery, dealer, or promoter and has never viewed his enterprise as commercial. In this regard, the book stands alone and has never fed into any broader effort.

All the painters received copies of the book except for Juan Camilo, who saw the book for the first time when I brought it to his house. He and his family were much more interested in the black-and-white photos in the back than in the pictures of the amates up front. They spent hours looking at the photos, trying to identify the people in them. Everyone in the family gathered around the book, the only time I have seen all of them preoccupied with the same concern. Juan's wife and eldest daughter were in particular keen to look at each photo and make fun of the clothing of the women and the expressions on their faces. The laughter and loud shrieking went on for hours.

Land Disputes with Other Nahuas

The dam dispute revolved around the land rights of the pueblo versus the claims of larger political units at the state and federal level. Now that the project has been set aside (at least temporarily), land rights among the pueblos have reemerged as the most important political issue in the region. San Agustín has quarreled with its neighbor, San Miguel, for centuries over land. These disputes have occasionally erupted into violence, and most Oapan villagers, including the three Camilo brothers, expect the issue to explode again.

Technically, land in Oapan is communally owned, but for most practical purposes, including bequests, land operates as private property. Since the eighteenth century, Oapan residents have been allowed to homestead land simply by working or building on it. (All the communal Oapan land is now taken, so Oapan residents must buy land from another person if they wish to increase their holdings.) Land boundaries across the pueblos, however, have never been fully sorted out. Land titles across the pueblos were in theory clarified in the original series of grants (extending from 1697 to 1716), but the relevant documents were ambiguous. One land dispute, between Oapan and San Juan Tetelcingo (lying to the west), began in the early 1700s but was resolved in the late nineteenth century, by mutual agreement. The land dispute with San Miguel, however, continues to the current day. Earlier residents of San Miguel believed that an early eighteenth-century visit by a land judge led to a settlement that unduly favored Oapan. Earlier Oapan residents believed that an 1802 decision unjustly gave some of their land to San Miguel (see Amith 2000, 1078). These grudges continued and multiplied over the years. In 1951 residents of San Agustín and San Miguel shot at each other with firearms, largely over the land issue, causing several deaths and injuries.[27]

Oapan residents claim that prior to the 1802 decision, they had been working the land since pre-Hispanic times. In their account, Oapan residents understood that they had to cede some land to their neighbors, but San Miguel residents kept on wanting to take more and more, eventually threatening the harvests and the lives of Oapan residents.[28]

Local legend has it that San Miguel residents arrived in the area relatively recently and have a different ethnic origin. It is rumored that they stem from the area of Tequicuilco (unlike other Alto Balsas peoples) and first came to the region for the fishing in the Rio Balsas. San Miguel residents have never painted amates and, earlier, did not play much of a role in the salt trade. Anthropologist Cathy Good believes that the conflict is as much ethnic and cultural as about the land. San Miguel residents are more mestizo and show less interest in Nahuatl and older customs. They buy thin, premade white tortillas, whereas most Oapan residents prefer homemade blue corn tortillas.[29]

Relations between the two pueblos remain tense. Oapan residents typically do not have close friends in San Miguel, even though the two pueblos are geographically very close and the cultures are very similar. Marriages between the pueblos are uncommon and would be viewed unfavorably by families on both sides. Oapan residents assert that San Miguel is prone to robbery, mysterious disappearances, and foul play. They stress that they themselves are a people of peace whereas the residents of San Miguel are more violent. They claim that San Miguel always has been and always will be better prepared for war.

Recently, an engineer was sent to the area by the state government to survey the land. In the eyes of Oapan residents, his measurements favored San Miguel. Oapan residents believe that this engineer was corrupt and was paid off by San Miguel. Felix Camilo complained that the San Miguel residents served the engineer venison when he visited the area, which he called a form of corruption. That being said, the final judgment was in fact relatively favorable to Oapan residents, who got almost everything they were asking for, short of seventy-seven hectares.[30]

The affected area in the land dispute runs the length of the Oapan–San Miguel border. The contested territory is between one and two hundred meters wide in most places, stretching to about eight hundred meters wide in a few places. San Miguel claims the entirety of this area, and the state capitol, Chilpancingo, has suggested that the two pueblos split the difference. (Marcial offers these estimates, based on a study of state-level documents from Chilpancingo.) Oapan residents have refused this compromise adamantly, as they believe it would amount to little more than theft. In essence, the communities are caught in a bargaining and rent-seeking game, with little hope for resolution through secure property rights.

Marcial, Juan, and Felix Camilo all own land in the contested area. Felix is especially upset, as he reports that San Miguel residents have been harvesting his land. Most commonly, he says they collect his watermelon without his permission, often holding arms for protection.

Marcial has plans to organize a protest movement around the disputed land. He would like to paint a large mural showing the nature of the dispute, perhaps in cooperation with other amate painters. He and others would then take this large mural and march on the state capitol, Chilpancingo, hoping to bring about a resolution of the dispute. He is hoping to replicate the successful protest strategies used against the dam, although it is not clear how he could interest anyone outside the village in the topic. Marcial nonetheless holds such a campaign as his current obsession. Even when I wished to talk about other subjects, Marcial frequently returned to the subject of the land dispute, often talking for hours, drawing maps, and explaining the nature of the conflict from his point of view. One wonders if the earlier struggle among the brothers over the family lands has made this an especially emotional topic for him.

Juan has a more philosophical attitude toward the land dispute. While he hopes that Oapan keeps the land (for reasons of obvious self-interest), he does not regard the inhabitants of San Miguel as any worse than those of Oapan. He thinks the matter is simply an issue of who is going to get the land, rather than an issue with a moral right and wrong. He believes that Oapan residents think of the San Miguel residents as evil simply because they do not know them. Juan thinks that neither side is morally superior to the other.

When asked about the validity of their claims to the land, Oapan residents continually reiterate the same phrase: "We have documents" [*tenemos documentos*]. In this rare display of legal positivistic reasoning, Oapan residents believe that if only the state authorities study the documents carefully enough and survey the land honestly, the justice of the Oapan claim will be obvious. Emotionally, they treat their land claim as virtually equivalent to a covenant with God. They do not, however, have good legal advice, nor do they have a good sense of where their claim stands in the broader Mexican legal system.

Felix Jimenez, Inocencio, and Roberto Mauricio do not hold land in the contested area, but the latter two have worked on the pueblo land commission, the *comisariado*.[31] This office governs the communal lands of Oapan, addresses conflicts over land, and deals with the state government in Chilpancingo over land issues. The office also measures land, oversees surveying, and issues land titles. The major issue in the *comisariado*, of course, is the dispute with San Miguel.[32]

The spread of land disputes to other pueblos has made the San Miguel issue harder to resolve. Oapan residents fear, probably correctly, that if they give in to San Miguel, they will face other claims against their land. For instance, the pueblo of Ahuelicán, lying to the north, at times has pressed land claims against Oapan and now is asking for its full legal independence from Oapan. Analco, the smaller pueblo directly across the river, has been seeking independence as well. For a while, Analco supported San Miguel in the land dispute with Oapan. Then San Miguel turned on Analco and tried to take some of its land as well, at which point Analco switched back to an alliance with Oapan.

Short of a full and fair land survey, it is impossible to tell how much each side stands in the right or if there is even a fact of the matter. The rhetoric used in Oapan suggests that Oapan probably does indeed hold legal title to the land under dispute. However, at the time of the title grants, many dating back to the eighteenth century, Oapan received more than an even share. Oapan residents claim that they deserve more land, arguing that they have been there longer and are the "first pueblo," from which the others have sprung. In essence, the other communities are seeking to revise this early settlement along more egalitarian lines, and Oapan residents are resisting.

Land and General Motors

The most recent controversy in the pueblo concerned a General Motors offer to buy village lands. In 2001 it became known that GM was negotiating to buy land in Oapan and San Miguel. GM would have used the land to construct a large track for testing new automobiles. The project would have occupied about two-thirds of the agricultural lands of the village and would have changed the entire way of life in Oapan.

The community voted resoundingly to reject the offer (neighboring San Miguel showed greater interest). Pueblo members expect that the outside world, especially the Mexican government, will lie to them. They simply did not believe the talk of how a GM test track would bring money and jobs to the town. Having heard many lies during the years of the dam struggle, they were suspicious from the outset. The price received by each family would have depended on its particular landholdings, but the base rate was seventy centavos (about eight cents) for a square meter. This would have put many families in the range of receiving somewhere between four hundred and a thousand dollars. To the villagers, this seemed like a small amount for giving up their way of life and their land.

All of the members of the Oapan painting group opposed the sale to General Motors, with Marcial taking the strongest leadership role. He spoke actively against the sale in a very public manner, and his words carried weight in the community. Marcial is known for being one of the most articulate and thoughtful Oapan citizens in a public forum.

In the final tally, fewer than fifteen villagers favored the project. The reality is that no substantial part of the community favors foreign investment. It is not that the residents have a well-formulated account of how such investment would make them worse off. Rather, they know that big changes of this kind would bring them under the scrutiny of the broader Mexican political establishment. From historical experience, they have very high levels of mistrust toward the state and central government. Today, they can live largely undisturbed and off the radar screen, so to speak. Since the villagers would not ever expect to receive the offer that is made to them, it is difficult for any constituency to favor such a project.

As mentioned earlier, while Oapan landholdings usually function as private property, the final land title is vested in the community. So the villagers never faced individual choices as to whether they might wish to sell to General Motors. Instead, the community as a whole produced a firm no through a town meeting, debate, and a vote.

The government pressured the villagers to take the GM offer, but to no avail. In fact, government pressure only made the villagers more suspicious. Roberto Mauricio and Marcial claim that the government promised to resolve the land dispute immediately with San Miguel if the villagers would sell the land. The negative vote remained firm, and GM moved on to look for other village lands to buy.

The villagers could not have expected to receive lucrative jobs from the test track. They do not have the literacy, skills, or education to contend for top or even midlevel jobs at such a concern. They might have received menial labor jobs for the Mexican minimum wage, but this would not have brought a significant improvement in living standards, by the estimation of the villagers.

Marcial claims that while the offered sum was small, money was not the chief reason why villagers turned down the offer. Marcial also cited the frequent automobile noises the track would have brought and the likelihood of delinquency in the village. Most of all, Marcial cited a fear of "contamination" from the outside world. The test track would have brought many outside influences to the village and would have hastened the disappearance of the traditional way of life. Not only would agriculture have disappeared, but within a generation, the pressure to speak Spanish rather than Nahuatl would have been strong.

The Oapan residents' desire to preserve the past and their suspicion of outsiders is not new. Decades before the GM offer, textile interests tried to set up commercial looms in Ameyaltepec, but the villagers refused to cooperate, in large part because of their suspicion of outsiders. Peggy Golde notes that villagers in the region often gave pseudonyms to their pueblos in the late 1950s, so that no one from the outside world could find or identify them.[33]

The CPNAB, which led the fight against the dam, played no real role in the General Motors dispute. Local opinion splintered almost immediately after the danger of the dam passed, and the villagers no longer perceive the council as representing their interests. The CPNAB continues to exist, but with no real mission or unifying purpose. It is simply a group of individuals with a historically important title but with no accountability and holding no general legitimacy within the pueblos. In fact, Oapan residents are suspicious that some CPNAB members have been "bought" by outside interests.

Although the GM sale fell through, the villagers do not regard the matter as closed. The villagers know that they sit on potentially valuable land, underused from the point of view of the Mexican government. The Mexican government would gain economically, if only through opportunities for corruption, if it could bring large economic projects into Guerrero and push out the villagers.

NAFTA and Trade

The General Motors episode shows why institutions such as the North American Free Trade Agreement (NAFTA) are problematic for many of the indigenous groups in Mexico. While the economic case for free trade is strong, politics matters as well. The long-run benefits of NAFTA, most of all for Mexico, are likely to dramatically outweigh the costs, but trade can worsen some political problems in the shorter run.

The core problem is that greater wealth sometimes brings greater confiscation in response. Both NAFTA and economic development more generally have attracted much foreign investment to Mexico. The land in Guerrero is suddenly more valuable than before—or at least potentially so. If better roads were in place, Oapan would be no more than two and a quarter hours from Mexico City. The Mexican government would like to get the villagers off the land, whether by legitimate means or not. The Mexican state and federal governments also favor foreign investment when the villagers do not. Any foreign investment that came into Guerrero would likely involve significant payoffs—of one form or another—to the various levels of government involved. The villagers would not expect to see any of this money. NAFTA has therefore increased the conflict of interest between the villagers and higher levels of Mexican government. For the reasons mentioned in the General Motors case, there is no significant contingent in Oapan that favors greater foreign investment.

The villagers may benefit economically from foreign investment by leaving Oapan and pursuing new lives elsewhere, such as in larger Mexican cities. It is harder to see how the village itself might have a brighter future. Except for agriculture and artisan work, village labor is unskilled and likely to remain so for the foreseeable future. The villagers, at best, have only very basic skills of reading, writing, and arithmetic.

At present, most of the Alto Balsas villages are in the process of becoming remittance economies. Oapan lags behind in this process (because outmigration has been slower), but it is headed in the same direction. Contact with the United States, then, can prove economically fruitful, but this appears to involve bringing Oapan residents to America rather than bringing American capital to Oapan. The combination of Oapan residents and American capital may succeed more under American legal and economic institutions than under Mexican ones.

Oapan nonetheless may prove resilient, as is illustrated by its rising living standards over the last forty years. Arguably, the situation appeared far bleaker in the 1950s, right before the amate boom. The village was much poorer and much smaller and had lost its traditional sources of income, such as the salt trade. A rapidly growing Mexican economy was encroaching on many traditional Mexican communities. Yet this is exactly when the village was on the verge of reaching its greatest heights of cultural achievement and its greatest burst of economic growth.

The Oapan amate painters remain pessimistic. As part of the interviews for this book, I asked each painter what could be done to improve the village and to improve village government in particular. Inocencio answered simply, "Less drinking." Roberto Mauricio demanded "justicia y derecho" [justice and right]. Marcial wanted an engineering project to raise the level of the river, so that the Rio Balsas could fertilize more of the surrounding territory. The others cited a desire for more unity and less fighting, a wish that all of the painters have expressed repeatedly in their discussions of village politics.

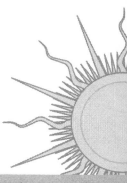

6 • Concluding and Summary Remarks

FEW OAPAN FAMILIES see the production of amate art as playing a significant role in their longer-term future. Many of the best amate painters are still working and using the full force of their talents, but the supply of painters is not being replenished. While the young in Oapan dabble in amate, few, if any, have come close to the best artists of previous generations. The young in Oapan no longer find that careful amate work yields sufficient returns. The older amate painters commonly charge that the young lack the necessary patience or discipline to perfect their skills. For the most part, the young agree with this interpretation.

The themes of liberty and power continue to shape the Oapan community, but greater economic opportunities are pushing Oapan residents in directions other than amate. As the community becomes wealthier and more diverse, residents have more options. For instance, crafts have become more profitable, because Mexico has grown, transportation technologies have advanced, and Oapan residents have improved their entrepreneurial and managerial abilities. If we consider the Oapan artists discussed in this book, only Marcial might earn more than does a typical family head with a good crafts business, and Marcial still earns considerably less than the most successful crafts merchants in Oapan. Marcial also faces riskier conditions and achieved his reputation only after toiling many years at lower wages.

In other cases, entrepreneurship manifests itself through external mobility. When the young in Alto Balsas communities think of riches, they think of migrating to the United States. Most ambitious young people would like to cross the border, though not everyone will have that chance. In 2003, it costs a pueblo member about fifteen hundred dollars to pay off a coyote for possible passage to the United States. In addition, the individual must endure hardships during the crossing itself, such as a four-day trek across desert with little water; facing snakes, coyotes, and bandits; or swimming the Rio Grande.[1]

Even if an individual does not make the trip, the mere prospect of leaving discourages investment in high-quality amate art. Many individuals will bide their time, hoping to pick up enough cash to cross over. These individuals are reluctant to invest in building careers and reputations that may pay off only in a longer run.

Houston, Los Angeles, Chicago, and Ontario, California (near Los Angeles), have all become centers of Alto Balsas migration, drawing mostly young men. The migrants commonly live in apartments housing three to seven people, who come and go on an irregular basis. Alto Balsas migrants tend to live together when possible, though they do not refuse roommates from other parts of Mexico. The migrants then seek out jobs of manual labor, typically paying in the neighborhood of seven to ten dollars an hour. They live as cheaply as possible and often send money back home. The richest home in Oapan has a camper and a large television antenna. The villagers claim that the family in this home receives money from several family members in the United States.

One top-rank amate painter (who does not wish to be named) migrated to Houston. He was a prodigy, producing superb amates at the age of twelve. His family runs one of the largest, best, and most successful amate-producing studios in Ameyaltepec. His father expressed great disappointment that his son did not stay in the village to work on his amates. The son now works evening hours in a Houston supermarket. In recent times, he has obtained access to amate paper and paints and has painted a few works. He has sold several good-quality amates to Americans, but they are not comparable to his best production from the village. His brother claims he suffers from a "trembling hand" syndrome that afflicts amate painters who take time off from their art. In any case, the artist cannot find many American clients at remunerative prices. He speaks no English and has no plan for marketing his work.

A well-known amate artist from Xalitla, Pablo Nicolás, also crossed the border, living in Los Angeles for several years. Martina Adame, perhaps the best-known amate painter in Maxela, claims that most of the best or would-be amate painters left Maxela and are now on "the other side" *[al otro lado]*, the Mexican euphemism for the United States.

Not all the migrants leave for strictly economic considerations. It is not obvious that they are happier in the United States, though they value the opportunity to send money back home. Since the migrants telephone back home frequently, the hardships of life in the United States are not a total surprise to each stream of new migrants. Though they are richer than back home, the migrants have few real opportunities for advancement. Most are torn between the decision to stay and a desire to go back home. Staying cuts off direct contact with families, language, and Nahua culture. Going back home means it is very hard to return to the United States. Given that most migrants have come to the United States within the last five or ten years, it remains to be seen how long they will stay. Those that return to Oapan, however, are seen as noisy, rowdy, and disruptive of the community.[2]

Boredom and the desire to escape are critical factors driving the decision to migrate. Many individuals see that they have no good opportunities in their villages, either economically or otherwise. They feel that nothing can be worse for them than a situation of few opportunities and high frustration, so they leave. Since they can always come back, the downside of this decision is not obvious. Many sense (correctly) that their opportunities in the United States exceed their opportunities elsewhere in Mexico. They would be outsiders in other parts of Mexico as in the United States, so they determine that they may as well go to the richer country and see more of the world.[3]

When Oapan residents are asked to name the best amate painters, the youngest individual they will cite is Salomón Ramírez Miranda. Salomón, who was forty years old in 2003, finds that high-quality amate does not pay its way. He is represented in the Jonathan Amith catalog with two political satires of high quality. Detailed black-and-white works are his preferred medium. Yet Salomón only paints a few such works in a year, largely for his own amusement. He does not expect to sell them, at least not for a remunerative price, and he feels he cannot justify the expenditure of time and effort. He says no one buys these works any more. Therefore, he spends most of his time painting more vivid and cheaper color amates for sale in the street or painting colorful ceramics. He would like to devote more time to high-quality amate but sees few prospects for the development of the market.

Amate painting has fared better in the pueblos of Maxela and Xalitla, in part because the painters there have sought different niches. Maxela has land of poorer quality than the other amate-producing villages, so agriculture plays a smaller role in that locale (this is reflected in the village's amates, which portray fieldwork with less frequency). Rather than working the fields, the men find commercial employment in the surrounding region. Given the proximity of Maxela to the main highway (five kilometers along a paved road) and the universal fluency in Spanish in the pueblo (since the 1930s and 1940s), the villagers have greater opportunities.

Maxela never developed the model of having male amate painters who work in the fields much of the year and otherwise paint. Instead, the women of Maxela took up amate painting as a household activity, usually to earn extra income for the family. Given that virtually all women in the village raise large families, Maxela has not developed full-time amate painters. Furthermore, unlike their counterparts from Oapan, Ameyaltepec, or Xalitla, the painters in Maxela make little effort to sell outside the village. Their family commitments make them less mobile, and their income is not important enough to the family to justify a several-week selling trip—as a woman from Oapan or Ameyaltepec might make. For these reasons, amates of good quality from Maxela are currently selling in the range of fifteen to fifty dollars, which is at the low end of the scale for quality work. Given the "hobbyist" nature of the amate-painting vocation in Maxela, the sellers tend to be more passive, and they fail to establish the highest reputations, even when they do very good work.

The village of Xalitla prices its quality amates in the middle range, with good works often going for fifty to one hundred dollars. Most (though not all) of the painters there are male, and many Xalitla families rely on amate and related crafts for their livelihood. The Xalitla painters have arguably the steadiest market, due to their location on the main highway between Mexico City and Acapulco. They also have been especially aggressive at participating in amate tournaments and cultivating outlets in Mexico City. Xalitla, however, unlike Oapan and

Ameyaltepec, has no clearly acknowledged village artistic leaders. No Xalitla amate painter has established a well-known "signature style," nor have the Xalitla painters received equivalent support from foreign patrons.

The Role of Pottery and Other Competing Forms of Artisanship

Increasing wealth and technological improvements have resurrected pottery as a competitor with amate painting. Whereas amate once displaced pottery, we now see new forms of ceramics displacing amate production. Originally, amate was a deliberate replacement for painting on pottery and drew the best painters away from the pottery medium. Now the opposite is more likely the case.

Pottery techniques, involving both construction and transportation, are becoming increasingly modern. Under the traditional methods, a ceramicist needs several days (not full-time) to produce a single piece. First the artisan must obtain mud, sand, and the appropriate binding substances from trees and animals; Oapan residents typically take the mud from the nearby Rio Balsas, carrying it by mule back to their homes. The mud is then combined with the sand and the binders until it is in easily workable form. Once the figures have been shaped, they are put in a burning pit to be fired. The pit reaches very high temperatures, and managing the pit is one of the hallmarks of an effective potter. After the cooking is done, the works are removed and soaked several times in water, so that the piece may dry and congeal properly.[4]

Though some Oapan potters still work in this tradition, it has not proven remunerative in recent years. It takes too much time and trouble relative to the available returns. A quick look at some of the remaining traditional potters shows how unprofitable this form of production has become.

The leading traditional potter in Oapan is Ángel Domínguez, but he makes only a limited amount of money from his work. He will sell high-quality small pieces to visitors for five to ten dollars and a four-foot painted water jug for less than one hundred dollars. Ángel finds it profitable to pursue a commercial strategy of seizing any immediate cash, rather than investing in a longer-term reputation. The villagers joke about Ángel's dealings with customers, dealers, and intermediaries. Those who leave money with Ángel for a commission find that Ángel simply keeps the money and then pretends that nothing happened. I have spoken with two ceramics dealers (in Taxco and Cuernavaca) who like to sell his work, but both describe his pieces as difficult to obtain. Cash and carry is the only way of doing business with Ángel, and his inventories are not usually high.[5] Ángel makes most of his living through his work as a *curandero*, or shaman. He is notorious for spending much of the day simply resting in his hammock. He receives many visitors who pay him about one hundred pesos (nine to ten dollars) for cures. When he wants some extra cash, he makes a few small ceramic pieces and waits for somebody to come by and buy them. Occasionally Ángel makes larger pieces for the villagers, typically for a wedding or to furnish a new household. The villagers wait until the item is ready before handing over any money. Felix Jimenez notes that Ángel no longer pursues his pottery craft with his previous interest or attention to quality.[6]

Carmen Camilo Ayala, sister of the Camilo brothers discussed in this study, is another skilled potter working in a traditional style. She grew up painting amates but moved away from the craft in the mid-1990s, when it proved unprofitable. Today, she spends most of her work time making pottery in the traditional style. In her most active year, she made approximately fifty pieces and sold them in the range of ten to twenty dollars apiece. Such a sum is not expected to support an entire family but provides extra spending money. She does not sell actively in markets but, rather, waits to be invited to exhibitions in Cuernavaca. Occasionally Felix Camilo takes her work around and markets it, though he has been unable to do this lately. She notes a personal preference for the older pottery style rather than the modern mass-produced works, but she believes the art is dwindling. Most people do not have the talent for the handmade work, and the market for it is not very large.

Given the limited profitability of traditional pottery production, most of today's ceramics activity follows the model cited in chapter 4: families buy premade ceramics from the town of Iguala and then paint the molds at home. Suns, masks, lanterns, small turtles, small boxes, and animal-shaped banks are popular at the moment. Most commonly, the items are painted a bright and sometimes phosphorescent blue. The entire household partakes in the painting, and the women have no special role in production or design, though they paint more commonly than do the men. Each piece is intended to be identical rather than unique, and a household tries to make as many items as possible.

These ceramic items are sold in Taxco, Cuernavaca, Acapulco, Cancún, and other tourist locales. In the streets of Taxco, a small piece of this kind might sell for between three and five dollars. Of that money, perhaps a dollar or two will go for the raw materials, and the rest will be kept as a return to labor. These pieces are typically attractive and charming, but they do not provide a base of skills that might be used for larger, better, and more ambitious projects. However, this kind of pottery is becoming more important to the economy of Oapan, at the expense of many other crafts, including amate painting.

Improved transportation has driven this reallocation of effort. Recall that amate first took off because the painters found it easier to transport the paper than ceramics. In those days, the pottery was carried down the mountain on burros and broke frequently. Arguably, tourist buyers have preferred ceramics all along, but only recently has it been easy for sellers to transport pottery. Now buses, trucks, and pickups leave the village on a regular basis. The ceramics are put in sturdy boxes and wrapped well with paper or plastic. This new ease of transport means that ceramics are displacing amate just as amate once displaced ceramics.

Many Oapan families are now involved in moving and selling this pottery en masse. Juan Camilo's oldest son, Leonardo, regularly takes trips to Cancún, traveling up to forty hours on the bus. He carries with him several thousand pieces of pottery, packed in fifteen or more cases, and usually manages to sell all of them. On a typical journey, not a single piece breaks underway.

Yet another economic factor has driven the switch from handmade to factory-made pottery. In earlier times, Oapan women had to make pottery for household uses, so they developed a great facility in pottery making. Once pottery skills were already in place, it was relatively easy to transfer them to a commercial arena. Today, households are stocked with mass-produced items to increasing extent. The younger generation of women does not need to learn the pottery arts with equal seriousness. It is easier for them to concentrate on painting premade pottery rather than modeling and casting figures from scratch.

Though pottery competes with amate for the attention of the young, pottery production has helped amate production in a few cases. For older painters already committed to amates, a family pottery business can help subsidize painting. Neither Marcial nor Inocencio Chino would have been able to continue painting had it not been for the pottery businesses run by their respective wives.

In addition to moving toward brightly colored, mass-produced ceramics, many Nahua artisans have invested increasing energy in jewelry made from semiprecious stones. The stones come from Mexico, Asia, and Eastern Europe. The artisans either purchase the stones they use to make jewelry or purchase intact necklaces and then break them up and rearrange them, often painting the stones in the process. These products have become especially popular in the main market in Cuernavaca.

Many of the young painters have switched to other nonamate media. Some paint on wood that is then laminated to form crosses or various household items. Others paint on wooden trays or plates, on wooden carved fish, or on burlap, gourds, leather, or rocks—usually in the form of small and convenient items for the household. Many of these works are quite pleasing and charming, but few of these artisans have gone on to bigger and bolder works of an artistic nature.

Other economic and technological changes have hurt amate markets in recent times. In the 1990s, the amate market changed fundamentally with the introduction of *sellos*, or copied sheets. Rather than drawing new amates, some producers figured they could make more money by copying amates that had already been made. Printing presses were set up, and extant designs for amates were copied in large numbers (often hundreds), as if they were lithographs. Once the design has been copied, children fill in the colors. In effect, amates are now mass-produced.

Residents of Oapan and Ameyaltepec attribute the development of *sellos* to the pueblos of Maxela and Ahuelicán. They claim that the inhabitants of those pueblos cannot draw amates well and thus must resort to copies. Furthermore, they resent that the sellers of *sellos* have spoiled their markets to large degree. The best painters also believe that *sellos* give amates a bad name and a low status and make it harder to market the better works.

Typically, the ordinary tourist buyer cannot readily tell the difference between a *sello* and an amate painted by hand, though they could tell if they spent a few seconds looking. The *sello* tends to be on thinner, more porous paper and of lower quality. On inspection, the drawing can be seen to be a multiple, not done by hand. The colors appear more artificial, less artfully done (even compared to a cheap street amate), and often fluorescent in nature. But buyers generally do not have these distinctions in mind when they buy. Furthermore, their expenditure is so small that most of them would not care much even if they knew the difference.

The rise of *sellos* is in part responsible for the weakening prices of street amates. For a hand-painted amate to be profitable, the seller might hope to get as much as five to ten dollars. *Sellos* can be sold profitably for much less, sometimes for as little as two or three dollars. The continuing survival of street amates in profitable form therefore requires that most buyers care enough about the difference to pay the extra dollars. Today, as the market has developed, only amate painters with established reputations can command superior prices from buyers.

We might mourn the displacement of quality amate, but Oapan shows a longer history of competing artistic forms. Just as ceramics are today displacing amate and as amate once displaced ceramics, quality mask production fell as quality amate production rose. The inhabitants say that the last Oapan masks were made about thirty years ago. Prior to this time, many Oapan families made good masks for their own use in fiestas. As prosperity grew and as amate painting became more popular, Oapan mask making died out. In essence, the economic and social division of labor increased. Since that time, Oapan residents commonly buy their masks from San Francisco Ozomatlán, where the masks are made for widespread commercial sale. Masks are now of smoother workmanship, but there is less unique vision. The masks of the San Francisco artisans are increasingly geared toward tourists and craft shops rather than for dancing and use. This "corruption" occurred precisely at the same time and for the same reasons that high-quality amate painting flourished.

More generally, Guerrero mask making peaked in the first half of the twentieth century. After this point, many fathers did not pass their skills on. While the best masks were made for local dances, this demand proved to be stagnant. Interest in the dances declined with modernization. Many outsiders and tourists demanded masks, so the mask makers switched into a high-volume, low-quality mode. Efficient workshop production displaced individual workmanship in the artistic sense. These same processes of modernization helped the market for amates get off the ground. Here again, we see close links between the creative and destructive sides of cross-cultural contact.[7]

Will Amate Be Canonized?

In recent times, we have seen amate increase its presence in the market for long-term fame and reputation. Commentators, curators, and collectors are processing the work and history of the amate painters with an eye toward determining where amate stands in the history of art and the history of Mexico. Obviously, this very book forms one piece of a much larger process.

Under the least optimistic scenario, amate painting will go down in history as one of the Mexican folk arts. It will be important to the history of Guerrero, but it will fail to advance significantly in terms of reputation.

Under the most positive scenario, amate and other high-quality Mexican folk arts are in a position analogous to the arts of the Native Americas early in the twentieth century. At that time, Native American art had some avid partisans but no established body of collectors, largely for social and class reasons. Most (non-native) Americans wanted to forget about America's Native American heritage rather than glorify it. Prices for Native American art skyrocketed only when white Americans decided to embrace Native American culture as part of the general American heritage and history. The attention given to Native American rights during the 1960s were critical in establishing this shift in attitude. In American society, Native artworks have gone from a sign of "primitiveness" to being a symbol of the sophistication and political conscience of the collector. This shift in political worldviews has caused Native American works to skyrocket in price. A reasonably good, but not spectacular, nineteenth-century Plains Indian drawing no larger or sturdier than an amate might easily sell for twelve thousand dollars in a Santa Fe or New York gallery. Fifty years ago, there would have been no real market for these works at all, save for the demands of a few eccentric collectors.

Over time, wealthier Mexicans may embrace the indigenous heritage of their country just as American collectors have turned to the Native American arts. It remains to be seen, however, when this turn-around might start, how many high-quality amates will survive to this time, and whether any amate painter will emerge as a historical leader for the movement.

The Smithsonian Institution has taken one small step toward can-onization with its decision to purchase amates for the opening exhibit of the National Museum of the American Indian. The museum, set on the Mall in downtown Washington, covers approximately 260,000 square feet just southeast of the National Gallery of Art. Perhaps because of NAFTA and the growing importance of Mexican-Ameri-can relations, it was decided that the museum would include the indigenous groups of Mexico. Native American delegates to the Smithsonian protested this decision, wanting to keep more space for North American works, but they have not prevailed.

The National Museum of the American Indian remained mired in dispute for years. Congress approved the museum in 1989, and the Smithsonian received the authority to acquire a collection of eight hundred thousand objects from the George Gustav Heye Foundation. Even after groundbreaking occurred, lack of funding and architectural disputes caused numerous delays. The museum opened, however, in September of 2004. The ability to raise funds from Native American casinos has been essential in completing the project, which faced few further obstacles as it approached inauguration.[8]

The contents of the museum have been determined by consultations with about thirty-five groups or "tribes," including the Nahua of the Alto Balsas region. Smithsonian authorities contacted the CPNAB, the pan-pueblo institution that led the region's fight against a dam in the 1990s (see chapter 5). The Smithsonian flew several CPNAB members to Washington at government expense to talk about what kinds of amates and other artworks from the region might be included in the opening exhibit of the museum.

The Xalitla members of the CPNAB tried to elevate the relative importance of their village in the history of amate. Xalitla now markets itself to outsiders as more indigenous than it actually is. The Xalitla representatives of the CPNAB told the Smithsonian that one of the amates should portray the "Indian market" in Xalitla. To anyone who knows the pueblo, this request borders on the absurd. To adapt an old saying about the Holy Roman Empire, the "Indian market" is neither Indian nor is it a market in anything but the most trivial sense. The so-called Indian market consists of a small number of Spanish-speaking mestizo Xalitla residents setting up stalls and selling small items, often nothing more exotic than beer or bubble gum. The Smithsonian, how-ever, took the bait and went off looking for photos and amates of Xal-itla's "Indian market."

In earlier times, the residents of Xalitla insulted the inhabitants of Ameyaltepec and Oapan and held them in low regard. They consid-ered them to be primitive Indians and made fun of their Nahuatl lan-guage and lack of proficiency in Spanish. Though the composition of Xalitla is mestizo, it is largely Nahuatl, but Xalitla citizens sought to distance themselves from Nahua culture. Today, the climate of opin-ion has changed. Xalitla residents envy the more indigenous status of the inner pueblos. They regard fluency in Nahuatl as an advantage and as something to be envied. Some Xalitla residents talk about learning Nahuatl, although no significant effort has been made in this direction.

The eventual decision of the Smithsonian reflected a greater inter-est in Oapan village politics than in Xalitla. Rather than choosing between Marcial and Nicolás de Jesús, the Smithsonian asked for two joint works, one on the struggle against the dam and another on the land disputes with San Miguel (both discussed in chapter 5 of this book). Marcial thus worked in collaboration with Nicolás and the two painted amates based on these themes. Marcial and Nicolás also have discussed whether they might market lithographs from this work.

During Marcial's subsequent visit to Washington in 2002, he sold another amate to the Smithsonian, this one a solo work, a black-and-white interior of an Oapan house. The Smithsonian talked of flying him to Washington again so he can paint part of a cupola that will be a permanent part of the museum.

Donation of the MIND Collection

The Thompsons, the leading collectors of the early work of the Oapan group, donated their collection to Ramapo College several years ago. It was then put on exhibit for several months in the school's art gallery.

The show did not generate significant external reviews, although it was well received within the campus community. Several years later, in the fall of 2001, Ramapo exhibited a portion of my amate and paintings collection, with an emphasis on the works of Marcial, though Juan was prominently represented as well.

Ramapo College is a state school of about five thousand students in northern New Jersey, near the New York State border. It is only a few miles from the house of Selden Rodman, and it is where Selden donated large parts of his collection. Just recently, the school opened a permanent gallery for Selden's works. Selden had pointed the Thompsons toward Ramapo as a potential home for the paintings. Selden felt that combining the MIND collection with his own donated works would make Ramapo a central locale for outsider art from Haiti and Mexico. Selden's own gift to Ramapo included some works from the Oapan group, and he wanted his Mexican legacy to be in the same place.

The Thompsons, unlike many art collectors, are not hoarders. They dispose of works, even very good ones, on a regular basis, through either sale or donation. They did not see that the works of the Oapan group were appreciating in value, so they decided to donate them. The Thompsons kept only two of the works for themselves: a painting by Marcial of his daughter Dahlia, holding a book upside down, and Felix Jimenez's *Cousins*, which portrays Felix and Marcial sitting together in a room, both playing guitars.

A recent exhibit in the Dallas Museum of Art entitled "Great Masters of Mexican Folk Art" included an amate from Ameyaltepec, which also has been reproduced in the eponymous catalog. The artist is Alfonso Lorenzo, one of the most talented amate artists. Lorenzo has been mentally ill since the early 1980s. His paintings reflect a fervent attention to detail, an almost pointillist use of dots, baroque elongated shapes, and skewed perspectives. He enjoys painting the obscene, painting furious owls, or painting God. For years, his family in Ameyaltepec dealt with his illness by chaining him to the wall; he currently resides in Clínica Cuernavaca, where he paints amates for a Dr. Guerrero in return for his treatment. After its opening in Dallas in October 2001, the show traveled to Chicago and New York, receiving enthusiastic reviews.

The French have shown a sudden interest in amates. Two Paris museums, including at the Parque La Villette, are organizing exhibits of amates involving the collections of Jonathan Amith and Gobi Stromberg (an American amate collector, patron, and resident of Cuernavaca). The interest of the French stems from earlier shows organized by Jonathan Amith (discussed in chapter 5), although it remains unclear what prompted this interest to come to the fore.

The painters take great pride in these events, which give them a sense of accomplishment. The early years with Rabkin aside, the outside world has sent them relatively few positive signals of their importance.

Summary Remarks

The introduction of this book raised the central theme of liberty versus power and the more specific topics of economic development and cultural globalization. Oapan and the painters provide only a single case study. Nonetheless, the investigation points toward greater support (as opposed to definitive demonstration) for the following conclusions.

1. Entrepreneurial economic development is possible under adverse conditions

The village of Oapan was not obviously poised for takeoff in the early 1960s. It was isolated, illiterate, and declining in population, and it had few, if any, political allies within Mexico. Yet Oapan residents have done a surprisingly good job of boosting their standard of living. Each generation has seen a much better life than the generation that came before it. The entrepreneurial energies of Oapan residents, most of all in the form of amate painting and craftwork, have driven this success.

The growth of Oapan living standards has come "off the books" for the most part. A look at the material culture of the village reveals how much living standards have gone up. No formal statistics mirror these facts, as real Oapan incomes are not measured in any direct way. For this reason, national income statistics sometimes underestimate the gains of the rural poor.

More generally, the economic study of Oapan should revise our opinion of globalization in an upward direction. Global markets, combined with tourism, have helped Oapan residents become richer and freer. Non-Mexicans have financed much of the amate movement, whether as tourists, art buyers, or art patrons. The American financial role, rather than corrupting or destroying Oapan, has served as a counterweight to mainstream Mexican culture. Oapan has persisted— rather than disappearing through migration or starvation—in part because of the amate arts and foreign finance.

2. Markets enable cultural voices

By driving the amate revolution, prosperity and cross-cultural exchange have given the Oapan painters their cultural voices. Through amate, Oapan residents have become more aware of their heritage and their uniqueness. Amates record the fiestas, dress, landscape, cuisine, social practices, agriculture, politics, and other aspects of Oapan life. The painters, by recording these details, also have become more self-conscious of their uniqueness. The outside world, as illustrated by scholars such as Jonathan Amith, has taken greater interest in the community. The amate arts also helped Oapan residents fight the Mexican government's plan to relocate the community to build a dam.

3. Artistic revolutions come and go through a process of "creative destruction"

Commerce, for all its benefits, does not guarantee a creative blossoming. Commerce, on average, boosts the chances of creative artists, but markets are blind to a number of preconditions for artistic achievement. It is not enough to simply bring together buyers and sellers, as markets are so effective at doing. An artistic revolution also requires sources of inspiration, extensive networks of training on the supply side, and favorable technologies. As these influences change, we can expect a market economy to bring a regular reshuffling of popular genres, styles, and art forms. Culture will never be static but, rather, is a process of growth, decline, and rebirth; in other words, culture is a process of creative destruction (Cowen 1998, 2002).

By increasing the quantity of available resources, markets can increase the likelihood of a strong artistic network. But in any particular instance, market forces eventually will discourage or work against a previously created art form, as we see with amate painting. The market economy thus will appear to be damaging human creativity. At the same time, though, we should not forget the broader perspective. A market creates more artistic opportunities in the first place, which in the long run means a greater number of declines as well.

4. The amate revolution has required geographic concentration and creative collaborative work

Cultural economics is—or ought to be—closely linked to economic geography. Spatial proximity, common training networks, and a common worldview have been critical to the amate revolution. It is vital that painters can learn from each other, and for this reason, we often observe painters working together or living in close proximity. Within Oapan, Marcial's role as group leader led to many more general connections to foreign buyers. It is no accident that good amates come from only four villages, all in the same general vicinity.

The extreme spatial concentration of amate production has made the production network especially dynamic but also vulnerable to extinction. A few small changes in technology or conditions in the pueblos can suffice to render quality amate production largely unprofitable. The amate story thus illustrates the beginnings of how an artistic genre can pass out of existence.

5. State power has oppressed the painters

The influence of power in the form of Mexican politics has been largely negative on the lives of the Oapan painters. The painters have had to deal with corrupt Mexican police, fight off threats to their land, and live in a general environment of political repression and legal discrimination. They are rightfully suspicious of political power and the Mexican state. Village politics has provided some public goods but also has drained the resources of the more productive community members, including Marcial. Life without politics is not possible, but the story of the Oapan painters does not show politics as the natural ally of the artistic spirit.

The Next Steps

It remains to be seen how the Oapan group will develop with time. Two of the painters featured in this study, Marcial and Roberto Mauricio, already have recurring health problems of a potentially serious nature. Mexican life is not very kind to an ailing person, with or without foreign financial support.

The Oapan pueblo itself, despite improving standards of living, is in a difficult situation. Many Oapan residents feel that the world is passing them by. Oapan residents, the painters included, are having to come to terms with their changing place in the region. In earlier times, Oapan led the immediate region as indisputably the largest and most important pueblo and one of the richest pueblos as well. Today, it is increasingly just another place. The hated neighbor San Miguel, historically poorer than Oapan, now appears somewhat wealthier, largely because its young men have been quicker to leave for the United States. Oapan still has deeper cultural roots and more young men in the pueblo, but these features no longer appear to be yielding new cultural returns, unless we count the ongoing work of the older amate painters, such as Juan and Marcial.

The painters discussed herein see this change in the relative local position of Oapan and rue it. Yet the same globalizing trends have increased the international stature—in a broader art world—of both Oapan and the painters. The Oapan painters, most of all Marcial, hope that external publicity for amates will help preserve the village. They know that their parallel lives remain where they started, embedded in Oapan but indisputably touched and mobilized by the outside world.

Felix Jimenez notes that the villagers had one set of gods during the pre-conquest period and that they now have a second set of gods. He says he likes the current gods and thinks they have done the village well. He wonders, however, whether they might someday be replaced by a third set of gods and what those gods might be.

Notes

CHAPTER I

1. Benjamin Barber (1995) offers a classic account of how larger cultures homogenize the world and wipe out many smaller cultures. Jeremy Tunstall (1977, 57) defined the *cultural imperialism thesis* as the view that "authentic, traditional and local culture in many parts of the world is being battered out of existence by the indiscriminate dumping of large quantities of slick commercial and media products, mainly from the United States." Fredric Jameson (2000, 51) wrote: "The standardization of world culture, with local popular or traditional forms driven out or dumbed down to make way for American television, American music, food, clothes and films, has been seen by many as the very heart of globalization."

2. I do not like any of these terms, which imply unities that do not exist, set these activities beneath high art (as with the term *folk art*), or define the activities only in a negative way, in terms of an opposition to something else (as with the term *outsider art*). For other studies of folk art production in Mexico and its economic aspects, see Cook and Binford 1990; Goertzen 2001. Barbash (1993) looks at the lives of some Oaxacan wood-carvers. Parezo (1983) studies the economics of Navajo sand painting.

3. Giorgio Vasari ([1568] 1991) pioneered the biographical approach to cultural economics. He presented the lives of the painters of the Italian Renaissance, comparing them to each other and seeking to confirm their fame. The comparative biographical approach of the present book also points to Plutarch's *Parallel Lives*, although Plutarch focused more tightly on the questions of what a good life consists of and whether one must live a philosophically aware life to be virtuous and to enjoy good fortune.

4. For instance, the lives of this study illustrate Vasari's maxim ([1568] 1991, 4) that most artists do not enjoy uninterrupted success but, rather, are subject to a wheel of fortune.

5. On the general topic of narrative in the social sciences, see, for instance, Mink 1970; Roth 1989.

6. Florence Browne is an elderly American retiree in Cuernavaca. She has known Marcial for over twenty years and was the first person to write an article about him.

7. See Good 1993 for the sea-level estimate (145) and for the population estimate (63). Many individuals are formal residents but spend little time in the pueblo, so the true population is difficult to estimate.

8. Nahuatl has over one million speakers, most of whom are located in central Mexico. Classical Nahuatl was formerly the lingua franca of the Aztec Empire. Many Nahuatl words are long, full of mellifluous syllables, and replete with sounds approximating our *sh* and *tl*. The vocabulary is rich and sophisticated and is believed by the villagers to be superior to Spanish. *Ki:xteyo:tia* means "he paints eyes on it," which refers to the last stage of painting an amate or picture. *Xtihkoto:naskeh* means "we will not snap the cord"—or, more metaphorically, "we will not give up growing corn." *To:naka:yo:tl* is used to refer to corn; it means both "our sustenance" and "that which results from the heat of the sun." The word *Nahuatl* itself means "clear speech." I learned the word for "he paints eyes on it" from Inocencio Chino, with assistance from Jonathan Amith. For the other words, I have drawn from Good 1993, 180–81, as amended by correspondence with Jonathan Amith. Amith's method of writing Nahuatl uses the colon to indicate vowel length. Classical Nahuatl offers such gems as *icnocuicatl,* which means "chants of orphanhood and deep reflection"; see León-Portilla and Shorris 2001, 30. León-Portilla and Shorris provide the etymology for *Nahuatl* as well (81, 661). Karttunen (1983) provides an analytical dictionary of classical Nahuatl. The dialect of Nahuatl spoken in Oapan is similar to classical Nahuatl, though speakers of the two would not find each other mutually intelligible in every regard. Jonathan Amith, who is currently assembling a dictionary of Nahuatl in Oapan, estimates that the difference is comparable to that between English in the time of Shakespeare and English today.

CHAPTER 2

1. For a variety of other treatments of poverty and inequality in Mexico, see Ravallion 1994; Tokman and O'Donnell 1998; Lustig 1998; Yúnez-Naude and Taylor 2001; De Janvry and Sadoulet 2001; Winters, Davis, and Corral 2002; Wiggins et al. 2002. For a general survey of the literature on global income inequality, see Firebaugh 2003. Legrain (2002, chapter 2) surveys the literature on how globalization alleviates poverty.

2. See Ochoa Campos 1964, 30–31. On poverty measures more generally, see Atkinson and Bourguignon 2000; Ravallion 1994. Reddy and Pogge (2003) criticize standard poverty measures.

3. An 1822 census noted that Oapan was growing corn, sugarcane, and *platanos* (plantains), in addition to making cheese (see Pavía Miller 1998, 92).

4. Venison is eaten, but deer are becomingly increasingly difficult to catch, due to depletion from overhunting.

5. Golde 1986, 75, and personal conversation with the author.

6. The colonizers sought to ease their rule by relocating communities and consolidating smaller pueblos into larger ones. But at the time, it was argued successfully that

many differing communities were needed to ease the crossing of the Rio Balsas at distinct points; thus, the pueblos remained intact. On resettlement resistance, see Gerhard 1993, 317–18; Amith 1995c, 133–35. On the arrival of nominal Spanish rule, see Ruiz de Alarcón 1984, 256 (the material added by the editors in appendix E).

7. See, for instance, Hassig 1985, especially chapter 13.

8. On the 1958 highway completion, see Good 1993, 196.

9. In addition to my talks with the villagers, see Hendrichs Perez 1945, 21–22.

10. At the end of her stay, though, Golde describes herself as wondering whether her home was really so different or whether the village simply seemed like a "caricature because it was not camouflaged or disguised by lofty phrases and implicit fictions." See Golde 1986 (for the quotations, 71 and 83). I also have drawn on my conversations with Peggy Golde for this account. Note that Golde spent most of her time in Ameyaltepec, the neighboring village, although she visited Oapan. Oapan is commonly considered to have a far more serious trust problem than does Ameyaltepec.

11. From oldest to youngest, the children are Fausto, Juan, Amalia, Marcial, Felix, Carmen, Vicenzia (who died young), and Francisca.

12. Marcial recounts playing in the river, a frequent source of danger to the young in the community. Often the current was high and swimming skills were not very reliable. Marcial's mother notes that her strongest memory of the boys' childhood was when a very young Marcial (seven or eight years old, by his recollection) nearly drowned swimming in the Rio Balsas. She felt compelled to beat him afterward for his daring, and she still remarks on his rebelliousness.

13. The Mexican government gives education scholarships, on the understanding that the recipients will later go to teach in the pueblos. Commonly the money is taken but the obligation is not enforced. So a teacher may be assigned to Oapan, but he or she will not be in residence very much. Michael Kremer (2003) provides a more general treatment of the lack of educational participation in Mexico.

14. In contrast to the production of Western paper, the production of amate paper preserves the longer fibers of the bark (Torres 1980, 25). This gives the paper greater durability, despite its porous nature. The production process determines what kind of amate will be made. The amate makers decide what kinds of trees to use, what kind of bark to put into the mix, and how much cloro and ash to add to the boiling process. Variations in the thickness of the paper depend on the amount of fiber beat with the stone and on the skill and intent of the papermaker. The age of the tree also influences the durability, flexibility, tone, and fiber of the paper. The marbleized appearance of many amates comes from variations in fiber color. The older the tree is, the darker and coarser will be the resulting paper. Longer cooking can make the paper finer. Corn kernels soaked in lime water result in a mixture that will make the amate paper yellow rather than white. Commercial bleach is used to lighten the color of the fibers or to introduce marble patterns into fibers that would otherwise be completely dark. See Bell 1988, 89.

15. See Bell 1988, 98; Von Hagen 1944, 22; Lockhart 1992, 40, 326. Amate paper is believed to have its origins in the tapa clothing of Central and South America, which was eventually modified to make amate. (Tapa paper is uncooked and pounded into shape; amate is cooked with alkaloids and then pounded.) The Maya appear to have developed amate paper in the fifth century A.D. and to have passed the technique

along to Toltec, Zapotec, and Mixtec peoples. The Mixtec (ca. A.D. 668 to 1450) inhabited parts of Guerrero and also painted on amate, often in mural form. Several different kinds of closely related trees are used for amate, including jonote colorado, jonote xalama, and jonote limon, among others. On the paper and its history, see Bell 1988, 77, 97–98. A number of scholars have cited the possibility that papermaking techniques came to Mexico from the South Pacific, which has the related tapa technique, but this view remains speculative.

16. See Sandstrom and Sandstrom 1986, 20, 31; Dow (1975) offers another account of this culture.

17. I am here indebted to the remarks of Max Kerlow in personal conversation.

18. On the early pottery history of the region, see Good Eshelman 1988; Good 1993; Hendrichs Pérez 1945, chapter 12. Ameyaltepec was settled by Oapan emigrants in pre-Hispanic times, and both villages specialize in amates and crafts. Nonetheless, Oapan has a different feel from Ameyaltepec. Ameyaltepec is almost medieval in setting, as it is built into a steep hillside. Oapan lies on the river, whereas Ameyaltepec does not. Oapan has about twice as many families. Oapan is considered to be more political and more contentious. It has a richer history and offers more large fiestas. Ameyaltepec is richer, cleaner, and more orderly. It does not allow its drunks to hang out in the town square or lie in the streets. Nor are pigs allowed to roam the streets, as they must be corralled and kept out of public view. The streets are swept every weekend.

19. See Amith 1995a; Kraig and Nieto 1996, 120. I also interviewed Max Kerlow and Felipe Ehrenberg. Kerlow and Felipe Ehrenberg differ on who actually introduced amate paper to the artists (Ehrenberg 1995 presents Ehrenberg's side of the story, which Kerlow explicitly denies). Kerlow describes Ehrenberg as his "assistant at the time," while Ehrenberg claims the artists were painting for him before he brought them to Kerlow. Cristino Flores, one of the first three amate painters, assigns priority to Ehrenberg. Under another version of the story of the origins of amate painting, an individual from Xalitla decided to paint on amate while working as a silversmith in Taxco. Some individuals in Taxco have reported that a Chato Castillo, an artist-designer who worked extensively in numerous media, brought amate painting to Xalitla. Some individuals have reported that the villagers had contact with amate paper as early as the 1950s, in craft markets, although it is nebulous whether they used this paper for painting. In general, Xalitla-based stories should be discounted, especially since the Kerlow version of the story appears to be consistent. Xalitla is closest to the main highway and, for this reason, might have appeared to outsiders as the original home of amate painting. The origins of amate painting are most likely between Kerlow and the artisans of Ameyaltepec. On these stories, see Stromberg 1982, 153. On the paper and cardboard experiments, see Good 1993, 197–98.

20. The several early exhibits of amate that Kerlow was also able to arrange include exhibition at the Galeria Jose Maria Velasco in Mexico City.

21. Ehrenberg's description here comes from my interview with him. In addition to consulting the account of Good Eshelman (1988), I have talked with several of the earliest amate painters in Oapan. The anecdote about the San Pablito merchants comes from Porfírio Morales.

22. In terms of quality, the Nahuatl-speaking Oapan and Ameyaltepec are the two clear leaders from the four main villages, with the Spanish-speaking Xalitla and Maxela next on the list. This ranking is robust whether we consider illustration in catalogs (Amith 1995a; Good Eshelman 1988), price commanded in the marketplace, or ability to command foreign buyers.

23. On collaborative circles, see Farrell 2001.

24. On clustering and location theory, see, for instance, Krugman 1997 and Fujita, Krugman, and Venables 1999.

25. Age estimates are from conversations. No formal birth records were kept. Even today, many pueblo residents do not know exactly how old they are.

26. On the end of the salt trade, see Good Eshelman 1988, 183–85; Amith 1995c, 143. For census data, see de la Peña 1949, 2:282. In colonial times, the villagers specialized in carrying and muleteering. Until Mexican independence, Asian goods arrived in Acapulco on a regular basis, frequently in December. Oapan villagers helped carry these goods and the trade with Peru to the rest of Mexico. Starting in the nineteenth century and continuing up until about 1939, many of the Alto Balsas villages specialized in salt commerce in addition to their subsistence agriculture. They bought sea salt on the Pacific coast, usually near Acapulco, and resold it in the interior of the state of Guerrero. This experience in the salt trade gave them commercial skills that later were used for marketing amates. The villagers knew how to establish outside trade contacts, how to deal with middlemen, and how to deal with a frequently hostile Spanish-speaking outside world. San Agustín and Ameyaltepec, two of the leading amate villages, also have strong backgrounds in the salt trade. Non-amate-producing villages tend to have weaker historical connections with the salt trade. On the role of the salt trade, see Good 1995. On the early economic history of the area, see Good Eshelman 1988; Good 1993, 75; Amith 2000.

27. I was not able to interview Francisca for this book, due to her distance from Oapan. The other family members claim she paints cheaper street amates, rather than higher-quality amates.

28. Felipe Ehrenberg narrates that Cristino Flores painted the first *historia*, which he did in black and white in Kerlow's workshop. Cristino drew on a popular song in Guerrero, rooted in medieval Spain, about a very thin woman. The amate sold rapidly, and Cristino did more like it (he still paints that song to this day). Ehrenberg relates words of the song as follows: "Delgadina se paseaba de la sala a la cocina . . . en vestido transparente . . . que su pecho le ilumina . . ." The next *historias* had religious themes, according to Ehrenberg.

29. These plots, while small, yield food year-round, rather than just during the harvest season, and are important for village nutrition.

30. Marcial's dreamy side showed itself early on. He notes that his strongest memory from childhood involves hearing music from the sky ("música celestial"). When he was seven or eight, he heard (or thinks he heard) a rising volume of "music" coming from the north for about ten or fifteen minutes. He was catching butterflies at the time but stopped out of fright. He narrates that an old lady heard the same music and screamed. He wanted to run and tell his parents, but they were out in the field working. To this day, Marcial still does not know whether he heard real music from the sky,

imagined the whole thing, heard some kind of unusual wind current, or perhaps heard a low-flying airplane or some other kind of machine. Once he began painting amates, Marcial had the chance to put his dreams down on paper.

31. See Lockhart 1992, 235.

32. On *nahuales* in the Balsas region, see Hendrichs Pérez 1945, chapters 14–15; Kraig and Nieto 1996, 114 (citing a talk with Livorio Celestino). On *nahuales* in earlier Nahuatl civilizations, see Le Clézio 1993, 105. On *nahuales* in other communities, see Ingham 1986, 118–19; Montoya Briones 1964, 175–77. Suspicion of witchcraft has diminished over time but remains nonetheless; Golde (1986, 77) reports widespread belief in witchcraft in Ameyaltepec in 1959.

33. I am indebted to group members for showing me photos of their early works, in addition to discussing them. The outside reader can get the best sense for this Ur-style from the Abraham Mauricio amates in Saldívar [1979] 1985 and on the Web site for my own collection: http://www.gmu.edu/jbc/Tyler/amate2.htm.

34. The earliest Ameyaltepec painters had signed their names for Max Kerlow and Felipe Ehrenberg, but the practice did not emerge in Oapan until the advent of *historias*. Note also that Juan Camilo was given the name *Tomás* at birth and signed that name on some of his early works. He later adopted the name *Juan*, partly because he likes the associated saint and partly as a conscious rebellion against his father's choice of name.

35. On Marcial and bargaining, see Lakehomer 1983, in addition to Marcial's own account.

36. On price trends, see Stromberg 1982, 51; Good Eshelman 1988, 35–36. Conversations with artists and Max Kerlow yield a consistent picture. The estimate from the early 1970s is from Roberto Mauricio and was confirmed by the other group members. The time trend in prices is not fully smooth, since supply problems with the amate paper led to repeated price spikes. The amate trees from San Pablito were overharvested, and the price of the paper rose until new sources of supply were found in other regions (in fact, the original amate tree was largely abandoned as a source of supply in favor of the jonote colorado tree). Note that the dollar-peso exchange rate remained fixed at twelve and a half pesos to the dollar until the middle of the 1970s. Good Eshelman (1988, 32–33) offers data on price spikes for amate paper.

37. One year in the early 1970s, the American Robert Walsh visited Oapan, specifically the home of Felix and Inocencio Chino. Inocencio had apologized and told him that the family was too poor to offer him anything more than rice and beans. Robert saw that the silo of the family was empty, as the harvest had been bad that year due to poor rain. At that point, Robert realized that the families needed amate sales to get by, especially when the rain did not come.

38. On the economics of rent creation, see, for instance, McChesney 1997; de Soto 1989.

39. "No estoy en otro país. Estoy en México. Yo puedo vender aquí . . . con mis paisanos . . ."

40. On Acapulco, see Good 1993, 271–74. Francisco Lorenzo, an Ameyaltepec artisan who sells in Acapulco, reports that the problem has eased greatly since the election of a PRD governor in Guerrero. Amate and craft sellers do have some capacity to

escape police harassment. They warn each other when an extorter is coming, the women hide their merchandise in large pockets sewn into their dresses, the sellers try to play off the extorters against each other, or they avoid carrying the money to pay the bribe.

41. De Janvy and Sadoulet (2001) provide more general evidence on the importance of nonfarm income in rural Mexico.

42. On this growth, see Thorpe 1998, 15.

43. On the miles of railroad track, see Haber 1989, 15; see also 21. On how the railroad boosted Mexican urban centers, see, for instance, Coatsworth 1981; Schmidt 1987; Buffington and French 2000.

44. See Cajigal and Asta 1994, 9 and passim; Lomnitz-Adler 1992.

45. See de la Peña 1949, 2:505–7; Jacobs 1982, 31–38.

46. On the rise of Taxco, see Oles 1993, 131–35. On Taxco as a backwater, see Jacobs 1982, 38–40. On the rise of the silver industry in Taxco, see Stromberg 1985.

47. On the Taxco road, see Oles 1993, 133. On the wood-burning train in Cuernavaca, see King 1970, 7. On the 1933 road, see Lomnitz-Adler 1992, 325 n. 12. On the roads in the 1950s, see Sherman 2000, 585–86.

48. On Acapulco, see Boardman 2001, 95 and passim; Sherman 2000, 586; Sullivan 2001. On the general history of tourism in Guerrero, see de la Peña 1949, 2:527–97.

49. On Mexican-American tourism during the 1970s, see Dinstel 1982, 53–55. Escobedo (1981, 147) provides the figure from 1960. Information and figures on earlier times are from Boardman 2001, 84–95.

50. On the developments of the 1920s and 1930s, see Delpar 1992; Oles 1993, 127–41.

51. In addition to my discussions with the group, I have drawn here on comments from Elígio Esteba and Porfírio Morales, two of the earliest amate painters in Oapan.

52. I am indebted to Florence Browne for this anecdote, which I have confirmed by talking to people in the village.

53. See Otero 1997, 916; Luboff 1999, 194–95.

54. See Luboff 1999, 193.

CHAPTER 3

1. See Salopek 1986.

2. On early retirees in Cuernavaca, see King 1970, 7, 19.

3. On the lag of several months, see Lakehomer 1983.

4. A wide variety of informal institutions enable local families to sell and lend each other land, animals, and labor. Not everyone wants to or is able to work the land every year, and these transactions allow community resources to be put to more efficient use.

5. On this episode, in addition to my talks with Marcial and Felix, I have drawn on Lakehomer 1983 and Rodman 1982 (201–2).

6. In the early days of amate, artists deviated from the amate medium at times,

largely due to periodic scarcities of amate paper. Overharvesting endangered the supply of amate trees. The more plentiful jonote colorado tree had not yet developed as a substitute, and the distribution network for amate paper was less well developed than today. When amate was periodically scarce, Alto Balsas artists painted on bristol board and sometimes on regular industrial paper. In the very early days, cardboard was an occasional medium. Nonetheless, the artists typically returned to amate paper as soon as it was possible to do so.

7. See Salopek 1986, 13–14.

8. See Saldívar [1979] 1985, 72, for one account of this fiesta.

9. Many modern amates use "Aztec" themes that are taken from modern, Western representations of Aztec culture rather than coming through past linkages to the Aztec Empire. Traditionally, these themes have been found only on cheap street amates; lately, though, some of the better amate painters (including Marcial Camilo, Carlos Ortíz of Xalitla, and Joel Adame of Maxela) have turned their attention to them. More generally, we have little systematic information about the painted visual arts in preconquest Nahua society, nor do the Oapan painters have any direct links to these traditions. Indirect influences run through the early mingling of Nahua artists with Spanish colonial styles. Nahuas painted various murals and frescoes in religious settings (churches, monasteries, etc.) for the Spaniards, though we do not know whether these painters were Nahua from the Alto Balsas region. These works mimic European styles of the time fairly closely, though they deviate in terms of various flora and fauna. Sometimes, preconquest glyphs and song scrolls can be found in these frescoes. Butterflies sip at the flowers, a preconquest motif expressing the joys that meritorious souls enjoy in the afterlife. Nonetheless, when Marcial Camilo paints butterflies today, which he does frequently, it is because there are many butterflies in the pueblo and the surrounding fields, not because he is drawing on pre-Hispanic inspirations. On frescoes, see Peterson 1993; on butterflies, see Lockhart 1992, 424. Robertson 1994 is one good source on early Nahua painting and manuscripts.

10. See Centeno 1997, 185 (on inflation in the 1970s), 204 (on the minimum wage estimate).

11. Maria reports that she almost lost touch with the artists around 1991, when her husband, Robert, died. Nonetheless, they have remained in touch, and Maria received a visit from them in Cuernavaca this last year.

12. Group members offer different accounts of the timing of Juan's departure. By Juan's reckoning, it came after two years of working with Rabkin and at times living in Rabkin's house. By Marcial's reckoning, it came several years later. The dates on Rabkin's inventory of pictures suggest a later date as well; one of his pictures by Juan Camilo that was put on eBay was listed as dating from 1979.

13. Browne n.d., 21.

14. On the positive side for women, the culture possesses strong matriarchical elements, and the status of women is relatively high. Women have a strong say in family matters. Female adultery, while hardly approved of, is not rare and does not make the woman an immediate social outcast (for this observation, I am indebted to conversations with anthropologist Jonathan Amith). Nor is it unusual for women to travel on their own to sell crafts. On the negative side, women's voice in the family comes

through their hard work. Women cook, raise the children, paint ceramics, make clothing, wash clothing, and care for the domestic animals. Once a marriage is forthcoming, the family of the male pays a dowry to the family of the female, currently in the neighborhood of thirty chickens and three to five pigs, perhaps with an ox thrown in. On one hand, this dowry reflects the positive status of the woman within the village. On the other hand, the dowry price is a market signal that the family is losing a member who contributes more to the household than she receives in return. At first, a newlywed couple usually lives in the household of the male's parents, though eventually they will strike out on their own. The dowry can be negotiated upward or downward. On the value of the woman, see also Good 1993, 405.

15. On the economics of quality certification, see Klein 2000.

16. I have not been able to track down the exact galleries. The list is from Browne n.d. ("Never in Their Wildest Dreams"), which I believe is a magazine article from a periodical called *Amistad: Magazine of the American Society of Mexico*. My copy of this article came from Marcial and does not include the original date of publication.

17. See Zacharias 1978.

18. See Browne n.d.

19. I have drawn this information from a conversation with Marsha Bol; from undated museum correspondence of Marsha Bol; and from a letter of March 12, 2002, from Barbara Mauldin, currently curator of Latin American art at the museum.

20. The peso figure is compounded over time and thus hard to convert into dollars. Marcial notes that he has in mind roughly twenty-six thousand "current pesos" (ca. 2001), which would place the sum at over two thousand dollars. This return stands in contrast to another book illustrated by amate paintings, *El ciclo mágico de los dias*, by Antonio Saldívar ([1979] 1985). Abraham Mauricio Salazar, brother of Roberto Mauricio, painted the illustrations for that book. He claims that the author promised him a percentage of the proceeds but gave him nothing beyond his original lump-sum payment for the work. To this day, he remains disillusioned. When I went to speak to him, Abraham's first question was whether he would receive a percentage of the proceeds of the present study.

21. In addition to one Mexican ethnographic survey published in 1945 (Hendrichs Pérez), an unpublished doctoral dissertation had been written by Peggy Golde at Harvard University in 1963 (see Amith 1995a, Golde 1986), but in both cases, the fieldwork predated amate painting in Oapan.

22. Taken from program notes, "Recuerdos de mi Pueblo."

23. Personal email communication, 2001.

24. "Recuerdos de mi Pueblo," program notes obtained from Marcial Camilo.

25. In addition to my conversations with dealers, I am drawing on the results from auctions held during this time at Parke-Bernet Galleries.

26. See *International Folk World* 1, no. 1 (1983), on the relocation of Galerie Lara.

27. See *International Folk World* 1, no. 1 (1983), on the masks.

28. See Centeno 1997, 185, 197; Haber 1989, 1.

29. On Castillo, see Ahlander 2001.

30. Email correspondence, 2001.

31. Email communications from Janie Burke, February 8, 2001.

CHAPTER 4

1. A 1979 painting by Marcial Camilo Ayala that depicts electrification is held in the Ramapo College collection.

2. The upper-end estimate is taken from a conversation with Marcial Camilo and validated by discussions with the families; the more typical estimate is taken from conversations with numerous village members. I have not found any family that keeps formal books or accounting. Good Eshelman (1998) estimates family income as somewhat higher, though she focuses on the richer community of Ameyaltepec. The estimate for the *topiles* and a day's labor is taken from the fieldwork of Jonathan Amith and from conversations with Marcial Camilo. For comparable estimates for other parts of rural Mexico, see Wiggins et al. 2002. Daughters are far less likely to cross the border, given the physical hardships involved.

3. On the more general history of telephone and telegraph connections in Guerrero, see de la Peña 1949, 1: chapter 4.

4. Golde 1986, 78.

5. Rabkin had told me the name of the village, and finally I found a map that listed it. I also called up Mexican information and received the village phone number, although no one who answered the village phone was able to tell me how to get to the village. So when I arrived in Mexico City, I chartered a taxi driver to help me find the village, at the cost of several hundred dollars. I now know how to take the bus, which costs virtually nothing.

6. I have not taken any profits from these deals and, in fact, have picked up some of the secondary expenses, such as shipping and phone calls.

7. Most of all, they ask about planes falling from the sky. Juan and his family see the planes from Mexico City to Acapulco flying over the village and have had the fear that the planes would crash and fall on the village. A few years ago, a small private plane did fall in the neighboring pueblo of Analco. Juan considers planes to be a very dangerous mode of transportation and frequently asks about them.

8. See Golde 1986, 87, for the quotation. Golde discusses marriage practices more generally as well.

9. See Golde 1986, 80–81.

10. An alternative translation for "although the vision is fading" is "one's vision also goes." Roberto wrote "la vista tambíen se acaba"; my translation relies on my conversation with him.

11. On the five thousand figure, see Burns 2001.

12. Kroll (1994) offers a brief exposition of the work of Inocencio Chino.

13. Inocencio estimates that his wife paints the equivalent of "fifteen cats a week."

14. The Ford Foundation will fund the continuation of this project.

15. These estimates include input from Inocencio in addition to Felix.

16. I am indebted to Alberto Wuggetzer and to Ana Luisa's daughter, Leonore Thomas, for this information.

17. There is a "health clinic" in Oapan, though it is poorly supplied and often unstaffed. It does little to make the villagers healthier.

18. Gruzinski (2002, 103, 168) details some similarities between Nahua and Euro-

pean classical pagan cosmologies. He writes that the Spanish colonists would encourage the Nahuas to compare their beliefs to the stories of Ovid.

19. Marcial uses email (ayala115@hotmail.com) to handle many of his orders. That being said, he does not have a reliable system for receiving messages, and he cannot always be expected to respond to a query, no matter how direct, pointed, or urgent.

20. On the deaths of Pablo and Pedro de Jesús, see Ehrenberg 1995, 21.

21. Oapan residents envy the extensive social networks of Ameyaltepec. When an Ameyaltepec resident travels to Cancún to sell wares, he or she can draw on an entire support network for this purpose; the same is true in Monterrey and other distant locales. An Oapan resident will not have access to similar help. Lower levels of trust mean that Oapan residents are more likely to work with other family members and hold a more limited circle of contacts. Oapan crafts merchants have only recently penetrated to these further locales, with the exception of Guadalajara.

22. This information is based on my interview with Nicolás and on Amith 1995b, 85.

23. See Kraig and Nieto 1996.

24. Like Marcial, Nicolás served as *comisario* of his pueblo. Nicolás also claims he did not finish a single work that year, due to the responsibilities of the job. Nonetheless, he wished to contribute to the success of his pueblo.

25. In reality, Nicolás was hearkening back to the very early days of amate painting. Felipe Ehrenberg notes that in the early days of amate, he and Max Kerlow, decided to have the painters, including Nicolás's father, Pablo, do some lewd works; Ehrenberg notes, "Man, they sold VERY well . . . little crazy figurines screwing all over the hills."

26. See http://www.handmadepapers.com, or look at the eBay offerings under the seller name of "barkskin."

CHAPTER 5

1. Good (1993, 314–16) discusses these services.

2. Serious crimes, however, are brought to the county seat at Tepecualcuilco. In Oapan, there are two *comisarios*, a primary *comisario* and a secondary *comisario*, the latter serving as an assistant. Each barrio of Oapan elects a *comisario* for a one-year term, and the two barrios rotate as to which chooses the primary or secondary *comisario*. Though the *comisarios* are formally chosen by election, "las autoridades" set the agenda by choosing the candidates. The elders cannot impose a candidate without popular support, but they also hold an effective veto right over major officeholders. On political institutions in neighboring Ameyaltepec, which are similar in form (if not always substance), see Good Eshelman 1988, chapters 6–9.

3. Each year, one *mayordomo* is drawn from each of the two barrios of San Agustín. Like the *comisario*, the *mayordomo* receives no pay and nothing from village fines.

4. The state and municipality attempt to regulate and control the politics of the pueblos. But Oapan ignores these stipulations for the most part and structures its own

political institutions. See Good 1993, 322. For an account of governance in another Nahua community, in the state of Puebla, see Montoya Briones 1964, 118–21.

5. In economic terms, note that the largely self-employed villagers cannot convert time into money at a fixed rate; thus, the greater scarcity of money can persist.

6. Tax assessments are made when a special project is required, such as fixing the bell in the chapel, but these assessments are frequently a matter of great contention (though less so in Ameyaltepec). In the last two years, the members of the "outside" party, PRI, have refused to pay their assessments. It would be very difficult to tax the people in the small Mexican villages a percentage of their income. A lump-sum tax would place a disproportionate burden on the very poor.

7. Greenberg (1981, chapter 1) offers a systematic survey of hypotheses about status and the cargo system. He does not consider the "optimal taxation" factors discussed here. Foster (1967, 207–11) offers an especially clear statement of the status hypothesis. Good Eshelman (1988, chapter 9) offers critical remarks about the status hypothesis for Ameyaltepec.

8. A number of *topiles* also help the *comisarios* implement their decisions. The Nahuatl word *topile* means "the one who has a rod"; in this context, it refers to the reach of the law.

9. Some writers have mentioned a redistributivist motive for the cargo system; see Greenberg 1981, 7–12. Brandes (1988, 55–56) offers some evidence against the egalitarian and "economic leveling" explanations of the cargo system.

10. "Porque me gusta la justicia."

11. Some older estimates, drawn from different (and probably poorer) Mexican villages, place the burden of a one-year cargo at several hundred dollars. See Greenberg 1981, 149. Cancian (1965, chapter 8) offers some yet earlier estimates, for the Mayan community of Zinacantan. Foster (1967, 209), studying communities in Michoacán, estimates the sum to range up to one thousand dollars a year.

12. The modern priest is based in Xalitla and visits Oapan only periodically. (Oapan was once the seat of the local parish, but Xalitla grabbed this position away in the mid-1960s, an act that earned Xalitla the continuing enmity of Oapan residents.) The traditional priest reports to the bishop in Acapulco. Some members of Oapan have recently converted and have become Jehovah's Witnesses (I know of one Mormon as well). This is considered a conscious decision to reject the traditions of the pueblo and to embrace at least some parts of the outside world. Many villagers object to the antipathy that these individuals hold to the traditional fiestas, costumes, and ceremonies.

13. I am indebted to Jonathan Amith for the observation about Nahuatl.

14. For a broader analysis of how and why democratization has come about in Mexico, see Weingast 2003.

15. Weingast (2003) argues that the North American Free Trade Agreement, the growth of Mexico, and increased immigration all raised the stakes for challenging the previously dominant PRI party in Mexico; this hypothesis is consistent with the evidence from Oapan.

16. See, for instance, Axelrod 1984.

17. Cowen 2004 discusses the relevance of this argument to peace in the Middle East.

18. On some related themes, in a more general context, see Cowen and Sutter 1999, detailing the "costs of cooperation."

19. In addition to interviews, I have drawn on Hindley 1999 for information about the dam.

20. On this history, see Weinberg 2000, 239.

21. The petition is reproduced and translated by Hindley (1999, 218).

22. In an email to me on July 23, 2001, Scott Guggenheim wrote: "it wasn't a very good dam in the first place, in that the economic case for it wasn't a very strong one. For the short term power needs, thermal (coal) made more sense, and for the longer term it was better to tie up to the North American power grid." He added that the World Bank considered the study of the social component of the project "incomplete" from the very beginning, largely due to lack of consultation with the communities.

23. On the Alto Balsas region during the revolution, see Good Eshelman 1988, 182. Peace has not always prevailed in the state of Guerrero more generally. The 1960s saw guerrilla activity in Guerrero, just to the south of the Alto Balsas region. A group known as the Armed Commandos of Guerrero organized a series of executions and kidnappings, largely to take revenge on federal police for a previous police massacre of unarmed citizens. The group was smashed, but small guerrilla actions recurred throughout the 1970s. Guerrilla activity heated up again in the early 1990s. Following the Chiapas insurgency, a group known as OCSS (Campesino Organization of the Sierra del Sur) began to operate in Guerrero. Controversy reached a peak on June 28, 1995, when police apparently massacred seventeen OCSS members and then tried to cover up their role, claiming self-defense. To this day, the police regularly patrol the roads of Guerrero. In theory, they are looking for drug gangs, but it is more plausible that they are hoping to contain future political troubles. See Weinberg 2000, chapter 12, for a partial history of guerrilla activity in Guerrero.

24. He finds it hard to work when staying with others in the village, given the ongoing distractions, lack of privacy, and loud music, which interferes with his taping work.

25. The artists retained the rights to the original drawings. Amith later purchased the amates by paying the artists three hundred dollars a piece for the items.

26. Although Amith later bought these protest amates, he has never shown much of an interest in collecting amates. He loves the artworks, but he lacks both the funds and the "collector's mentality." To this day, his amate collection is extremely small, though very high in quality. He talks of how he would like to have more amates by a variety of painters, especially his closest friends (Inocencio, Marcial, and some of the Ameyaltepec painters), but he owns little more than the original collection of protest amates from the dam fight.

27. In 1716 Oapan received formal recognition of its land, through a *composición*, as part of a systematic Spanish colonial effort to define land titles and raise more revenue. Over the course of the eighteenth century, however, several villages (Ahuelican in 1717, Ameyaltepec—then called Amayotepec—in 1757, and San Miguel Tecuciapan in 1786) separated formally from the municipal seat (*cabecera*) of Oapan (Amith 2000, 183, 1079). Jacobs (1982, 56–57) offers a slight amount of information on the nineteenth-century land disputes, which were not restricted to Oapan. See also Guardino 1996.

28. For one version of this account, see Stromberg 1982, 72, which complements my talks with Oapan residents.

29. I am indebted to conversations with Henry Kammler, a German anthropology student who is doing work in Oapan and San Miguel. See also Good Eshelman 1988, 195–96.

30. I have had less success getting residents of San Miguel to present their side of the story to me. I am identified by my contacts as being a friend of Oapan and thus am considered an unsympathetic outsider—to be excluded from any discussion. The interpretation of the latest settlement as favorable to Oapan comes from Jonathan Amith.

31. Inocencio served first in the *comisariado*, for three years in the early 1990s. Roberto also served for three years (1996–98).

32. Roberto claims that his stint on the commission opened his eyes to the extent of corruption in Mexico—not only in San Miguel, but also in Oapan. It made him more cynical but also gave him new ideas about how to make the world better and gave him more courage.

33. See Golde 1986, 79.

CHAPTER 6

1. The information on migration is based on several interviews. For obvious reasons, the sources wish to remain nameless. For a more general study of the difficulty of crossing the border, see Eschbach et al. 1999. This source gives a conservative estimate of sixteen hundred crossing-related deaths for 1993 to 1997, almost one a day.

2. For the content of this last sentence, I am especially indebted to my conversations with Jonathan Amith and to his migration project, discussed in chapter 5 of the present study.

3. Personal factors play a role as well. The amate prodigy mentioned earlier left for personal reasons in addition to economic ones. In part, he left because he impregnated a local girl whom he did not wish to marry. (This surprised the community, who thought the eccentric son would be lucky to marry at all and would jump at the chance to marry this girl. The family ended up having to make a payment to the girl's family for her abandonment). Others have speculated that the son was tired of remaining under the thumb of his father—a strict disciplinarian and stern taskmaster—in the amate workshop at home.

4. This information about pottery is taken from visits to Ángel Domínguez; see also Stromberg 1982, 76–77.

5. Ángel's untrustworthiness in these matters is in contrast to the character of most of the amate painters, who are generally honest in meeting commissions and encounter their biggest trust problems when required to deal with each other.

6. Traditionally, the town potters have been women. The townspeople consider Ángel to be homosexual or a hermaphrodite. He is well into his mature years and has never married. He also spends much time on his sewing machine (again rare for a male in the village) and speaks with a lisp. Anthropologist Henry Kammler, who has spent much time in the village, is convinced that there is homosexuality in Oapan, though

usually between married men. Ángel is the only Oapan male who openly flaunts his different sexuality.

7. On the history of Guerrero mask making, see Cordry 1982; Good Eshelman 1988, 42–43. Jonathan Amith (oral communication) relates how the decline of mask making is also linked to a growing scarcity of the wood needed to make good masks.

8. On the museum, see Trescott 2001.

Bibliography

Ahlander, Leslie Judd. 2001. "One Hundred Years of Mexican Art: 20th Century Painters and Sculptors from the Pollak Collection." In *Travels in the Labyrinth: Mexican Art in the Pollak Collection*. Philadelphia: University of Pennsylvania Press, 2001.

Amith, Jonathan D., ed. 1995a. *The Amate Tradition: Innovation and Dissent in Mexican Art*. Chicago: Mexican Fine Arts Center Museum.

Amith, Jonathan D. 1995b. "The Creation of Indigenous Images: From Private Nightmares to Public Protest." In *The Amate Tradition: Innovation and Dissent in Mexican Art,* edited by Jonathan D. Amith, 41–100. Chicago: Mexican Fine Arts Center Museum.

Amith, Jonathan D. 1995c. "The History of the Balsas River Basin Nahua Communities." In *The Amate Tradition: Innovation and Dissent in Mexican Art,* edited by Jonathan D. Amith, 129–44. Chicago: Mexican Fine Arts Center Museum.

Amith, Jonathan D. 2000. "The Möbius Strip: A Spatial History of a Colonial Society: Central Guerrero, Mexico, from the Sixteenth to the Nineteenth Century." Ph.D. diss., Yale University.

Andreski, Stanislav. 1966. *Parasitism and Subversion: The Case of Latin America*. New York: Pantheon Books.

Arias, Ron. 1978. "Marcial Camilo Ayala." *Southwestern Art* 7, no. 1 (fall): 40–43.

Atkinson, Anthony B., and Francois Bourguignon, eds. 2000. *Handbook of Income Distribution*. Vol. 1. Amsterdam: North Holland.

Axelrod, Robert. 1984. *The Evolution of Cooperation*. New York: Basic Books.

Barbash, Shepard. 1993. *Oaxacan Woodcarving: The Magic in the Trees*. San Francisco: Chronicle Books.

Barber, Benjamin R. 1995. *Jihad versus McWorld*. New York: Times Books.

Bell, Lilian A. 1988. *Papyrus, Tapa, Amate, and Rice Paper: Papermaking in Africa, the Pacific, Latin America, and Southeast Asia*. McMinnville, Oreg.: Liliaceae Press.

Boardman, Andrea. 2001. *Destination México—"A Foreign Land a Step Away"; U.S. Tourism to Mexico, 1880s–1950s*. Dallas: Southern Methodist University.

175

Brandes, Stanley. 1988. *Power and Persuasion: Fiestas and Social Control in Rural Mexico*. Philadelphia: University of Pennsylvania Press, 1988.

Browne, Florence Reine. 1977. "And Now There Are Six." *Amistad: Magazine of the American Society of Mexico* 2, no. 19 (May): 16–21.

Browne, Florence Reine. N.d. "Never in Their Wildest Dreams." N.p. Photocopy.

Buffington, Robert M., and William E. French. 2000. "The Culture of Modernity." In *The Oxford History of Mexico*, edited by Michael C. Meyer and William H. Beezley, 397–432. Oxford: Oxford University Press.

Burkhart, Louise. 1989. *The Slippery Earth: Nahua-Christian Moral Dialogue in Sixteenth-Century Mexico*. Tucson: University of Arizona Press.

Burns, Scott. 2001. "Mexico or Bust: Retire Rich on a Peasant's Savings." *MSN Money*, March 23. http://moneycentral.msn.com/articles/retire/style/6550.asp.

Cajigal, Sergio Estrada, and Ferruccio Asta. 1994. *Crónicas de Cuernavaca, 1857–1930*. Veracruz, Mexico: Ediciones Asta.

Cancian, Frank. 1965. *Economics and Prestige in a Maya Community: The Religious Cargo System in Zanacantan*. Stanford: Stanford University Press, 1965.

Carrasco, Pedro. 1961. "The Civi-Religious Hierarchy in Mesoamerican Communities: Pre-Spanish Background and Colonial Development." *American Anthropologist* 63, no. 3:483–97.

Centeno, Miguel Ángel. 1997. *Democracy within Reason: Technocratic Revolution in Mexico*. University Park: Pennsylvania State University Press.

Coatsworth, John H. 1981. *Growth against Development: The Economic Impact of Railroads in Porfirian Mexico*. DeKalb: Northern Illinois University Press.

Cohan, Tony. 2000. *On Mexican Time: A New Life in San Miguel*. New York: Broadway Books.

Cook, Scott, and Leigh Binford. 1990. *Obliging Need: Rural Petty Industry in Mexican Capitalism*. Austin: University of Texas Press.

Cordry, Donald. 1982. *Mexican Masks*. Austin: University of Texas Press.

Cowen, Tyler. 1998. *In Praise of Commercial Culture*. Cambridge: Harvard University Press.

Cowen, Tyler. 2000. *What Price Fame?* Cambridge: Harvard University Press.

Cowen, Tyler. 2002. *Creative Destruction: How Globalization Is Shaping the World's Cultures*. Princeton: Princeton University Press.

Cowen, Tyler. 2004. "A Road Map to Middle Eastern Peace? A Public Choice Perspective." *Public Choice* 118:1–10.

Cowen, Tyler, and Daniel Sutter. 1999. "The Costs of Cooperation." *Review of Austrian Economics* 12:161–173.

Cowen, Tyler, and Alex Tabarrok. 2000. "An Economic Theory of Avant-Garde and Popular Art, or High and Low Culture." *Southern Economic Journal* 67, no. 2: 232–53.

De Janvry, Alain, and Elizabeth Sadoulet. 2001. "Income Strategies among Rural Households in Mexico: The Role of Off-farm Activities." *World Development* 29, no. 3:467–80.

de la Peña, Moises. 1949. *Guerrero Economico*. 2 vols. Chilpancingo: Government of the State of Guerrero.

Delpar, Helen. 1992. *The Enormous Vogue of Things Mexican: Cultural Relations between the United States and Mexico, 1920–1935.* Tuscaloosa: University of Alabama Press.

De Soto, Hernando. 1989. *The Other Path: The Invisible Revolution in the Third World.* New York: Harper and Row.

Dinstel, Edward Ray. 1982. "United States Investment, Trade, and Tourism Involving Mexico: A Study of Selected Problems of Dependency during the Administration of President Luis Echeverría (1970–1976)." Master's thesis, Baylor University.

Dow, James. 1975. *The Otomí of the Northern Sierra de Puebla, Mexico: An Ethnographic Outline.* Lansing: Latin American Studies Center, Michigan State University.

Ehrenberg, Felipe. 1995. "Nahua Art and the Antinomies of Mexican Aesthetics." In *The Amate Tradition: Innovation and Dissent in Mexican Art,* edited by Jonathan D. Amith, 17–22. Chicago: Mexican Fine Arts Center Museum.

Elster, Jon. 1998. "A Plea for Mechanisms." In *Social Mechanisms: An Analytical Approach to Social Theory,* edited by Peter Hedström and Richard Swedberg, 45–73. Cambridge: Cambridge University Press.

Eschbach, Karl, Jacqueline Hagan, Nestor Rodriguez, Ruben Hernandez-Leon, and Stanley Bailey. 1999. "Death at the Border." *International Migration Review* 33, no. 2 (summer): 430–55.

Escobedo, Eugenio Macdonald. 1981. *Turismo: Una Recapitulacion.* Mixcoac: Editorial Bodoni.

Farrell, Michael P. 2001. *Collaborative Circles: Friendship Dynamics and Creative Work.* Chicago: University of Chicago Press.

Fehrenbach, T. R. 1995. *Fire and Blood: A History of Mexico.* New York: Da Capo Press.

Firebaugh, Glenn. 2003. *The New Geography of Global Income Inequality.* Cambridge: Harvard University Press.

Foster, George M. 1967. *Tzintzuntzan: Mexican Peasants in a Changing World.* Boston: Little, Brown, and Company.

Fujita, Masahisa, Paul Krugman, and Anthony J. Venables. 1999. *The Spatial Economy: Cities, Regions, and International Trade.* Cambridge: MIT Press.

Gerhard, Peter. 1993. *A Guide to the Historical Geography of New Spain.* Rev. ed. Norman: University of Oklahoma Press.

Glaeser, Edward L., and Janet E. Kohlhase. 2003. "Cities, Regions, and the Decline of Transport Costs." Economic Department, Harvard University.

Goertzen, Chris. 2001. "Crafts, Tourism, and Traditional Life in Chiapas, Mexico: A Tale Related by a Pillowcase." In *Selling the Indian: Commercializing and Appropriating American Indian Cultures,* edited by Carter Jones Meyer and Diana Royer, 236–69. Tucson: University of Arizona Press.

Golde, Peggy. 1986. "Odyssey of Encounter." In *Women in the Field: Anthropological Experiences,* edited by Peggy Golde, 65–93. Berkeley: University of California Press.

Good, Carl, and John V. Waldron. 2001. *The Effects of the Nation: Mexican Art in an Age of Globalization.* Philadelphia: Temple University Press.

Good, Catharine Louise. 1993. "Work and Exchange in Nahuatl Society: Local Values and the Dynamics of an Indigenous Economy." Ph.D. diss., Johns Hopkins University.

Good Eshelman, Catharine. 1988. *Haciendo la Lucha: Arte y comercio nahuas de Guerrero.* Mexico, D.F.: Fondo de Cultura Económica.

Great Masters of Mexican Folk Art: From the Collection of Fomento Cultural Banamex. 1998. New York: Harry N. Abrams.

Greenberg, James. 1981. *Santiago's Sword: Chatino Peasant Religion and Economics*. Berkeley: University of California Press.

Gruzinski, Serge. 1989. Man-Gods in the Mexican Highlands: Indian Power and Colonial Society, 1520–1800. Stanford: Stanford University Press.

Gruzinski, Serge. 1993. *The Conquest of Mexico: The Incorporation of Indian Societies into the Western World, Sixteenth through Eighteenth Centuries*. Cambridge, Mass.: Polity Press.

Gruzinski, Serge. 2002. The Mestizo Mind: The Intellectual Dynamics of Colonization and Globalization. New York: Routledge.

Guardino, Peter F. 1996. *Peasants, Politics, and the Formation of Mexico's National State, Guerrero, 1800–1857*. Stanford: Stanford University Press.

Haber, Stephen H. 1989. *Industry and Underdevelopment: The Industrialization of Mexico, 1890–1940*. Stanford: Stanford University Press.

Hassig, Ross. 1985. *Trade, Tribute, and Transportation: The Sixteenth-Century Political Economy of the Valley of Mexico*. Norman: University of Oklahoma, 1985.

Hedström, Peter, and Richard Swedberg, eds. 1998a. *Social Mechanisms: An Analytical Approach to Social Theory*. Cambridge: Cambridge University Press.

Hedström, Peter, and Richard Swedberg. 1998b. "Social Mechanisms: An Introductory Essay." In *Social Mechanisms: An Analytical Approach to Social Theory*, edited by Peter Hedström and Richard Swedberg, 1–31. Cambridge: Cambridge University Press.

Hendrichs Pérez, Pedro R. 1945. *Por Tierras Ignotas: Viajes y Observaciones en la Region del Rio de las Balsas*. Mexico, D.F.: Editorial Cultura.

Hindley, Jane. 1999. "Indigenous Mobilization, Development, and Democratization in Guerrero: The Nahua People versus the Tetelcingo Dam." In *Subnational Politics and Democratization in Mexico*, edited by Wayne A. Cornelius, Todd A. Eisenstadt, and Jane Hindley, 207–38. La Jolla: Center for U.S.-Mexican Studies, University of California, San Diego.

Ingham, John M. 1986. *Mary, Michael, and Lucifer: Folk Catholicism in Central Mexico*. Austin: University of Texas Press.

Jacobs, Ian. 1982. *Ranchero Revolt: The Mexican Revolution in Guerrero*. Austin: University of Texas Press.

Jameson, Fredric. 2000. "Globalization and Strategy." *New Left Review*, July–August, 49–68.

Karttunen, Frances. *An Analytical Dictionary of Nahuatl*. Austin: University of Texas Press, 1983.

King, Rosa E. 1970. *Tempest over Mexico: A Personal Chronicle*. New York: Arno Press.

Klein, Daniel B., ed. 2000. *Assurance and Trust in a Great Society*. Irvington: Foundation for Economic Education.

Kraig, Bruce, and Dudley Nieto. 1996. *Cuisines of Hidden Mexico: A Culinary Journey to Guerrero and Michoacan*. New York: John Wiley and Sons.

Kremer, Michael. 2003. "Randomized Evaluations of Educational Programs in Developing Countries: Some Lessons." *American Economic Review Papers and Proceedings* 93, no. 2 (May): 102–6.

Kroll, Martin. 1994. "Inocencio Jimenez Chino: The Emergence of an Amate Painter." *Latin American Art* 6, no. 1:54–55.

Krugman, Paul. 1997. *Development, Geography, and Economic Theory*. Cambridge: MIT Press.

Lakehomer, Leona. 1983. "Marcial Camilo and His Aztec Family." *International Folk World* 1:2.

Le Clézio, J. M. G. 1993. *The Mexican Dream; or, The Interrupted Thought of Amerindian Civilizations*. Chicago: University of Chicago Press.

Legrain, Philippe. 2002. *Open World: The Truth about Globalisation*. London: Abacus.

Leibsohn, Dana. 1997. Review of *The Amate Tradition*, edited by Jonathan D. Amith. *American Anthropologist* 99, no. 2:460–61.

León-Portilla, Miguel, and Earl Shorris. 2001. *In the Language of Kings: An Anthology of Mesoamerican Literature—pre-Columbian to the Present*. New York: W. W. Norton.

Lockhart, James. 1992. *The Nahuas after the Conquest: A Social and Cultural History of the Indians of Central Mexico, Sixteenth through Eighteenth Centuries*. Stanford: Stanford University Press.

Lomnitz-Adler, Claudio. 1992. *Exits from the Labyrinth: Culture and Ideology in the Mexican National Space*. Berkeley: University of California Press.

Luboff, Ken. 1999. *Live Well in Mexico: How to Relocate, Retire, and Increase Your Standard of Living*. Santa Fe: John Muir Publications, 1999.

Lustig, Nora. 1998. *Mexico: The Remaking of an Economy*. 2nd ed. Washington, D.C.: Brookings Institution.

McChesney, Fred S. 1997. *Money for Nothing: Politicians, Rent Extraction, and Political Extortion*. Cambridge: Harvard University Press.

Mink, Louis O. 1970. "History and Fiction as Modes of Comprehension." *New Literary History* 1:541–58.

Montemayor, Carlos. 1999. "Guerrero: La Guerrilla Recurrente." In *Guerrero, 1849–1999*, vol. 2, edited by Édgar Neri Quevado, 279–87. Guerrero: Gobierno del Estado de Guerrero.

Montoya Briones, José de Jesús. 1964. *Atla: Ethnografia de un Pueblo Nahuatl*. Mexico City: Instituto Nacional de Antropología e Historia.

Nash, June C. 2001. *Mayan Visions: The Quest for Autonomy in an Age of Globalization*. New York: Routledge.

Ochoa Campos, Moises. 1964. *Guerrero: Análisis de un Estado problema*. Mexico, D.F.: Editorial F. Trillas.

Oettinger, Mario, Jr. 1995. "!Santiago y a ellos! Folk Art as an Agent of Change." In *The Amate Tradition: Innovation and Dissent in Mexican Art*, edited by Jonathan D. Amith, 101–12. Chicago: Mexican Fine Arts Center Museum.

Oles, James. 1993. *South of the Border: Mexico in the American Imagination, 1914–1947*. Washington: Smithsonian Institution Press.

Oppenheimer, Franz. [1908] 1999. *The State*. Reprint, New Brunswick, N.J.: Transaction Books.

Otero, Lorena Melton Young. "U.S. Retired Persons in Mexico." *American Behavioral Scientist* 40, no. 7 (June–July): 914–922.

Paradis, Louise Iseult. 1995. "The Precolumbian History of the Mezcala Region." In *The Amate Tradition: Innovation and Dissent in Mexican Art*, edited by Jonathan D. Amith, 113–28. Chicago: Mexican Fine Arts Center Museum.

Parezo, Nancy J. 1983. *Navajo Sand Painting: From Religious Art to Commercial Art*. Tucson: University of Arizona Press.

Pavía Miller, Ma. Teresa. "Origen y Formación." In *Historia General de Guerrero*, 3:13–146. Chilpancingo: Instituto Nacional de Antropología e Historia.

Peterson, Jeanette Favrot. 1993. *The Paradise Garden Murals of Malinalco: Utopia and Empire in Sixteenth-Century Mexico*. Austin: University of Texas Press.

Porter, Michael E. 1998. *The Competitive Advantage of Nations*. New York: Free Press.

Putnam, Robert D. 2001. *Bowling Alone: The Collapse and Revival of American Community*. New York: Simon and Schuster.

Ravallion, Martin. 1994. *Poverty Comparisons*. Langhorne, Pa.: Harwood Academic Publishers.

Reddy, Sanjay G., and Thomas W. Pogge. 2003. "How *Not* to Count the Poor." Working paper, Columbia University and Barnard University, http://www.socialanalysis.org.

Robertson, Donald. 1994. *Mexican Manuscript Painting of the Early Colonial Period*. Norman: University of Oklahoma Press.

Rodman, Selden. N.d. "Marcial and His 'Aztec' Family." New York: MIND.

Rodman, Selden. 1982. *Popular Artists in Tune with Their World*. New York: Simon and Schuster.

Roth, Paul A. 1989. "How Narratives Explain." *Social Research* 56:449–78.

Ruiz de Alarcón, Hernando. 1984. *Treatise on the Heathen Superstitions That Today Live among the Indians Native to This New Spain, 1629*. Translated and edited by Richard Andrews and Ross Hassig. Norman: University of Oklahoma Press.

Saldívar, Antonio. [1979] 1985. *El ciclo mágico de los dias: Testimonio de un poblado indigena mexicano*. Illustrated by Abraham Mauricio Salazar. Mexico City: Consejo Nacional de Fomento Educativo.

Salopek, Paul. 1986. "Vision: Marcial Camilo Is an Aztec Farmer Who Paints His Dreams." *IMPACT, Albuquerque Journal Magazine*, December 16, 13–14.

Sandstrom, Alan R., and Pamela Effrein Sandstrom. 1986. *Traditional Papermaking and the Paper Cult Figures of Mexico*. Norman: University of Oklahoma Press.

Schmidt, Arthur. 1987. *The Social and Economic Effect of the Railroad in Puebla and Veracruz, Mexico, 1867–1911*. New York: Garland Publishing.

Sherman, John W. 2000. "The Mexican 'Miracle' and Its Collapse." In *The Oxford History of Mexico*, edited by Michael C. Meyer and William H. Beezley, 575–607. Oxford: Oxford University Press.

Smith, Waldemar R. 1977. *The Fiesta System and Social Change*. New York: Columbia University Press.

Stromberg, Gobi. 1982. *El Universo del amate*. Mexico City: Museo Nacional de Culturas Populares.

Stromberg, Gobi. 1985. *El Juego del Coyote: Platería y arte en Taxco*. Mexico, D.F.: Fondo de Cultura Económica.

Sullivan, Kevin. 2001. "Acapulco's Faded Magic." *Washington Post*, October 11, C1, C8.

Taylor, William B. 1979. *Drinking, Homicide, and Rebellion in Colonial Mexican Villages*. Stanford: Stanford University Press.

Thorpe, Rosemary. 1998. *Progress, Poverty, and Exclusion: An Economic History of Latin America in the Twentieth Century*. Baltimore: Johns Hopkins University Press.

Tokman, Víctor, and Guillermo O'Donnell, eds. 1998. *Poverty and Inequality in Latin America: Issues and New Challenges*. Notre Dame, Ind.: University of Notre Dame Press.

Torres, Bárbara. 1980. "El papel del amate historia y significado." In *El Universo del amate*, edited by Gobi Stromberg, 13–30. Mexico City: Museo Nacional de Culturas Populares.

Trescott, Jacqueline. 2001. "Tribe Gives $10 Million to Indian Museum." *Washington Post*, June 5, C1, C7.

Tullock, Gordon. 1967. "The Welfare Cost of Tariffs, Monopolies, and Theft." *Western Economic Journal* 5 (June): 224–32.

Tunstall, Jeremy. 1977. *Media Are American*. New York: Columbia University Press.

Urrutia, Cristina, and Marcial Camilo Ayala. 1984. *El Maíz*. 2nd ed. Tizapán, D.F.: Editorial Patria.

Vasari, Giorgio. [1568] 1991. *Lives of the Artists*. Reprint, Oxford: Oxford University Press.

Von Hagen, Victor Wolfgang. 1944. *The Aztec and Maya Papermakers*. New York: J. J. Agustin.

Weckmann, Luis. 1992. *The Medieval Heritage of Mexico*. New York: Fordham University Press.

Weinberg, Bill. 2000. *Homage to Chiapas: The New Indigenous Struggles in Mexico*. New York: Verso Books.

Weingast, Barry R. 2003. "The Performance and Stability of Federalism, Mexican Style: An Institutionalist Perspective." Working paper, Stanford University.

Wiggins, Steve, Nicola Keilbach, Kerry Preibisch, Sharon Proctor, Gladys Rivera Herrejón, and Gregoria Rodríguez Muñoz. 2002. "Agricultural Policy Reform and Rural Livelihoods in Central Mexico." *Journal of Development Studies* 38, no. 4 (April): 179–202.

Winters, Paul, Benjamin Davis, and Leonardo Corral. 2002. "Assets, Activities, and Income Generation in Rural Mexico: Factoring in Social and Public Capital." *Agricultural Economics* 27:139–56.

Yúnez-Naude, Antonio, and J. Edward Taylor. 2001. "The Determinants of Nonfarm Activities and Incomes of Rural Households in Mexico, with Emphasis on Education." *World Development* 29, no. 3:561–72.

Zacharias, Maria C. 1978. "A World Where God Shines: An Important New Group of Mexican Naïve Painters Enters the International Art Scene." *Americas* 30, nos. 6–7 (June–July): 32–36.

Index

183

Titles in the Series (*continued*)